GOD SAID:
LET THERE BE WOMAN

1

GOD SAID:

A Study of Biblical Women

James A. Fischer, C.M.

ALBA · HOUSE   alba house   NEW · YORK

SOCIETY OF ST. PAUL, 2187 VICTORY BLVD., STATEN ISLAND, NEW YORK 10314

Library of Congress Cataloging in Publication Data

Fischer, James A
   God said, Let there be woman.

   Includes bibliographical references.
      1. Woman (Theology)—Biblical teaching. I. Title.
BS680.W7F57   261.8'34'12   78-21117
ISBN 0-8189-0378-3

Nihil Obstat:
Joseph P. Penna, J.C.D.
Censor Librorum

Imprimatur:
Joseph T. O'Keefe
Vicar General, Archdiocese of New York
November 26, 1978

The Nihil Obstat and Imprimatur are
a declaration that a book or pamphlet is considered
to be free from doctrinal or moral error. It is not implied
that those who have granted the Nihil Obstat and
Imprimatur agree with the contents,
opinions or statements expressed.

Designed, printed and bound in the United States of
America by the Fathers and Brothers of the
Society of St. Paul, 2187 Victory Boulevard,
Staten Island, New York, 10314, as part of their
communications apostolate.

1 2 3 4 5 6 7 8 9 (Current Printing: first digit).

DEDICATION

In gratitude to my friends,
the Vatterott Family,
for the leisure of a cabin in the Ozarks
to write of beautiful things.

CONTENTS

INTRODUCTION

And God said: "Let there be woman." And that, in the opinion of some, is where all the trouble started. Such badly jocose comments reveal more about our prejudices than our formal statements. Prejudices not only get packaged in quasi-biblical language; they are unwittingly justified by supposed Biblical teachings.

Much of our cultural response to women still depends on a strain of fundamentalistic Biblical interpretation within large segments of the population. Reading or knowledge of the Bible may be minimal, but the "folk wisdom" is carried on. Under the veneer of male civility, sometimes under the patina of ecclesiastical propriety, there does often lurk a conviction that the Bible portrays woman as the eternal seductress. Oddly, the Bible never uses that word about women except of such people as Jezabel whom everyone would admit was corrupt to the core. It is often airily assumed that women in the Bible, especially in the Old Testament, were considered as properties of the men. The women whom the Bible portrays in some fullness do not look that way to me. In the New Testament Paul is popularly pictured as the great anti-feminist, standing outside a delivery room, listening with satisfaction to the screams, and commenting: "Women shall be saved by child-bearing." In domestic quarrels it is all too easy for the male to say that women should obey their husbands: the Bible says so and that is that. The male use of such clichés is ancient and irrational. The female use of the Bible for claiming such things as equal rights or erecting a glorified picture of the liberated woman may be equally distorted.

My professional colleagues do not inspire me with a great deal more confidence. They tend to dismiss the apparently anti-feminist sayings as merely "time-conditioned," or as anachronistic middle class attitudes. That women can no longer be constrained to wear hats in church or to keep quiet seems an eminently time-conditioned conclusion. However, settling the problem in this way smacks of finding the easy solution which can be applied to everything we don't like. We should also throw out such "time-conditioned conclusions" as holy war; or perhaps since we have declared holy war on poverty we should throw out the observation that "the poor you have always with you."

From time to time I have commented on various passages concerning women in the Bible. Now I want to make an honest attempt, inadequate as it must be, to consider the whole Biblical attitude toward women. My approach is somewhat unusual, if I may judge by most of what goes on in trying to solve this problem, whether popularly or scholarly. On the scholarly side, I shall use methods of research which individually are rather ordinary. I seem to have put them together in a somewhat unusual way. I call this method the "wisdom approach," though a good number of my colleagues will dispute the precision of the term or the validity of using it so extensively. Having said this, I feel that I have conformed to the "honesty in advertising" regulations.

It is well known that all the ancient Semitic cultures produced a good deal of literature which is properly termed "wisdom." It ranges from simple folk sayings about agriculture to sophisticated dialogues about the meaning of life. It is extensive both in the amount which still exists and in the areas from which it came. The Bible has a good number of books which have been traditionally called

the Book of Proverbs, the Wisdom of Ben

were essentially observers of life.

preference on the actual experiences rather than on theories, covenants or voices from heaven. At times they gathered up the experience of the ages before them and thus influenced the way in which people acted in the future. Yet they were not essentially rule-makers. Especially, they were not policemen for the establishment. Some of them, such as Job and Qoheleth, defied all established views. Their principal value was that they continuously asked what life was all about. Even when they seemed to function as rule-makers, this was not the destination of their thought, but only the way-station to further inquiry. They accepted life as the raw material for wise understanding of the ways of God and man, and they always wanted to eat of the Tree of Knowledge and so learn how to get to the Tree of Life—an imagery which they themselves created or at least popularized.

When we look at the bottom line of what they said, we are often tempted to see it as a conclusion from some grand principle. Our minds have been conditioned by our Western culture to think in terms of principles and conclusions. It is difficult for us to accept that other peoples were deliberately satisfied to think in other ways even though we do it often enough ourselves. When we sit down to do some serious thinking, we tend to reduce to ethical judgments matters on which they were inclined to be satisfied with wry and quizzical observation.

Perhaps it is this very attitude which is the truest

signature of the Wise Men. Irony, biting or benign, pervades their writings.

> *Like a golden ring in a swine's snout*
> *is a beautiful woman with a rebellious disposition. Pr*
> *11:22*

It offends us. It is probably true, but it is not a cliché, that most obvious of conclusions. It has something to say and it is deliberately provocative. Parables are like that, too. Qoheleth tells this one: "Against a small city with few men in it advanced a mighty king, who surrounded it and threw up great siege works about it. But in the city lived a man who, though poor, was wise, and he delivered it through his wisdom. Yet no one remembered the poor man" (Ec 8:14-15). So also their story-telling is quizzical. The long account about King David ends with an ironic twist when the upstart son of the adulterous wife becomes the heir of the promise that David's house would rule forever—a consummation devoutly not to be wished for if Solomon was the pattern.

It is, in fact, these odd twists, these unexpected endings, these concentrations on the mystery behind events which is the most distinctive mark of the Wise Man. It is impossible to tie him down to one literary form such as proverb or parable. His mark can be found in stories which are distinctly psychological in their inner workings. Whether the stories are factual or fictional seems to make no difference. Even laws have a good deal of it in their origin or purpose. As we go through this book, I shall point out more specifically how this "wisdom tradition" operated in various passages of the Bible. I should not want to suggest that all of the Bible is governed by this attitude. But much of the material concerning women from simple proverbs to apocalyptic symbols certainly is. I have tried to include enough to insure that I am not making a prejudiced sampling of the material. I can only assure my readers that I have tried to include all of the most important material here and that I have studied most of the rest. How well I have succeeded in portraying the whole sweep of Biblical attitudes on the subject of women is

understanding is revealed—and the author is revealed either as a secret scoundrel or as an insightful commentator. I confess that I as a man and a celibate at that have struggled often to understand these Biblical women and the women who have formed part of life. There is no easy solution short of unrealistic idealism or equally unrealistic cynicism. The women whom I know and I myself are wrapped up in too many paradoxes. I will settle for reality, however disturbingly untidy it may be.

In the writing of this book I have benefitted from the advice and criticism of women whom I have met in the ministry and whom I esteem as women, as human beings and as competent lay commentators on the Bible. In particular, I want to thank Sister Mary James de Ste. Helene, L.S.P., Sister Mary Rose McPhee, D.C., Mrs. Eileen Catoni, Miss Martha Flick, Mrs. Arvella Moneck and Mrs. Agnes Stern.

The translation used throughout is that of the New American Bible except as noted.

PICTURES IN A GALLERY

The women of the Bible who are mentioned by name run the gamut from unknowns whose name alone appears as if on a plaque to those who are given full length portraits. There are fewer of them than the men, but they seem to be cut from the same cloth of heroines and villains, from the charming girl Ruth to that ruthless seductress Jezabel. There are great moments for them. Huldah sits in her home in the Second Quarter of Jerusalem and advises King Josiah who must consult her; Esther dresses in her royal gowns to save her people by her beauty. There are frightening scenes such as Jael nailing Sisara's head to the ground or Jephthah's daughter being sacrificed because of her father's oath. There is Lydia of Philippi offering her house to Paul when all the men were afraid to do anything, and Magdelene recognizing Christ as Rabboni while all the disciples doubted. And then there is the darker side. Delilah seduces Samson (who, to tell the truth, is a very odd sort of "hero"), Athaliah climbs to the throne of Judah by killing off her whole family, Rebecca deceives Isaac. Also there is the witch of Endor, a shadowy figure in her cave who spoke the truth to Saul. Altogether they are as mixed a bag of human beings as the men.

My interest lies not with the historical facts so much as with how the authors of these various pieces portrayed the women they found essential to their story line. That may tell us far more about the actual attitudes of the Bible than any study of the legal documents or the ancient Semitic law codes. So I propose to make a sampling of women who are presented to us in some detail. I must pursue my way obliquely; I do not think that these characters are presented to us in order to define the role of women; they are presented as individuals who had an important role in God's story of saving his people, or whose adventures said something compelling about mankind's relation to God.

1. Naomi

The Book of Ruth is widely known, if only for the poignant lines of its heroine: "Wherever you go, I will go, wherever you lodge, I will lodge; your people shall be my people, and your God my God" (Rt 1:16). The story is simple enough. Naomi left Judah with her husband Elimelech and her sons to escape a famine. They settled in the pagan land of Moab and there prospered as family and farmers. The two sons happily married Moabite women, Orpah and Ruth. But then disaster struck. Elimelech died. Then the sons. The family business collapsed when a famine came upon Moab. Naomi determined to return to her homeland and told the two daughters-in-law to go back to their families. They were good women and had a future yet before them. But Ruth could not be put off; she not only wanted to stay with Naomi, she wanted to be a Jewess and so professed her faith.

The two women arrived back in Bethlehem at the time of the harvest, penniless outcasts. To scrape together enough food, Ruth went out in the fields to glean after the harvesters. She happened upon the field of Boaz, a wealthy farmer, who was much taken by her charm and gave her a free hand, generously supplying Naomi with all the two women needed. Naomi saw a sudden opportunity in this. She remembered that Boaz was actually a kinsman of hers. She boldly advised Ruth to push her advantage and go out to the threshing floor in the evening dressed in her best finery and sleep at the feet of Boaz. As she had anticipated, Boaz, who

wanted to buy it until he found a marry the girl. So in a solemn scene Boaz bought the property and acquired the right to marry Ruth. Soon the happy pair had a boy child and the story closes with the women of the town celebrating the birth of the boy whom the grandmother Naomi held in her arms. To this some later author appended a genealogy which connected Boaz and his son Obed to King David.

As far as scholars can tell at the present time (and their telling is not at all unanimous), the story as we have it now goes back to between 950-700 B.C. It is from a circle of writers who began presumably during the Davidic and Solomonic times (circa 1000 B.C.) to recast ancient tales in a brilliant new style. Simply as literary artists, these unknown authors rank among the top word-crafters of all times. They produced such exquisite compositions as the Adam and Eve story, the Joseph Stories and the Succession Narrative which tells the dramatic tale of David's sin and subsequent disasters.

Technically, this is the Yahwist Tradition. It is so called because the authors preferred to use the name Yahweh for God rather than the more generic El or Elohim. It used traditional materials, pre-existing stories which often had a substantial basis in fact. The achievement was to recast these records into living stories. The characters became vividly human; the interest centered not so much in the events as in what happened to the people. So they were dramatic, psychologically oriented, effortless in their apparent

simplicity and yet subtly crafted. Here the Yahwist
Tradition and the Wisdom Tradition came together.

What is the point of the story of Ruth? There is no moral
drawn: the author leaves that to each reader. So we must look
to the story as story. For Ruth and Boaz everything works out
well; they are good and loving people who do the things we
would like to do. But without Naomi the story would be
boring. The old woman supplies the drama. Ruth professed
her faith in God in a touching scene; but then Ruth had
never been let down by God. Naomi zeroed in on God as the
cause of all her trouble. "I went away with an abundance,
but the Lord has brought me back destitute" (Rt 1:21). So
Naomi took matters in her own hands and made them come
out right. She pushed Ruth into cultivating Boaz; she sent
the girl out in her best finery at evening to sleep alongside of
him, flaunting all custom. She manipulated Boaz by her
control of the piece of family property which carried with it
the right to marry Ruth. She waited in the background for
the inevitable to happen, and finally the child of the
marriage was placed in her lap. The shrewd plans of the
bitter old woman came to fruition. And then the women said
to her:

> Blessed is the Lord who has not failed
> to provide you today with an heir. Rt 4:14

As one reads the story, the air is heavy with questioning as
the old woman sits there. Who had provided? Is Naomi the
counterpart of Job? The same problem of good and evil,
reward or gift is presented in both cases. Like Job with his
restored fortune, Naomi knew that she did not control either
the taking away or the providing.

For the story-teller, it seems not to have mattered that a
woman was the center-piece of the drama. Both books, Ruth
and Job, meditate on the rather abrasive relations of human
beings with God. Both leave the final solution hanging for
the reader to discern as best may be. The implicit praise in

both stories is for the man or woman who challenged God to prove that he is faithful. Sex makes no difference in the

[illegible — text obscured]

on, does recognize that conviction. So also Ruth appears among the four women who are mentioned in the genealogy of Christ as given by Matthew (Mt 1:5). Ruth was not a Jewess by birth. Somehow her confession of true faith and her acceptance into the ranks of the Chosen People ("your people, my people; your God, my God") did make a point for the early Christian community. Acceptance into the ranks of the Chosen People depended on taking the proper stance before Israel or the church.

What shall we make of the story of Naomi for our purposes? Should we resent Ruth being made part of a package-deal with some real estate? That is not the direction the story takes and it mangles a work of art for the sake of simplistic prejudice. The story must be taken as a whole. It is not notably religious in itself. Yet it appealed to the Hebrews and was accepted by them for centuries as part of their religious heritage. It said something to them of how the ways of God became known to human beings. In Ruth and Boaz it described how human beings can grow in loving concern for one another as God is always lovingly concerned. In Naomi it posed the great mystery of how God and a woman crossed paths and how the woman finally came to realize the provident action of God behind all the seemingly improvident ways of acting. It did not matter much whether the characters were portrayed as men or women. Somehow they needed to accept their dependence on God and to accept their own proper role in the society of his Chosen People.

Note on Ruth

The best commentator on Ruth is Edward F. Campbell, Jr., *Ruth* (Anchor Bible, New York: Doubleday, 1975). Campbell has surveyed all the previous work and has handled the matter with a sure and deft hand. Somewhat similar, though much briefer, is Wesley J. Fuerst, *The Books of Ruth, Esther, Ecclesiastes, The Song of Songs, Lamentations* (Cambridge Bible Commentary, New York: Cambridge University Press, 1975). Other commentaries of older vintage and lesser value may be found in the Jerome Biblical Commentary, John Mckenzie, *Dictionary of the Bible* (Milwaukee: Bruce, 1965); G.A.F. Knight, *Ruth and Jonah* (Torch Bible Paperbacks, London: SCM Press, 1966), Otto Eissfeldt, *The Old Testament* (New York: Harper and Row, 1965) 477-483.

---

2. The Jewess' Tale — Judith

To luxuriate in a bit of certitude which is not entirely justified but certainly possible, let us read the book of Judith as a good Pharisee might have read it after the Roman occupation of 63 B.C. Harsh times and a new set of gods had again invaded Jerusalem. People looked back to the good old days when that most proper lady, Queen Alexandra, had reigned (78-69 B.C.). How this new tyranny would all come out, no one knew. But someone had to say the ancient truth that if Jews lived piously Yahweh would always protect them.

Fortunately, someone did say that in a story, not in a sermon. Possibly he himself was a Pharisee. He invented "the Jewess," for so "Judith" reads, and modeled her a bit on that prim Queen Alexandra. Then he stirred together some popular history about Nebuchadnezzar and an invasion of Palestine, not being overly concerned about the facts since this was a story. He zeroed in on the old tale of Jael killing

...omething like that his great dramatic
...ther and her beauty and
...ll of this

exchan...
substitutes a widow ...
Jerusalem.''

But to the story itself. Nebuchadnezzar sent his general
Holofernes with a huge army to punish the Western nations
for refusing to support him in his war against the Medes. All
bowed down before Holofernes and admitted that
Nebuchadnezzar was indeed "the great king" and their god;
all, that is, except a small group of Israelites who holed up in
the mountains of Judah and defied the great army.
Holofernes, therefore, beseiged the town of Bethulia which
controlled the mountain passes to Judah. There the
beseigers and the beseiged sat, waiting for the water to run
out.

However, a new dimension is added to the story of
military strategy. Achior, an Ammonite chieftan who had
been previously captured, advised Holofernes that this
people could not be overcome if they were living according
to their religion. He suggested that he be sent as a spy to find
out if the Jews were actually doing so. Holofernes sent him
to the Jews, but not as a spy. He threw him out before the
Jewish lines to be captured and killed with the rest when the
irresistable army slaughtered the Jews. So Achior lived with
the beseiged, wondering if his confident analysis of the faith
of Israel was really true.

The water did run out in time and the brave leader of
Bethulia, Uzziah, finally bowed to pressure in the streets and
resolved to wait only five more days for God to act. At this
desperate moment Judith appeared. She was a wealthy and
beautiful widow living on her estate outside Bethulia. She

summoned the men and upbraided them for trying to dictate
to God when he shall act. Then she took over and put her
own secret plan into operation. One evening she and her
maid crossed the no-man's land between the armies and were
captured. Judith dazzled the enemy soldiers and especially
General Holofernes. She told him that Achior was perfectly
right; the Jews could not be conquered unless they broke
their own laws. Then she confided to Holofernes that they
were on the point of doing this; they were going to eat the
priestly food which was not permitted. Besides, she also
knew a secret path to the city. Holofernes was looking more
at Judith than listening to her; he agreed to let her go out
each evening to pray between the lines of the armies. For
three days Judith lived her chaste life as an untouchable
beauty. Then Holofernes could stand it no longer; he invited
her to a party in his tent. Unfortunately, he got drunk.
Judith took his sword and cut off his head. She had her maid
put it in the usual bag of provisions and went out for her
nightly prayers. But this time Judith simply went back to
Bethulia and told the Jewish soldiers: "my face seduced
Holofernes to his ruin." She produced the bloody head and
had it spiked on the wall. But who could be certain that the
gruesome trophy was really the head of Holofernes? One
man knew, Achior the Ammonite. He was summoned—and
fainted.

In the morning the Jews made a noise as if to attack and
the Assyrians discovered the horrible truth that their leader
had been murdered. In the confusion they were slaughtered.
Judith joined in the victory dance and sang a great song
celebrating God's powerful action. Then she returned home
and, always the proper lady, lived a long life as a widow.

Now, what can we learn about woman's role from this
tale in late Judaism? Obviously, the story was not written as
an epic of woman's new role in that society. But the story was
about a woman. Presumably, the author could have made
the same point by telling a story about a man; the author of 2
Machabees had done that in the century preceeding. Making
a woman the heroine must have been acceptable in the

...blic mind of Judaism, both in Palestine and in the
... Jews used the story of the victory of
... ...kkah

games w...
cut off Holofernes' head (and in a j...
story mutilated his body); Achior fainted when he saw the
bloody head. Those lusty males in the Assyrian camp
drooled over her beauty and lost all common sense; Judith
ruthlessly held out the bait for them never allowing them to
touch her.

This woman was truly a seductress and a cold-blooded
one at that. But the readers were expected to accept it because
she used her seduction for a good purpose. The story must
have appealed because that kind of woman appealed—
strong, beautiful, pious. That she took charge of the men
was accepted unblinkingly. That was the way good women
acted and the way men accepted them. It may not have been
legal, but it was what happened.

Note on Judith

Scholars have not paid much attention to the Book of
Judith. The Jews never accepted it as part of their sacred
books although they used it at the feast of Hannukkah.
Christians accepted it only with misgivings and so it is listed
as "deutero-canonical" by Catholics and "apocryphal" by
Protestants. The only recent commentary is by Morton S.
Enslin, *The Book of Judith* (Leiden: Brill, 1972). I have
relied much on Enslin's very brief, but perceptive notes. I
have accepted his dating of the book after 63 B.C. and its
provenance in Pharasaic circles. The literary dependencies
on the Jael story, on Esther and perhaps Daniel are clear.

Most authors make a point that the basic theme is the same as the Exodus story; namley, deliverance by God. For this, cf. Patrick Skehan, "By the Hand of Judith," CBQ 25 (1963), 94-100. Enslin raises the interesting question as to why the heroine should be a widow, but he does not answer it.

---

3. The Lady Killer — Jezabel

Lest I be suspected of leaning over backwards, I include here the story of Jezabel, the very epitome of feminine wickedness.

She came as a princess of Sidon to marry Achab, King of Israel in 869 B.C. as part of a political deal. What the political manipulators didn't count on was the kind of kitten they got. Jezabel had designs not only to wrap Achab around her finger but to make Israel into a pagan nation of her own. She brought with her priests and prophets. That was expected, but four hundred prophets was rather much. She had hardly become queen when she launched a bloody persecution of the bands of preachers and enthusiastic worshipers of Yahweh who were also known as "prophets." Many of them simply gave up their preaching; some of the hardier fled to the hills. But many paid with their lives. Obediah, the pious prime minister, managed to save one hundred and fifty of them by hiding them in caves, but he knew that he was taking his own life in his hands.

Unfortunately for Jezabel, one prophet was not cowed. Elijah the Tishbite swept in from the desert, a gaunt prophet-soldier sworn to the uncompromising way of the Nazarites, an extremely militant Levitical group. He could not be silenced. In fact, he challenged the Jezabel prophets to a trial of bringing down fire from heaven, and when they failed, they were all murdered by an enraged populace. Elijah simply vanished back into the desert.

Next Jezabel offended all decency by having her weak husband seize the property of a defenseless neighbor,

Naboth. By threatening the nobles and elders Jezabel had Naboth condemned for impiety and done away with. Achab [illegible] next door in which to [illegible] of Achab. [illegible] commander, Jehu. That did it. Jehu matched Jezabel in ruthlessness. He slaughtered the army and drove on to Jezreel. As he entered the gate, he saw Jezabel trying to seduce him from her second story window. He had her thrown down and ran over her with his chariot. Later at the victory celebration he told his men to bury "that accursed woman." They found nothing but a few bones. The dogs of Jezreel had done their work.

In dealing with this story we should note first of all that it is not really a single story. From the first note about Jezabel to the end of her life the matter is scattered over sixteen chapters. She is a bit player, so to speak. Moreover, the information comes from various sources — court records, prophetic interventions, legends of the prophets and others, each of which has its own viewpoint and purpose. Moreover, this material has been rather poorly stitched together so that at times we cannot be sure of the chronology, the precise source and viewpoint, or the amount of material which has been omitted. For example, the first entry under Jezabel is simply:

> *"He (Ahab) even married Jezabel, daughter of Ethbaal, king of the Sidonians, and went over to the veneration and worship of Baal" (1K 16:31).*

Along the way we read at the death of Ahab:

> *Indeed, no one gave himself up to the doing of evil in the sight of the Lord as did Ahab, urged on by his wife Jezabel (1K 21:25).*

Although these two sayings appear approximately in the same vein, one comes from the court record as interpreted by the Deuteronomist authors and the other from a cycle of prophetic stories about Elijah. The final story which I have related comes from a cycle of Jehu stories.

However, there is a certain consistency: nobody had anything good to say about Jezabel. It wasn't that she was a woman; she was just rotten. She was a pagan princess who did not know her place. She tried to influence the history of Israel by pushing it into paganism. She used her womanly wiles to do it; even at the end she defiantly played the seductress. It was all right for Ruth or Judith to use beauty to influence men to accomplish God's purpose; it was definitely not right for Jezabel to use the same beauty to defy the words of the prophets. Beyond that, not much can be learned from this story as to how the Jews looked at their womenfolk.

Note on Jezabel

The standard commentaries seem to cover the matter sufficiently. Among others I have depended on John Bright, *A History of Israel* (Philadelphia: Westminster, 1959) for the historical data and on Otto Eissfeldt, *The Old Testament* (New York: Harper and Row, 1965) for the literary analysis.

---

4. The Women of the New Testament

[illegible] mentioned

greetings. So the choice

separate themselves into Christ's women and Paul's women—and there is a curious difference in tone. Christ's women are very feminine. The most constant thing said of them is that they "fear." The word needs interpretation; say for simplicity's sake that these are women in awe of some wondrous event. Paul's women are strong and practical, like Priscilla, the wife of Aquila, who is eventually called by her more intimate name of Prisca and made the first half of the Prisca-Aquila team. Such also are Lois and Mary ("who was more than a mother to me") and Damaris, the seller of purple in Philippi.

Out of them all I have chosen three. The first is the Samaritan woman; the second is Mary during the public life of Jesus; the third is Magdelene. We shall come back to Mary the mother later under symbols. By the time the Gospels were written Mary the person shed so much light on the true significance of Jesus that her story had become intermingled with theological insights that saw her as a symbol of God's saving action among men. Here we shall simply consider one of the few brief paassages which refer to her without much overlay of theological reflection.

5. The Samaritan Person — Jn 4:4-30

One day, presumably in spring, Jesus stopped at the well of Jacob in Samaria and sent his disciples into town to buy something to eat. There came to the well a Samaritan woman. She has no name, but she had a reputation; she was the village vamp. She desperately tried to play the role. So when he asked her for a drink of water, she feigned shock that he would speak to her. Then when he told her that he would give her living water, she had to make a game of it and asked how he could reach the water without a bucket. When he told her that the water he would give would become a fountain of life within the drinker, she tossed this off laughingly with: "Give me this water that I may not thirst, or come here to draw water."

But he would not let her go. He told her brusquely, as she had hoped that he would, to go get her husband. She had ready the coquettish invitation that she had no husband. But he cut her off with: "The fact is that you have had five, and the man you are living with now is not your husband."

Clearly, she had lost that game which she was so accustomed to playing, so she had refuge in the impersonal religious cliché so dear to those who would avoid serious talk. They were standing at the foot of Mt. Gerazim where the Samaritans had once built a temple to Yahweh. It had not been a very imposing temple and it did not stand for much. The Samaritans said that it was the most ancient sanctuary of God. So the woman brought forth the ancient one-liner about Jerusalem being an upstart religious center. But he said something which brought the matter back to personal involvements: "An hour is coming, and is already here, when authentic worshipers will worship the Father in Spirit and truth. Indeed, it is just such worshipers the Father seeks." He had spoken the truth which they both knew; the old argument over Jerusalem was a fraud. God is a spirit and cannot be confined to a place. But God was seeking her. Something broke within her and she said the first honest thing that day: "I know there is a Messiah coming. When he comes, he will tell us everything." Jesus replied: "I who speak to you am he." She had come to the well seeking a man; she found one, not the one she had planned to meet in her role as the village vamp, but the one who appealed to the real woman.

The disciples came up at that moment. They were

As the final scene tells, they found a man whom they
believe. So the Samaritans went out of their way rather
ungraciously to tell the woman that they wouldn't believe
her, but they did believe him. It did not seem to matter to her.

To retell the story in this way is, perhaps, to romanticize
it and many have done that before me. The question is
whether this retelling points the story in the direction which
it was intended to have. So first of all, we must ask what the
story is doing in the Johannine Gospel. Perhaps it is a
"foundation story" of the beginning of the Samaritan
church. However, it is too good a story to be simply a record
of facts. Some have diagnosed it as a very brief account in the
first few verses leading up to the pronouncement that Jesus
would give living water. The rest would then be a collection
of sayings of Jesus to bring out what that meant. This
supposes that the Johannine way of explaining teachings
was rather abstract, and it does not fit the facts. As far as we
can tell, we have here a complete story which grew slowly out
of years of preaching by John and his missionary band in
Asia Minor. At what stage of that development the story as it
now stands was written we do not precisely know, but it is
rather far along. What we have then is a superbly crafted
story which must be fitted into the style in which this Gospel
tells stories. If we examine others in the Johannine Gospel,
we find that many of them concentrate on the way in which
people reacted rather than on the logic of the argument. In
this story the climax comes when Jesus says: "I am he." No

explanation is added. The "I am" sayings in John always end in incident. The end is the revelation of a person, not of a point in an argument.

If we look at this matter more broadly, we find that we have here a type of story-telling which centers on the psychological development of character. This is generally true of the stories which cluster around the wisdom tradition and John is certainly in that tradition in many sections. From that tradition came the stories of the Garden of Eden, the Joseph Narratives, the Ruth story, etc.; all of these are studies in human psychology. They all say: this is how people react to the sudden revelation that God has touched them. The dialogue is secondary: it reveals enough to define something, but not enough to be a complete answer.

If this be admitted, then the explanation of the story even in paraphrse must center on what happened to the woman psychologically. I have pictured her here as a "strange woman," trapped in her own cloak of disrespectability. She had to live up to the reputation which she had planned for herself. What Christ did was to free her to be herself. Under the veneer of a bad reputation lived a real woman of faith who was afraid to tell herself that she believed. Then he risked telling her who he was. Nothing more needed to be said than "I am he."

If we ask what this says about our theme of how the Bible portrays women, we should certainly not zero in indignantly on the implied custom that women should not talk to strange men. We do not really know if that was a custom, and it is obviously not the point of the story. The point of the story is that somebody deliberately selected a story about a woman to carry along these wise words of Christ. There is more. She is the first one to whom Jesus in the Johannine account clearly reveals that he is the Messiah. She is the first messenger of the Good News outside the chosen group. Samaria later became an important center of evangelization. The origins of that church apparently went back to this woman. Her story was important. It was also important to the story that she be a woman; without her

... .ld be no story. The Christian com-
....d no surprise over a

John is Raymond ......
(New York: Doubleday, 1966, 2 vols.). .....
followed Brown's theory of the origin and development of
John 4. Brown's diagnosis of this story differs from mine;
however, Brown does admit much more of the wisdom
influence in John than previous commentators; cf., *op cit*, I,
cxxii-cxxvii on Wisdom motifs. The theory that this story is
a literary development from a pronouncement story is that of
J. Bligh. Commentaries on John are numerous and any
general commentary will give a listing of the more
important ones. I am probably influenced indirectly by C.H.
Dodd and not at all by R. Bultmann.

---

6. The Incident of the Allegations of the Scribes—Mk 3:20-35

One day the Scribes accused Jesus of having a devil and
of casting out devils by the prince of devils. It is a counter-
attack which would probably not occur to us today and we
tend to dismiss the whole incident as an echo from a more
superstitious and simplistic age. However, the incident is
related quite soberly in all three Synoptic Gospels (cf. also
Mt 12:22-50 and Lk 11:14-23). No reasonable doubt exists
that an historical report lies at the basis of the three stories.
For our purposes, it is the only incident in the common
proclamation of the Gospel in which Mary, Christ's mother,
appears. John does not have this incident, though he gives
additional information about Mary at Cana and at the foot of

the Cross. But those are uniquely Johannine stories.

Mark is unique in the way in which he ties the Mary incident into the accusation that Jesus has a devil. Before the story of the accusation, he has a scene in which some of Christ's "familiars" (literally, "those of him") come to bring him home because they said: "He is out of his mind." After the accusation Mark pictures Jesus as preaching to the crowd seated around him. His mother and brothers arrive and stand outside. The story concludes: "Whoever does the will of God is brother and sister and mother to me." This is called Mark's "envelope technique," and it must be considered seriously in the point which it makes.

If we take a look at the story of the accusation as told by all three Evangelists, we must note the apocalyptic images used. Jesus is accused of being in league with other-worldly powers such as appear in apocalyptic writings. Mark had previously referred to such imagery in his story of the cure of the paralytic at Capharnaum (Mk 2:12). There Jesus himself had used the well-known images by claiming to be the "son of man" who had "power on earth" (Mk 2:10). In apocalyptic writings "son of man" was sometimes used to designate the divinely appointed hero who led the forces of good in the battle in the heavens. He was definitely a heavenly figure. Jesus shocked the Scribes not only by accepting that title for himself, but by claiming to have "power on earth." Perhaps the Scribes sought to exploit this as a weakness by another bit of apocalyptic lore. In those stories the most dangerous enemy was often a demon who concealed himself as an angel of light. Such an understanding would make the accusation that Jesus was not the "son of man," but a secret devil much more reasonable. Jesus' answer finally centers on his own conclusion that they are blaspheming against the Holy Spirit.

But Mark gives a further proof (and perhaps a warning to the second generation Christians) by using his envelope technique, to present the plausibility of the argument of the Scribes. But when the dispute is over, Mark has Jesus seated calmly preaching a very traditional doctrine of placing God above family to a group of people who obviously respect

incident. Only then does he put ...

brothers and mother of Jesus standing outside the house. Putting the stories together that way seems to say: "you Pharisees have never really believed or done what is right— these people do." Luke puts the story in still another context. First he has Christ relate several parables, concluding with the one about the lampstand. Then he has the story about the brothers and mother of Jesus, as if to say: "This is what lamp-people are like" (Lk 8:19-21). We can only explain this wide diversity of uses by presupposing that the incident of the brothers and mother never had a very definite locale in the oral tradition about Jesus. Each of the Evangelists was somewhat free in arranging the matter as best suited his plan.

Too much cannot be read into such a brief reference to Mary to give any great illumination on our problem. Since the stories are so loosely structured, we cannot attribute to Mary the sentiments of "the familiars." However, as all three Evangelists have used the final story, Mary and the brethren are in some way vindicators of the probity of Jesus. Mark is clear in his arrangement of the matter. Perhaps one other negative note of some importance can be added. Whatever the basis for the later exaltation of Mary the Mother, it certainly did not spring from an over-sentimentalized portrayal of her.

Note on Jesus and the Allegations of the Scribes

The analysis of the Markan story as I have given it parallels to a degree that of Vincent Taylor, *The Gospel according to St. Mark* (London: Macmillan, 1955), which remains a landmark commentary on Mark. I have relied on D.S. Russell, *The Method and Message of Jewish Apocalyptic* (Philadelphia: Westminster, 1964) for the data on apocalyptic concepts. Many other commentaries, of course, have been written.

---

7. Mary Magdelene—Jn 20:11-18

Mary Magdelene appears by name among the women at the Crucifixion scene (Mt 27:26,61; Mk 15:40,47; Jn 19:25) and at the early morning scenes on resurrection day (Mt 28:1; Mk 16:1,9; Lk 24:10; Jn 20:1,18). She is also mentioned among the women who accompanied Jesus and is described as the one "from whom seven devils had gone out" (Lk 8:2). Various other stories about unnamed women have clustered about her name, but we have no assurance that they belong to her story.

The one complete story about her occurs in Jn 20:11-18. Here Mary alone remains behind at the tomb and meets Jesus. She first mistakes him as a gardener and then recognizes him when he calls her "Mary." She calls him "Rabbouni" and embraces him. He tells her not to cling to him and sends her on a mission to his brothers to say: "I am ascending to my Father and your Father, to my God and your God."

All the stories about the resurrection are difficult to trace in their origins, confusing in their chronology and mysterious in their theological import. There seems to have been no one way of telling the stories which formed the basis for the various Gospel accounts, such as often happens in the rest of the Gospel material. Rather, each tradition has come

A Study of Biblical Women

23

... an independent witness. The Magdelene story ... it seems to parallel in some ... Thomas,

empty. They are ... brethren. The reaction of the men is doubt or incredulity.

Secondly, it is very important for the theological meaning to pay attention to the descriptions of how Christ looked. If the meaning was that the Crucified is now the resurrected Victor, we should expect his physical appearance to be described in terms such as are used in the Transfiguration scene or the Ascension scene. It is not. Christ appears to Mary Magdelene, to the disciples on the way to Emmaus, to the apostles fishing on the Lake of Galilee and presumably to those in the Upper Room as a quite ordinary man. He is so ordinary that they do not even recognize him at first. There are no rays of light, no attending angels, no diaphanous appearance. That familiar figure has been changed in some way, but changed to appear more ordinary. In each case he must speak to them in personal terms before they recognize that he is the Jesus with whom they had associated. Somehow this is crucial before they can believe. The resurrected Jesus is described not as overwhelming his followers with physical evidence, but as calling them on a very personal level to believe that it is he.

So in the story of Mary Magdelene she first identifies him as the gardener. It is no mere momentary lapse. John has a rather lengthy conversation in which Mary speaks to him as the gardener. Even when she turns around and looks at him "she did not know him." He must call her by her name—simply, Mary—before she knows who he is. Her answer does not identify him as some other-worldly person or even as "Lord" or "Christ" as the developing theology of the Church named him in much of the New Testament. To her he is still the Wise Man who had first revealed to her who she was and who she could be. "Rabbi" is a term which only John uses of Jesus; "Rabbouni" is a personalized form of the word which only one very intimate with the Teacher would use. Just what action Mary then took is not recorded in John; in Matthew's account the women fall down before Jesus and embrace his feet and do him homage, but John says nothing like this. Instead, Jesus says in an obscure phrase: "Do not cling to me!" That Mary should have embraced him affectionately is quite understandable; his reason for telling her to let go is quite mysterious: "for I have not yet ascended to the Father." Of all the attempts to untangle this curious reason, the best seem to center on some understanding of the ascending. This comes into the next verse: "Rather, go to my brothers and tell them, 'I am ascending to my Father and your Father, to my God and your God.'" John has no ascension scene in his Gospel; resurrection and ascension are combined. Certainly both are unique events in human history; yet it is the commonality of Jesus with the people he knew which is stressed. It is not simply "my Father," "my God" to whom he is ascending, but "my Father and your Father," "my God and your God." That and the very ordinary human appearance of Jesus have something important to say to Mary and the brothers.

In retelling the story of the Samaritan woman I have stressed the psychological factors in the story as decisive for the kind of story-telling which John preferred. The crux of the story depends on a sudden revelation of the internal realization which comes upon the one to whom Jesus speaks. In his revelation of who he is the other person comes to realize who she is (or he—the technique is used in other places in John, such as the Nicodemus incident, or the conflict with the Jews in Jn 10:32-39). The emphasis is on what happens to the human being when confronted with a situation which can be met either by accepting or rejecting absolute faith.

So if we look at the resurrection stories as they were presented to the early Christians we can see how they were ⟨...⟩ from the readers. It was up to

⟨text obscured⟩

living beyond death on the lips of women ⟨...⟩ umbrage. It is the men who doubt and question. The problem as John describes it is not with Jesus but with the rest of us. That a man should rise from the dead by the power of God is not, within the context of the Biblical teaching about the wondrous deeds of Yahweh, something which defies acceptance. That it should involve us in the same way is indeed difficult to accept. We can live with an odd fact; we cannot live comfortably with a demand for personal faith. In that respect the Evangelists commonly and John particularly in the story of Mary Magdelene found it most fitting to put the proper response in stories about women. So apparently did the early Christians find it most appropriate.

Note on Mary Magdelene

Raymond Brown, *The Gospel According to John, XIII-XXI* (Anchor Bible, New York: Doubleday, 1970), 979-1017 summarizes the research of the past and proposes his own diagnosis of the passage. I have followed Brown in the details which I have used. However, the basic interpretation of the story as a psychological drama is my own and follows the methodology which I have previously used in this book.

---

8. Summary

The stories which have been retold and analyzed here reveal nothing immediately applicable to our topic of the place of women in the Biblical teaching. Conclusions must be reached by implication.

The first implication which is immediately evident is that in the crucial questions about human life, the believing community accepted stories about women as the principal actors without any demure. True enough, such stories are not as frequent by far as those about men. They are "exceptional stories," if one may put it that way. Rarely do women enter into the main-stream of the story told about the pilgrimage of the Chosen People. They are bit actors in the play. Only Jezabel in the Old Testament stories we have reviewed is part of the "sacred history," and she is a rather dismal part. Ruth and Judith are occasional pieces which stand apart from the official record. In the New Testament the Samaritan Woman and Mary Magdelene are more part of the official record, but they are in it only as told by John. Elsewhere the main action occurs among men. Yet one should not pass over lightly the community acceptance of the stories which do often appear on the periphery. On any supposition that the people of the Bible were anti-feminist, the stories would never be there at all. Nothing in the narratives or the history of the acceptance of the books indicates that there was a problem in accepting the stories simply because the principal actors were women.

Secondly, it should be noted that the stories do bring out an insight into reality which is peculiarly feminine. Nobody but Naomi, a woman, could have appreciated how God had acted in a woman's concern for her family. One could hardly make a story at all about Jesus and the Samaritan person. Only Mary Magdelene responded with such personal familiarity when she realized what she was being asked to believe. Doubting Thomas is pictured almost as a Byzantine icon, formally professing faith in "My Lord and my God." As Marshall McLuhan says: "The medium is the message."

ESSAYS ON WOMEN IN GENERAL

Introduction

I am tempted to call this chapter "Instructions" in order to strike a balance of one word sub-titles: stories, instructions, symbols. However, it will not do since it will give a false emphasis.

The Biblical passages which I shall cite do not instruct women in how they should act. At least, this does not seem to be the first thing intended. The data which the Bible uses is observation of the way in which women act. That data was drawn from social custom. Social custom, of course, has instructional value. Parents do hand on their experience to children, teachers to students and the Wise Men of Israel and early Christianity did set down for the future what they had seen of value in such customs. Obviously, they expected that they would be listened to. But it was not the specific ways of acting which were mandated, but the insights and attitudes which were handed on.

For example, Israel as well as Mesopotamia and Egypt had instructions about children obeying parents. One is tempted to call that a natural law, so widespread is it in society. But the Wise Men saw much more to it than a law. Israel's law was phrased thus: "Honor your father and your mother that you may have long life in the land which the Lord, your God, is giving you"(Ex 20:12). The first part of this customary law is straightforward and clear. The second part is mysterious. There is no evidence that obedient children live longer than disobedient ones and there is no evidence that the Israelites interpreted the law in that way. If we may be permitted a guess as to how the motive got into the law, we can reflect upon the Shechemite war in the time of the Judges circa 1200 B.C. In that civil war families were divided; sons betrayed fathers and wiped out their own families. The lesson was obvious. The man who broke faith with his own parents could expect no better from his own children. Moreover, the promise of God that he would give the land of Palestine to the Chosen People amounted to nothing if people killed off their own families. One had to imitate the life-giving God who gave the land freely for the use of all. In some such way the saying, which was common in all societies, functioned as a religious insight among the Israelites. It was not a newly given rule; that already existed. It was an insight. So also when Paul cites "the first commandment to carry a promise" (Ep 6:2), he was addressing people who knew the custom of taking care of elderly parents, but who now had a new understanding of why and how they should do this "in the Lord."

Doing things "in the Lord" involved a great deal of freedom. The shape of the world was determined by a free act of God. The ancient law dictated that the Sabbath should be kept holy. There is no reason in the world why one day should be more holy than another. There is a reason in heaven, as the ancients saw it: God liked it that way. Man's acceptance of this one rule, as of all the things which were commanded, was seen as an opportunity to excercise freedom in accepting God's will. That is what is ultimately behind all the laws, rules, customs and instructions as the Chosen People saw them. To be able to follow God's will was for them the greatest exercise of freedom, especially considering how often they were prevented from doing so by oppressors or their own weakness. So the great hymn of Zachary celebrates this freedom:

> *(He) remembered the holy covenant he made,*
> *the oath he swore to Abraham our father that he*
> *~~would grant us~~*

cumscribe the way in which life was to be lived. Social customs do so for all peoples whether Chosen or not. What the sacred writers wanted to know was how much of the image of God could be seen in men and women as they lived within the conditions which life imposed. The distinction is of no small importance. In our day we speak of ethics and think of rules of conduct which must be practiced. Sometimes the temptation is great to read the Bible in this way. Unfortunately, we are seldom consistent in our acceptance. If the domineering husband likes the Biblical injunctions that women are to be submissive, he probably dislikes the injunction that he should be the leader of prayer in his house. Scholars are inclined to accept Biblical sayings as imperative models when they agree with predetermined opinions, such as that Jesus was a pacifist; they are inclined to reject them as "time-conditioned conclusions" in such matters as slavery. Both attitudes seem to miss the point which the essays in the Bible are making.

In the work which follows I hope to tie together the consideration of the social institutions which formed the starting point of the reflections with the larger vision of men and women striving to be like God.

1. Women in the Book of Proverbs

The Book of Proverbs is an anthology of popular

sayings, most of which have no specifically religious content. How long this collection was in the process of formation no one can say; the final edition seems to date from the early part of the fifth century B C., and the first nine chapters are apparently the most recent addition.

Proverbs 5-9 contains a lengthy instruction to a young man on adultery. It is presented as parental advice about youthful temptations and the joys of honorable mariage. So Pr 6:20-35 begins a new section:

> *Observe, my son, your father's bidding,*
> *and reject not your mother's teaching. Pr 6:20*

The advice then given is rather earthy: an adulteress may be pretty, but she is a trap; men get burned and they may be beaten up like a thief. Perhaps the mother added the observation that the adulteress is a trap, or, as R.B.Y. Scott translates it: "she hunts with a keener appetite." There is nothing religious about this; it is the kind of advice which parents have always passed on to children and it has its effects. A father's observation, "Son, stay away from red-headed women" may not have much depth, but it is the kind of thing which young men are apt to remember much longer than the most solemn commandment.

The way of the Wise Man may be seen to perfection in a brilliant little instruction in the seventh chapter of Proverbs. At the beginning stands an admonition to seek wisdom: "Say to Wisdom, 'You are my sister!' Call Understanding, 'Friend!' " This is as elevated as the thought gets. What follows is such a delightful eye-witness account of the adulteress at work that it is too good to pass up.

> *For at the window of my house,*
> *   through my lattice I look out—*
> *And I saw among the simple ones,*
> *   I observed among the young men,*
> *   a youth with no sense.*

Going along the street near the corner,
    then walking in the direction of her house—

and with an impudent look says to him.
"I owed peace offerings,
    and today I have fullfilled my vows;
So I came out to meet you,
    to look for you, and I have found you!
With coverlets I have spread my couch
    with brocaded cloths of Egyptian linen;
I have sprinkled my bed with myrrh,
    with aloes, and with cinnamon.
Come let us drink our fill of love,
    until morning, let us feast on love!
For my husband is not at home,
    he has gone on a long journey;
A bag of money he took with him,
    not till the full moon will he return home."
She wins him over by her repeated urging,
    with her smooth lips she leads him astray;
He follows her stupidly
    like an ox that is led to slaughter;
Like a stag that minces toward the net
    till an arrow pierces its liver;
Like a bird that rushes into a snare,
    unaware that its life is at stake. Pr 7:6-23

One can just hear some imaginative father reconstructing the scene for his son. Nothing more need be said. The final admonition does not carry the advice further except to add: "her house is made up of ways to the nether world, leading down into the chambers of death" (Pr 7:27). That may mean no more than that the adulterer can get syphilis.

The arrangement of the book would hint that these sayings arose in post-exilic Judaism. We cannot be more precise although there is a hint that this lecture is in some way connected with pagan cult. The woman is not just an adulteress; she is a "strange" or "stranger" woman; she has "fullfilled her vows." Apparently, she is a pagan wife who has sacrificed to some goddess of fertility and now is looking for a seducible Israelite to help her carry out the last act of her ritual.

These admonitions against adultery are found mostly in the first part of the book (cf. Pr 5:1-14; 6:20-35; 7:1-27; 9:13-18). Only one stray proverb on this topic occurs in all the rest of the work. It is squeezed in between the numerical riddles of Chapter 30 and simply observes: "Such is the way of an adulterous woman; she eats, wipes her mouth, and says, "I have done no wrong" (Pr 30:20).

The other unpleasent sayings about women are so shot through with humor that one can only laugh. The hen-pecked husband observes "For a persistent leak on a rainy day the match is a quarrelsome woman" (Pr 27:15; the same appears almost exactly in 19:13 from an earlier collection). His wife's tongue drives him to take refuge in the empty guest room even though he is the "master": "It is better to dwell in a corner of the housetop than in a roomy house with a quarrelsome woman" (Pr 21:9 and 27:15). He finally decides: "It is better to dwell in a wilderness than with a quarrelsome and vexatious wife" (Pr 21:19). There is even a resigned good humor in the married man's discovery that: "Like a golden ring in a swine's snout is a beautiful woman with a rebellious disposition" (Pr 11:22).

This is all that is said about "bad" women in the hundreds of proverbs in the book. There is certainly no prejudice in the "strange woman" sayings; that kind of woman, especially a pagan devotee, is bad for society and indeed the same can be found in the "international wisdom." The shrug of the shoulders' resignation of the ̲ ̲ ̲ ̲ ̲ ̲ ̲ ̲ ̲ ̲ ̲ ̲ ̲ ̲ ̲ understandable enough. Perhaps the

in life and that was that.

The sayings about the adulteress are a minor part of the book; the ribbing of nagging wives is infrequent. Both are quite common in the non-Biblical literature of the times. What is different about the Book of Proverbs is the counterpoised reflections on the Good Wife.

We have studied the "strange woman" in Proverbs 7. That is a non-religious essay on adultery, but it is embedded in a larger context that runs from Pr 5:1 to 7:27. Pr 5:1-14 is the usual instruction to a young man about avoiding adultery. It is balanced by advice to a young married man on what he should find at home that satisfies him.

> *Drink from your own cistern,*
> > *running water from your own well.*
> *How may your water sources be dispersed abroad,*
> > *streams of water in the streets?*
> *Let your fountain be yours alone,*
> > *not one shared with strangers.*
> *And have joy of the wife of your youth,*
> > *your lovely hind, your graceful doe.*
> *Her love will invigorate you always,*
> > *through her love you will flourish continually,*
> *When you lie down she will watch over you,*
> > *and when you awake, she will share your concerns;*
> > *wherever you turn, she will guide you,*

> *Why then, my son, should you go astray for another's*
> *wife*
> > *and accept the embraces of an adulteress? Pr 5:15-20*

The sudden shift to this delicate imagery is quite notable against the direct and earthy language which preceded it. Since the author found nothing about good wives in the international admonitions against adultery, he had to create his own beautiful, if somewhat obscure, pictures. The man, too, wants to be a life-giver; he expresses that under his image of the running water. His wife must be his alone, otherwise he is never certain that he is the life-giver. The wife of his youth gives him far more than any transient adulteress can give; she gives him not only children but a vigorous and satisfying life.

Then for the first time in these observations on life Yahweh is mentioned. He sees all, even the most intimate embraces.

> *For each man's ways are plain in the Lord's sight;*
> > *all their paths he surveys.*
> *By his own iniquities the wicked man will be caught,*
> > *in the meshes of his own sin he will be held fast.*
> *He will die from lack of discipline,*
> > *through the greatness of his folly he will be lost. Pr*
> *5:21:-23*

And so the young man is back to the need for the wisdom which his elders can give him. It is a discipline, but a discipline which finally uncovers for him the presense of God in the virtuous life and the self-made destruction which follows on folly.

I omit here any mention of Pr 8-9, though it too stands as a counterpoise to the whole discussion on the adulteress. However, that poet has carried his observations on the good married life into the realm of symbol and that demands a further treatment later in this book. I mention it here,

to indicate the the direction from which the symbol
move down from the rarified

12:4). A gra
virtue is covered with shame" (Pr 11.10,
half might be translated: "but aggressive men grasp
riches"—such are the vagaries of translations at times).
However, these are pedestrian observations that anyone
could make; the proverb-maker's real insight comes out in
such a saying as: "Home and possessions are an inheritance
from parents, but a prudent wife is from the Lord" (Pr 19:14
and cf. also Pr. 18:22). There is here a religious faith which
understands that love and marriage are a very chancy game
and a happy outcome is not due to any human prudence.

The final poem in the book is the hymn to the worthy
wife.

> *When one finds a worthy wife,*
> *her value is far beyond pearls. (Pr 31:10)*

This wife is no meek little house-person; she is an efficient
manager of a large household and business enterprises. She
runs a cloth-making business, she buys property and plants a
vineyard, she is happily busy at providing her house and
servants with all they need. She is the woman behind her
important husband in town.

> *She is clothed with strength and dignity,*
> *and she laughs at the days to come.*
> *She opens her mouth in wisdom*
> *and on her tongue is kindly counsel.*

She watches the conduct of her household,
   and eats not her food in idleness.
Her children rise up and praise her;
   her husband, too, extols her;
Many are the women of proven worth,
   but you have excelled them all.
Charm is deceptive and beauty fleeting;
   the woman who fears the Lord is to be praised.
Give her a reward of her labors,
   and let her works praise her at the city gates.

                                              Pr. 31:25-31

It is quite exceptional. No other literature has a similar poem in praise of a worthy wife. If we had only the laws to go on, even such enlightened laws as the Code of Hammurabi, we would never have suspected that a woman could fill a place like this in society. Yet Judith did, and she was very like this worthy wife. Two religious ideas come into the poem; the worthy wife "reaches out her hands to the poor"; and she is a woman "who fears the Lord." One can hardly imagine this robust woman quaking in fear before the Lord; indeed, the expression is one of the most frequently used terms in the book of Proverbs and says that the beginning of wisdom is a reverential attitude toward life and a fear of failing to see God in all its variegated forms. The woman who fears the Lord is a wise woman; and that is the highest accolade the Wise Man could bestow.

Note on Proverbs

The most meticulous commentator on the Book of Proverbs is William McKane, *Proverbs* (Philadelphia: Westminister, 1970). R.B.Y. Scott, *Proverbs, Ecclesiastes* (Anchor Bible, New York: Doubleday, 1965) is satisfactory, but not nearly so detailed or so sure in its perceptions. The variant translations I have given are from Scott.

---

2. The Sober Sided Sage

better moments the ...

Sirach but a revelation of the person of God. Wisdom is always "she," a lady who lives with God. Unlike Pr 5-9, however, these poems are dissociated from Ben Sirach's consideration of women as he knew them.

Jesus ben Sirach does not have a great deal to say about women in his lengthy book. Si 9:1-9 is the old warning against adultery, repeated in a pedestrian fashion. Si 25:12-26:18 is his one major treatise on women, good and bad. One is tempted to suspect that Sirach had two marriages, except that Proverbs had also balanced off good women against bad. There is a difference in tone; whereas the occasional comments about nagging wives in Proverbs are light and humorous, ben Sirach has failed to see the humor in a strident spouse. For him, "No venom is greater than that of a woman" (Si 25:14); "There is scarcely any evil like a woman" (Si 25-18). It must be understood that even ben Sirach does not mean that about women in general, but about wives who drive men crazy. Some later copyist added a verse which Sirach would have approved: "A strident, garrulous wife is like a trumpet sounding the charge; in a home like hers a man lives in the tumult of war" (Si 26:27 in the Lucian recension). Moreover, ben Sirach makes these comments without a single religious reflection and certainly without adducing any religious "principles" which justified him in thinking this is what women were by nature. It is in this context that we must understand his saying: "In woman was sin's beginning and because of her we all die." It sounds as though ben Sirach was blaming women for all sins in the world, and 1Tm 2:14 seems to confirm the idea that "original sin" came into the world through a woman. Whatever 1Tim may mean, Si 25:23 is simply an observation that a venemous, sullen, railing, evil wife is a source of sin for everybody who lives in the house with her. Sirach advises giving her her walking papers (Si 25:25), and perhaps he did. This attitude pervades most of ben Sirach's occasional comments on evil woman (cf. Si 7:19, 26; 19:2; 23:22; 28:15; 30:21; 31:28; 27:11; 41:20, 21: 42:6).

On the other hand, the praises of the good wife are expressed more delicately, with greater religious insight and with fewer words.

> *Happy the husband of a good wife,*
> *twice-lengthened are his days;*
> *A worthy wife brings joy to her husband,*
> *peaceful and full is his life.*
> *A good wife is a generous gift*
> *bestowed on him who fears the Lord;*
> *Be he rich or poor, his heart is content,*
> *and a smile is ever on his face. Si 26:1-4*

The recognition that a good wife is a gift of God apparently came down from the earlier saying in the book of Proverbs (cf. also Si 36:21-27; 40:19-23 where the same sentiment is expressed). In a later comment in this same chapter 26, ben Sirach likens the good wife to the sun rising in the Lord's heaven (Si 26:16); it also doesn't hurt if she is shaped like a woman (Si 26:18). Such a woman is indeed a prize.

> *Though any man may be accepted as a husband,*
> *yet one girl will be more suitable than another.*
> *A woman's beauty makes her husband's face light up,*
> *for it surpasses all else that charms the eye;*
> *And if, besides, her speech is kindly,*
> *his lot is beyond that of mortal men. Si 36:21-23*

Ben Sirach shows more social prejudice in his treatment of
daughters than of wives. The old man was a stern
_____ daughters were a worry

_and a j___g_

This is not very elevating; it has no speck of religious
sentiment. But then neither had the traditional piece of
advice to sons about avoiding adultery. It was simply a
record of what that society learned by experience. Nothing is
said about this being commanded by God; nothing is said
about God at all. It is hardly possible to say that this is the
teaching of the Bible on what we must do; it doesn't seem to
be anything more than what the social manners of the time
held as useful. Whether it was or was not is even beside the
point. Why it got into the Bible at all is more to the point.
Apparently, it was carried along by much more in the book
which was of supreme worth, as the great lyrical poem on
God in nature which follows in the 42nd chapter.

Note on Sirach

Sirach (or Ecclesiasticus, as the Greek name has it) is not
a book which is commented on frequently. John G. Snaith,
Ecclesiasticus (Cambridge Bible Commentary, London:
Cambridge University, 1974) is the latest. Si has a curious
history. It was written in Hebrew and then translated into
Greek. Rabbinic Judaism denounced the book and the
Hebrew copies were destroyed. A Hebrew copy showed up at

Qumran, dated from about 800 A.D., and then the copies were again destroyed about 1100 A.D. The Hebrew text remained unknown after that until a copy was discovered in Cairo in 1896 and later at Qumran. Some people obviously disliked Sirach with vigor, but the reasons are not clear even to Jewish commentators. It seems a very traditional Jewish view of life. The Greek text itself comes in several versions and I have quoted one of the variant translations.

---

3. The Love Song

The title of the book called the Canticle of Canticles means simply "the greatest song." Appropriately, it is a love song. Having said that, we are immediately bogged down in perplexities about this book. The words in the book indicate that some of the verses are spoken by a girl and some by a boy and some apparently by "we." The ancient Greek translation helped to clarify the dialoque by adding appropriate names for the speakers. In the same spirit some modern commentators have elaborated on the stage directions and turned the poems into a drama. The problem with such an approach is that no other drama appears in ancient Near Eastern literature; the only thing resembling drama is the cultic acting out of the myths, and the Canticle is definitely not a myth. Others have seen it as a collection of popular love songs, perhaps from a typical wedding celebration. Many passages do appear to be rather disconnected fragments of songs (cf., 6:11-22 and the whole ending in 8:8-14).

If a story line must be traced, the Canticle tells of a young girl who has fallen in love with a boy, that she wants to give herself to him completely, but he keeps disappearing and she must search him out before she can finally be united to him. However, complications arise when all the material is forced into this plot. There are those disconnected fragments mentioned before. Then "a king" is mentioned in

1:4 and 3:6-11. Some have supposed that a "king and queen
for a day" game is involved in the marriage ceremony such as
... celebrations. However, it is a

the story to smooth ...
tries to account for everything, the less the Canticle seems to
hold together.

The Canticle has most often been interpreted as a
parable of God's love for Israel. Such a view has a long
tradition in the theme of Yahweh's love for his faithless
spouse which Hosea, Jeremiah, Deutero-Isaiah and Ezechiel
preached. Perhaps the Canticle is such a parable. But, oddly,
God and Israel are never mentioned and certainly nothing is
said about a faithless lover, which is the theme of the
prophetic sayings. Nor are there any references to the
covenant, the Law, and the cult which are almost the
constants of Hebraic religion. If the Canticle is a parable to
us and to many generations before us, it apparently was not
so in the beginning. Somebody had to see that connection
because it isn't in the book. In fact, one might ask what is
religious about the Canticle.

For all such problems I have no answer. The least
exposed position seems to be that someone at some time
wrote or gathered a set of remarkably sensitive love poems.
The basic theme was the total commitment of the lovers to
one another. By "total" I mean "totally human." They range
from the delightfully erotic to the depth of identity.

> *I am a wall,*
>> *and my breasts are like towers,*
> *So now in his eyes I have become one to be welcomed.*
>> *Cant 8:10*

The only recurrent refrain which occurs introduces a note of prudence.

> *Do not rouse, do not stir up love*
> *before its own time. Cant 2:7; 3:5; 8:4*

And then there is thrown in a most arresting wisdom saying:

> *For stern as death is love,*
> *relentless as the nether world is devotion. Cant 8:6*

Death was often enough personified as a Hunter who eventually tracks down everyone. That is a cliché, however vivid. To see love in the same way is to make a superb act of faith in someone.

The poem is in the Bible and the community of Israel certainly saw in it something which expressed their religious view of life, whatever that view may have been. We grope for the insight which they accepted. Certainly, the poems began in a human way; they said: "This is what being totally in love can mean." Somehow that human experience was seen to have a religious point.

For our purposes one should note that this love affair was no brokered marriage. Being completely human meant being completely free; the girl chose her boy because she wanted him. It was accepted as right because it involved total commitment. Presumably such love affairs were approved in ancient Israel. Whatever our sober-sided research may say about the inequality of the marriage contract in ancient Israel, the popular imagination could see the picture presented in the Canticle as possible and desirable.

Note on Canticle of Canticles

To be honest, there is no definitive commentary on the Canticle and few that are truly insightful. The Jerome

Biblical Commentary and other such general works probably do as much for it as one can expect by listing the

You married women must obey your husbands, so that any of them who do not believe in the word of the gospel may be won over apart from preaching through their wives' conduct. They have only to observe the reverent purity of your way of life. The affectation of an elaborate hairdress, the wearing of golden jewelry, or the donning of rich robes is not for you. Your adornnment is rather the hidden character of the heart, expressed in the unfading beauty of a calm and gentle disposition. This is precious in God's eyes. The holy women of past ages used to adorn themselves in this way, reliant on God and obedient to their husbands—for example, Sarah, who was subject to Abraham and called him her master. You are her children when you do what is right and let no fears alarm you.

You husbands, too, must show consideration for those who share your lives. Treat women with respect as the weaker sex, heirs just as much as you to the gracious gift of life. If you do so, nothing will keep your prayers from being answered. 1 P 3:1-7

Such is the New American Bible's translation and it follows the same pattern as found in most English translations of the past four centuries. One may legitimately ask whether it has become entangled in some unexamined prejudices. The net effect of such key words as "must obey," "weaker sex,"

"obedient to their husbands" is to shift the emphasis to a
teaching on the subordination of women to men. In all
honesty, this is not the intent of the original text in the Greek
language. A somewhat duller, but more literal translation
would read:

> *Similarly (to what you experienced in your conversion),
> wives take their place toward their husbands in order
> that, even if they disbelieve the word (of the Gospel), they
> will be gained over through the way of living of their
> wives even apart from the word (when) they consider the
> faultless and respectful way of living (of their wives). 1 P
> 3:1-2*

> *Similarly (to the way Abraham respected Sarah),
> husbands live with their wives in understanding, giving
> honor as to the weaker wifely vessel and as to ones fellow-
> chosen for the gift of life, in order that your prayers may
> not be blocked. 1 P 3:7*

The "must obey" has disappeared. "Must" was not in the
Greek text to begin with and could be read in only on the
presupposition that the statement set down a rule. "Obey"
has been transformend into a simple "take their place." All
languages have a common word for obey; Paul uses it of
slaves and children, but not of wives. So also Peter seems to
be relying on a new Christian vocabulary in using a very odd
word to describe the relationship of wives to husbands. The
word basically connotes a proper order in accepting a status
which God has assigned to one. It is used of Christ in various
texts such as 1Cor 15:25, 27; Heb 2:7; Ep 1:22 and 1P 3:22.
    This change in the translation and the understanding
of wise reflections which we have been using enables us to see
the whole passage in a new light. The Wise Men of the Old
Testament had many sayings about family life, but none of
them ever said that a wife must obey a husband. Presumably
that was the normal ordering of things, but nobody ever tried

to make a religious maxim out of it. If any insight was to be gotten out of the husband-wife relationship, it had to start ⟨...⟩ translation "take their place" implies, it

⟨illegible obscured text⟩

were making themselves obnoxious to government officials by ignoring the law (1P 2:13-15). Things go much better and in a more Christian way among those who respect officials (1P 2:16-17). He has observed that some Christian slaves no longer want to obey their masters or to obey only reasonable masters (1P 2:18-20). He can see good in obeying un-reasonable masters; Jesus suffered unjustly and there must be some value in that. He ends with the fact of experience which they all know: "At one time you were straying like sheep, but now you have returned to the Shepherd, the Guardian of your souls" (1P 2:25).

Similarly, he looked at the marriages of Christian women to pagans and saw that some of these marriages were being torn apart because the wife was parading in all of her finery to the Christian meetings and affronting her husband by doing so (1P 3:3). On the other hand were those strong Christian wives who simply went about being better wives since they had become Christians. They preached the Gospel very effectively in this way. He saw the same thing happening in the lives of Christian men who had a Christian wife. It was far better for them to respect their wives as equals in the Christian vocation, called to a new life just as much as the man, than to harp on wifely virtues. It certainly made for a more prayerful attitude at home (1P 3:7).

These were the facts. The importance of the author's observation, however, was in the interpretation which he gave to the facts. Married women took their proper place at home as Christians "in order that" their husbands might be won over to the Gospel through their wives' conduct (1P 3:1). Husbands did live with their Christian wives in mutual understanding "in order that" their prayers might not be hindered. Something different was going on at home since one or both had been converted. There was a new purpose to life, an understanding that the Gospel was being preached in these homely ways between husband and wife. Perhaps externally life went on much as before—except for those parading wives. But it went on with a new understanding that brought a greater unity.

The previous sections on citizens and slaves had looked at life in precisely this way. The good Christian had been a good citizen before his conversion; he continued to be but for a different reason. "In a word, live as servants of God" (1P 2:16). The slave who had put up with a harsh master before his conversion continued to put up with him afterwards but for a new reason. "When a man can suffer injustice and endure hardship through his awareness of God's presence, this is the work of grace in him" (1P 2:19). Christianity did not add new rules; neither did it preach social revolution. It accepted the customary ways of life, but it changed the people who continued to live according to the customs. So in our passage the point is not that "wives must obey their husbands." Everybody in that society expected that they would. The point was that a Christian woman found something new in the customary way of acting, a missionary work of evangelization that made her an apostle at home.

Seen in this way the basic message is truly sensible and uplifting. However, it must be admitted that the sentences still carry with them a certain measure of social prejudice. There is an international saying in Persian, Greek and rabbinic literature in which a man gives thanks that he is not a woman or a slave. Women are here called "the weaker wifely vessel," a more earthy expression than our contemporary "weaker sex." The man is expected to lead the family prayers; the wife is to do her preaching by "the reverent purity of your way of life." Make of it what you will. It was a

way of life which experience at that time said was a good way
~f life. It was not a conclusion that things must be done thus
[text obscured] ~ion at all but the simple

[text obscured]

The Epistles of J... ,
York: Doubleday, 1964). Unfortunately, Reicke adopts
usual approach of demonstrating that women were inferior
in Roman and Jewish law and then must consider this
passage a "time-conditioned conclusion." As justification of
my translation of 1P 3:1-7, I refer the reader to Nigel Turner,
Grammatical Insights Into the New Testament (Edinburgh:
Clark, 1965), 165 and the article on *hypotassomai* in the
Theological Dictionary of the New Testament, I, 776.

---

5. Paul and Women

a. Preliminary Remarks

Before venturing into the shoal waters of Paul, let me
say a word about what I intend to do and how I intend to do
it. The only extended statements of Paul on women occur in
1 Cor 7, a general treatment of various problems concerning
tensions in the Christian community of Corinth circa 54
A.D.; 1 Cor 11, a statement about the place of women in that
Christian assembly; 1 Cor 14:34-36 on women speaking in
public meetings; and two passages on "household duties" in
Col 3:18-19 and Ep 5:22-33. Apart from this, women are
mentioned only in passing in such texts as Rm 7:2; 1 Cor 5:1;
Gal 4:4, 26, and these present no considerable difficulties.

From the bits of biographical data scattered in New Testament writings, it is evident that Paul was on good terms with many women and acknowledged with sensitivity that they were among his most loyal and appreciated co-workers.

I shall consider the major passages mentioned above, using the method of wisdom techniques which have been my principal diagnostic tool throughout. Paul on his own word was educated as a Pharisee in the school of Gamaliel in Jerusalem. A broad stream of tradition connects the Wise Men of the Old Testament to the later rabbinic literature of the Midrashim, the Targumim, the Talmud, etc. It is certainly not all of one piece and its methods changed as social, political and religious needs changed. But one thread does run through it all; the whole approach was earthy, tied to concrete facts and always seeking insight behind the real-life experiences. The technical data establishing that Paul in his methodology is in the mainstream of this way of looking at life is beyond the scope of this chapter and I have detailed it elsewhere. However, the validity of these interpretations can be measured to a certain extent by how well they clarify otherwise obscure texts.

b. Paul on the Tensions in Corinth—1Cor 7

Paul's essay on the tensions in Corinth is notoriously overlaid with difficulties in translation from early times. The chapter begins in the New American Bible: "A man is better off having no relations with a woman." This is not exactly what the original text said; as a matter of fact, it is a paraphrase of an ancient Latin version. The hand of a Roman administrator is apparent in making an ethical imperative out of what seems to have been a simple observation: "it is beautiful for a man not to touch womenfolk." The new Christians in Corinth seem to have been amazed by the discovery that living a chaste life could be beautiful. The translations, however, seem to have taken off

in the direction that there was something bad about sex and
to have ended up almost inevitably with a put down of

necessity of having sexual relations and of having time ...
for prayer (1Cor 7:1-7); they were concerned about who could
or could not get married (1Cor 7:8-11); they argued about
freedom to leave an impossible spouse (1Cor 7:12-15); they
profited by people who had remained virgins and in the
service of the church, but they would not let them get out of
the situation (1Cor 7:36-40). In all of these matters the basic
problem was of freedom versus necessity. Paul threw in a few
of his own examples. What should a Christian slave do? Was
he bound to use every means to become a freedman? What of
the circumcised Christian who looked like a Jew at the
public baths? Should he seek out a doctor to restore his
"uncircumcision" (1Cor 7:15-24)? Most of all, Paul called
attention to the self-imposed necessity of busyness (1Cor
7:25-35). It affected every class in the Corinthian church,
whether virgins in church service or married people. That
this is the central concern of the chapter can be seen by
looking at the contrasting words with which the chapter is
loaded: "not bound," "free," "freeman," "free of all
worries," "no restrictions" as against "bound", "fettered",
"slavery", "schema."

Paul's insight into all of this is that God is a God of
peace and wants his children to be serene whatever
necessities of life may hold them. The cords that bind, bind
only when we pull on them. So he says: "Were you a slave
when your call came? Give it no thought. Even supposing
you could go free, you would be better off making the most of

your slavery. The slave called in the Lord is a freedman of the Lord, just as the freeman who has been called is a slave of Christ." Once Paul has made clear that freedom is first of all an internal condition, he can say quite bluntly: "The general rule is that each one should lead the life the Lord has assigned him, continuing as he was when the Lord called him."

The key to the chapter is in a series of exuberant paradoxes which certainly should not be interpreted as sober-sided rules.

> *I tell you, brothers, the times are tight.*
> *It remains that those who have wives should be as if they did not have them,*
> > *those weeping as not weeping;*
> > *those rejoicing as not rejoicing;*
> > *those buying as not possessing;*
> > *and those who use the world as not abusing it;*
> *for the tight pattern of this world is passing.*
> *I want you to be unbound:*
> > *The unmarried man binds himself down by the Lord's busyness*
> > *how he may please the Lord;*
> > *The married man binds himself down by the world's busyness*
> > *how he may please his wife—and he has become bound;*
> > *All—the wife, the husband and the virgin bind themselves down*
> > *by the Lord's busyness in order that these things may become*
> > *holy both in body and spirit.*
> > *(The wife binds herself down by the world's busyness*
> > *how she may please her husband).*
> *I say this for your own good,*
> > *not to throw a noose over your heads,*
> > *but that you may arrange your life in good order*

*and with a constancy toward the Lord without
distraction. 1Cor 7:32-35 in my own translation.*

experience come under ...

trap in each. Those who are fervent are trapping themselves
in a rarified asceticism which will exceed their strength;
those who are struggling to be virgins or widows may be
demanding more of themselves than they are capable of;
those who are trying to patch up a bad marriage with a
pagan because they think that they must sacrifice everything
to do so may be simply destroying the peace which God
wants all of us to have; slaves may be spending their energies
trying to become free when they should be devoting those
energies to acting as free Christians; virgins are an obvious
benefit for the Corinthian community both because of their
example and the work they do for the church; but they may
be trapping themselves in a self-made imperative to conform
to public opinion. Most of all, everyone, the virgins as well
as the married folk, may be binding themselves down by a
quota of productivity—and it matters not whether it is the
Lord's work or the world's work—and so losing the freedom
which rightly belongs to them. They should have a "live for
the day" attitude since all this rigid system of the world in
which we live is already passing away.

The insight is consistent in that it makes no distinction
between men and women. Both have the same freedom as
they have the same temptations. Married men are as much
tempted to these rigidities as are married women. So are
virgins, male or female.

c. Covered Women—1Cor 11:2-16

In 1 Cor 11:2-16 Paul speaks of women wearing some sort of head-covering at the Christian assemblies. The passage can be made dreadfully bad simply by turning it into a selective "principle-conclusion" statement; i.e. women are inferior to men; therefore, they must wear something on their heads to show it.

The passage in question is only part of a larger section which deals with abuses at the celebration of the Eucharist. The abuses were truly enormous. Some men first visited the pagan shrines and had sexual intercourse with the temple prostitutes; then they came down from the pagan temple and shared in the body of Christ. Some were such strict Christians that they not only abstained from going to the pagan temples; they refused to eat with Christians who had bought some meat which had been offered to idols and then sold in the common markets. At some of the celebrations of the Eucharist the rich took a place to themselves, scorned the poor, and got into loud and drunken arguments with one another over the Lord's table. In all these matters Paul first lays the facts on the line. Then he points out the horrible lack of faith understanding in such conduct. Finally, he points to good Christians whose actions reveal the true beauty of the realities. He does not say that the good Christians are acting in the only way that is acceptable; he looks at what they are doing and interprets what it says about the dignity of men and women who are "in Christ."

Among the ways of acting which had caused disturbance in the Christian community was a new trend among some women to come to the Eucharist celebrations without dressing up for the occasion. Social custom among both Greeks and Jews dictated that women should wear some sort of head-covering when they appeared in public. The custom was apparently of long standing and well-observed. So Paul notes at the beginning that he is simply handing on a tradition which existed in the churches, and at the end he mentions again that this is a custom in all the churches,

European as well as those in Asia Minor. It is important to
note that Paul is not making up any new rules. It was
.......................they seemed to have changed the

convention which bespeaks an order in creation. Christ is the
"head." All Christians know that, and it gives them their
own dignity. "I want you to know that the head of every man
is Christ, the head of a woman is her husband, and the head
of Christ is the Father." "Head" doesn't mean "boss"; it
must be taken in Paul's usual sense of the one who gives
power and life. Now Paul is aware of a visual picture in this.
When Christian men get up in the assembly of the faithful to
pray or "prophecy," they stand boldly without a prayer
shawl or a hat. Paul sees it as a sign of Christian fearlessness
in proclaiming the Gospel. Their wives can be proud of
them. "Any man who prays or prophesies with his head
covered brings shame upon his head" and "A man, on the
other hand, ought not to cover his head, because he is the
image of God and the reflection of his glory."

If a woman prays or prophesies in church, she ought to
keep her head covered. Paul says if she were to act otherwise
she would be acting as badly as the doxies in the street who
went around with shaven heads. So what we have thus far is
simply an attempt to see what a Christian could discern
behind the usual social practises.

But having gotten off on the tack of talking about the
image of God which is within us, particularly within the
male, Paul became involved in a consciousness that he also
had to say something about the image of God in the woman.
Woman's place in church was to reflect the image of God in
her husband who fearlessly proclaimed his faith, yet she also

reflected the power of God. "Power" was not only the power
to preach, but also the power to give life. Paul calls attention
to the obvious fact that men cannot even come into the world
without women. But perhaps he has in mind that power to
give life in the Gospel which 1 Peter had mentioned.
Certainly, women have their own power. In one of his most
baffling one-liners, Paul says: "For this reason a woman
ought to have an *exousia* over her head because of the
angels." I leave the crucial word untranslated rather than
mangle it by some such translation as "a sign of
submission." *Exousia* literally means *power, authority*. It is
used many times in the New Testament, though it is difficult
to say what it means here, except that we must preserve the
basic idea of authority. In the Asian cities of the Roman
Empire coins were authorized which had on them a figure of
the patron goddess of the city. She always had a distinctive
headdress or crown. This was called an *exousia*, the sign of
her authority. Apparently in a flight of fancy Paul pictured
Christian women, the life-givers, with their modest headdress appearing to the angels as goddesses. The explanation
is not as solid as I would like it to be; however, it does take
into account the essential meaning of the word and has some
visual evidence to back it up.

Having gotten thus far, Paul has vindicated power and
authority for both men and women. Both are images of God.
"In the same way that woman was made from man, so man is
born of woman; and all is from God." Yet there is a certain
"proper place" for each, and this is what he tries to read into
the social customs. Women of the time wore their hair long
and gloried in it. For Corinthian men it was dishonorable to
wear their hair long. Paul does not argue that a certain
hairstyle is required; he simply cites the custom. At the end
he adds a rather petulant word that he will not argue the
point; the custom prevails in all the churches and people get
along very well when the custom is observed.

The important thing to note for our purposes is that
Paul is not imposing rules on the Corinthian community.
The customs already existed. Paul was not adverse to

changing customs. As a Jewish boy he had learned to pray with his head covered. He accepted the quite different

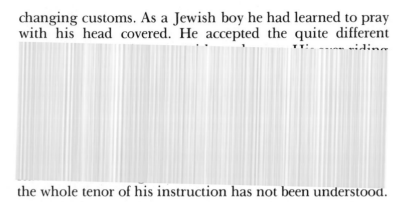

the whole tenor of his instruction has not been understood.

d. Order in Family Life—Col 3:18-4:1 and Ep 5:22-6:9

Col 3:18-4:1 and Ep 5:22-6:9 draw a picture of a well-ordered and kindly family life. Both passages have lists of people involved and both are arranged the same way.

1. Wives—"obey" your husbands (Col 3:18; Ep 5:22)
2. Husbands—love your wives (Col 3:19; Ep 5:25)
3. Children— obey your parents (Col 3:20; Ep 6:1)
4. Fathers—do not nag your children (Col 3:21);
      do not anger your children (Ep 6:4)
5. Slaves—obey your masters (Col 3:22-25; Ep 6:5-8)
6. Slave-owners—deal justly with your slaves (Col 4:1);
      stop threatening them (Ep 6:9)

Similar lists in this same order can be found in the non-literary papyri of Egypt and in the Greek and Roman moral writers, such as Epictetus and Marcus Aurelius. Scholars call such lists by the German word *haustafeln* and seek an understanding of the author's intention by studying the special literary form. The study does not seem to throw any great light on what Paul has to say. Every society sets down orderly ways of acting which express how the human experience has summarized what seems to work best, and there is nothing very religious in this.

So the real message of Paul cannot be found by considering these as his "rules" since he did not create them. His distinctive contribution must be sought in the insights which he brings to the orderly ways of acting in society. That children need discipline and a good education is both an imposed necessity and a wish everywhere and at all times. Paul goes beyond this to expound why children should obey and why parents should provide. His insight is expressed in pithy phrases such as "in the Lord." Thus children should obey "as the acceptable way in the Lord."

What did such a saying mean in practical terms in Christian communities of Asia Minor circa 62 A.D.? The children had heard about "the *Lord* Jesus" from an early age. He was the "lord of history," as we say, or the Father who had arranged all things for our good. The orderly fulfillment of chores and the showing of reverence toward parents was an acting out of respect for the beauty of the God of Order who created human society to be what it was at its best.

Slaves, whom Paul advised to remain slaves as a general rule (cf. 1Cor 7:21), should sanctify their work by carrying out orders cheerfully and taking pride in honest workmanship because the Master in heaven had appointed them to this work in his world. The only true freedom came from within when they recognized that God had given each a work to do and they could accept it freely or simply drudge along under necessity.

It is in this context, however uncomfortable it may be to us, that we must look at what is said about wives. First of all, the very brief statements about wives "obeying" must be interpreted in the same way as that word is used in 1 Peter. Although children and slaves are called to obey, wives are "submissive"; i.e., they accept their proper role in the family. The same peculiar word is used by Paul as is used in 1Peter when wives are mentioned. The word does not imply that a husband's word is final in the household or that a wife must

put up no arguments, or that she is unequal, etc. Paul simply
says that wives should freely embrace the proper role which

acceptance of a given role as a free choice, however it may be
fulfilled in any definite society, can she advance along the
road to Christian dignity.

Ep 5:22-23 has an extraordinary expansion on these
succinct sayings about husbands and wives. The usual
saying about wives being submissive is expanded by
"because the husband is head of his wife just as Christ is head
of his body the church, as well as its savior. As the church
submits to Christ, so wives should submit to their husbands
in everything." Now if one considers the actual situation of
the churches to which the letter was addressed, it does not
appear that these wifely churches were submitting to Christ
very well at all. Ephesus was no immaculate bride, meekly
silent before her Lord. The Ephesian church in 62 A.D. (or
possibly a whole group of churches) was torn by dissension.
It pained Paul no end. He had dreamed of a world united,
one in which there were no barriers between Jews and
Gentiles, Greek and barbarians, slave or free, men or women
(cf. Gal 3:28). Now he found his churches tearing themselves
apart. A lesser man might have despaired; Paul was a man of
faith who could read what was really going on here. The
unity really did exist; it was struggling to make itself evident
despite human weaknesses. What was most important for
the readers of this Epistle to discover was that it was Christ
who gave them unity, not their own clever arguments which
were expected to silence the opposition.

So also husbands were to love their wives as Christ loved

the church. Christ did not love the church as though it were a perfect woman and neither could husbands reserve their love until the moment when their wives became perfect. "He gave himself up for her to make her holy, purifying her in the bath of water by the power of the word, to present to himself a glorious church, holy and immaculate without stain or wrinkle or anything of that sort." The power to unify, whether in marriage or in the churches, came not from human beings but from Christ the Head; yet one had to understand that the involved human beings had to prepare themselves for receiving such beauty by taking their proper stance before God.

The essential comparison here is one taken from the Old Testament. Israel was God's bride. He had chosen her freely that she might manifest the holiness of her spouse, God. As the story of Israel unfolded, it was evident that she advanced toward this happy state not by perfect conformity, but by her many falls and disgraceful ways as a prostitute. Yet she always remained God's bride, and she was conscious of it through the centuries. That held the Chosen People together. The book of Isaiah had strongly interpreted this faith in God the savior, particularly in the Servant Poem of Is 53 where God sends another servant to his servant Israel to redeem her from her shamefulness and make a holy and sanctifying people. This is precisely what Paul sees Christ doing in the church.

But then Paul shifts to another image from the tradition. The whole business of men and women being different had haunted the human race for an explanation from the beginning. As the experience was summarized in Gen 2-3, the Hebrew had found married life a most mysterious as well as a most satisfying experience. He noted, as we note, that children want to grow up and become independent. And then just when independence from parents was somewhat achieved, a man freely tied himself down again to a woman. Something inside him said that he was incomplete without her. He could not be like God all by himself. So the author of Gn 2-3 added a footnote to his story

[illegible obscured text] of Eve from Adam; "That is why a man

himself. Observe that no one ever hates [illegible]

nourishes it and takes care of it as Christ cares for the church—for we are members of his body. 'For this reason a man shall leave his father and mother, and shall cling to his wife, and the two shall be made one.' "

Now if one looks at this expansion of the usual saying that husbands should love their wives, one can see the realities of Christian marriages as well as the use of symbolic figures intertwining and mutually enriching. Although the text abounds in "shoulds," it is not really a set of rules which is being proposed. Certainly the quoted Genesis text was never understood as a rule that husband and wife should cling together, but an observation that they tended to do this because God made them that way. So also this text penetrates into the reality which lies behind ways of acting which are often very beautiful though sometimes so disfiguring that the wrinkles show. Christ works to make the church "holy and immaculate without stain or wrinkle or anything of that sort." If Christians would only look at the glorious possibility in their marriages, they would be spurred on to live up to them. That, after all, is the ultimate imperative.

For our purposes, we should note that Paul has here for once cleared up what he means by saying that wives should be submissive. First of all, "submissive" means accepting one's proper role in creation, especially in the creation which sanctifies. In this passage it is the wife who is the sanctified; however, in a somewhat similar cultic expression in 1Cor 7:14 it is either the wife or the husband who is the sanctifier in mixed marriages. "The unbelieving husband is consecrated by his believing wife; the unbelieving wife is consecrated by her husband. If it were otherwise, your children should be unclean; but as it is, they are holy." The sanctifying power could not be confined to one sex.

One may object that Paul never says that husbands should be submissive to wives, but only to Christ. On the other hand, he never says that wives should love their husbands. One cannot learn much from such omissions. They testify to the incompleteness of all these pictures. As the Corinthian text indicates, either the husband or the wife could be the sanctifier. In the Ephesian text he has simply used the normal pattern of Christian life. No more can be drawn from it than that.

Note on Paul

For technical explanations to this somewhat unusual approach to the Pauline sayings see James A. Fischer, "Pauline Literary Forms and Thought Patterns," CBQ 39 (1977), 209-23; "Ethics and Wisdom," CBQ 40 (1978, July issue); "I Cor 7:8-24—Marriage and Divorce," BR 23 (1978, to be published), "Paul on Virginity," The Bible Today 7 (1974), 1633-38. Among the commentators whom I find most perspicacious on these passages are C.K. Barrett, *A Commentary on the First Epistle to the Corinthians* (New York: Harper and Row, 1968) and Markus Barth, *Ep 4-6* (Anchor Bible, New York: Doubleday, 1974).

---

6. The Pastor's Point

The two Epistles to Timothy and the one to Titus have long been called "Pastoral Epistles." They are more concerned about practical problems in the church than most of the other writings which have Paul's names on them.

Today a tendency exists to consider them letters by an
unknown author to Pauline churches after the

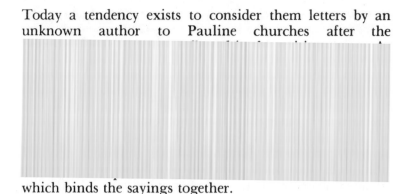

which binds the sayings together.

a. Women as Teachers—1Tm 2:8-15

*It is my wish, then, that in every place the men shall offer
prayers with blameless hands held aloft, and be free from
anger and dissension. Similarly, the women must deport
themselves properly. They should dress modestly and
quietly, and not be decked out in fancy hair styles, gold
ornaments, pearls or costly clothing; rather, as becomes
women who profess to be religious, their adornment
should be good deeds. A woman must learn in silence
and be completely submissive. I do not permit a woman
to act as a teacher, or in any way to have authority over a
man; she must be quiet. For Adam was created first, Eve
afterward; moreover, it was not Adam who was deceived
but the woman. It was she who was led astray and fell
into sin. She will be saved through childbearing,
provided she continues in faith and love and holiness—
her chastity, of course, being taken for granted.*

Before we begin to resent the injunctions in this
passage, let us establish some ways in which we shall go
about understanding the text. Let us presume first that the
Pauline author is trying to give an insight into existing

customs and secondly that his insight proceeds from the Yahwist's story of the creation of Adam and Eve. The presumptions are reasonable. The old Jewish custom was that only men prayed aloud in the synagogue and that only men studied Torah at home. There is ample evidence for this in rabbinic sources. We have no great evidence that the Christian communities continued the practices, but 1Cor 14:34-36, 1P 3:1-7 and the *haustafeln* to a lesser degree point in that direction. Only 1Cor 11:5 which speaks of women prophesying in the Christian assembly gives a hint that women were beginning to talk up publicly. In Tt 2:4 widows are urged to be "good teachers of younger women" but only by their example. So it would seem reasonable to suppose that the social custom of the Jews persisted even though it was being mildly challenged. The passage we are considering would not exist if there had not been some discussion about it going on.

Secondly, it cannot be seriously questioned that Gn 2:18-24 is the opening insight of 1Tm 2:8-15 since verse 13 alludes to it specifically. Gn 2-3 is a rather paradoxical and ironic view of the human condition; the male seems to have all power in his hands, but he does not have the power to give life by himself. Adam is not a complete man without Eve; he will surrender father and mother and give away his youthful independence to become "one self" with his life-giving wife. Such is the paradox as the Wise Man expressed it in an aside in Gn 2:24, and that saying dominates all the New Testament reflections on marriage.

Now if this be the essential thought, the passage falls into place. The men offer prayers; no point is made about that since it is accepted custom. The author wishes that they do it with blameless hands and a heart free from anger and dissension. Women deport themselves modestly, not with ostentatious dress; the author hopes that it will be good deeds which are their ornament. "A woman must learn in silence in her proper stance (our old word *hypotassomai* is used here as a noun). I do not permit a woman either to teach or domineer over a man, but to be in silence" (vv. 11-12 in my

own translation). The Pauline author has not set up a rule;
⸺⸺⸺⸺ ⸺⸺⸺ The question is what meaning a
⸺⸺⸺⸺⸺⸺⸺⸺⸺⸺⸺⸺⸺⸺⸺⸺ ⸺⸺⸺⸺ first.

author of 1Tm to add. ⸺⸺⸺⸺⸺,
deceived, but the woman. It was she who was led astray and
fell into sin." In the Pauline comment in Rm 5:12 it was:
"through one man sin entered the world." The ancient
comment in Gn 2 on the sharing of God's power by the lord
of creation and the mother of all living stressed the
interdependence of the sexes, not their subordination. Yet
there is an order for the *ish*, the male, and the *ishah*, the
female. "She will be saved through child-bearing." The
male will be saved through the sweat of his brow (Gn 3:19).
That could have been said if the context had concerned men.
However, the passage concerns how women should appear
in modest dress. So the author adds, lest he be trapped into
approving any child-bearing, "provided she continues in
faith and love and holiness—her chastity, of course, being
taken for granted."

One may object that this is a white-washing the text. It is
not my intention to do so. The customs are undoubtedly
discriminatory, as we are inclined to look at such things. But
the point of the passage is not primarily to canonize the
custom as an immutable law; it is to grasp an insight into the
existing custom. After nineteen centuries we hope that our
social customs reflect more of the dignity of men and women
than did theirs. It is not a self-evident state of affairs, nor are
our reasons for our customs or changes of custom entirely
clear. The author of 1Tm was more concerned about his
insight into the nature of human beings as images of God
than about an action program. Subsequent generations of

Christians canonized the Biblical insights into the then prevailing customs as the word of God. That has not happened to our insights or principles as yet.

b. Widows as Church Workers—1Tm 5:3-16

The instruction on widows in 1Tm 5:3-16 does not add much to our project; it is as uninspiring as a set of union regulations on retirement. It contains no deep religious insights. So we can look at it rather dispassionately.

In Judaism widows were usually provided for by their families. It was a sacred obligation. When family help failed, the Jewish community provided. The evidence is clear that Jews took a very serious view about the community's obligation to provide and that in the Jerusalem of the first century a well-organized system of financial aid to widows existed. The Christian churches seem to have adopted the system. (cf. Ac 6:1). 1Tm 5:3-8 stresses the family and community obligation.

However, among these church supported widows were some who were "enrolled" and paid salaries for services they performed. The work is described as caring for children (not their own), taking care of Christian visitors, making house calls and a generic "good works." It is understandable enough that abuses crept into such work. 1Tm 5:11-16 scores young widows who have been hired for the job, but have proved to be lazy, gossipy, suspected of adultery before and of looking for another man now, and (possibly) of distorting the Gospel teaching. It lays down a rule that henceforth such widows must be sixty years old and screened for good reputations and good works.

There is nothing anti-feminist in these prudential rules learned from sad experience. The same emerges in the early experience about promoting men to be "bishops" and deacons. The list of qualifications (1Tm 3:1-13) implies that some of the early ones had been drunks, brawlers, poor fathers and greedy.

Two rather minor observations may be made for our
~~~~se. First. in this passage we are dealing with
~~~~~~~~~~~~~~~~~~~~~~~~~~~~~~~~~~~~~ ~~~mined were

they were ~~~~~~~~ ~~~~~~

c. Deaconesses—1Tm 3:11

In a section dealing with the qualifications for
"bishops" and deacons (1Tm 3:1-13) a curious phrase
occurs. "The women likewise should be honorable, not
slanderous, sober, reliable in everything." The next verse
says that "deacons should be the husband of one wife," and
verse 11 is often interpreted of the deacon's wife. However,
this is a curious way to say such a thing. The qualities are
described before the deacon's wife is mentioned. Verse 10 had
spoken about a period of probation for deacons and then
verse 11 is introduced: "The women likewise . . . ." One is
tempted to argue that women likewise were deacons. After
all, deacons were primarily engaged in social services and the
salaried widows of 1Tm 5:9-10 were similarly employed.
However, one verse so curiously suspended in the text cannot
lead to an absolute judgment.

d. Other Sayings

2Tm 3:6 refers to "silly women." It is not a blanket
judgment on all women. Indeed, it occurs in a scathing
denunciation of men—"treacherous, reckless, pompous,
lovers of pleasure rather than of God" (v. 4). They "worm

their way into homes and make captives of silly women burdened with sins and driven by desires of many kinds." It is hardly the kind of text to cause problems to either feminists or anti-feminists. Titus 2:3-5 has some advice for older women which fits into what has already been said in this chapter without adding anything new. "Similarly, the older women must behave in ways that befit those who belong to God. They must not be slanderous gossips or slaves to drink. By their good example they must teach the younger women to love their husbands and children, to be sensible, chaste, busy at home, kindly, submissive to their husbands. Thus the word of God will not fall into disrepute." Granted the pattern of life at that time, one cannot fault it. It is conscious that such normal ways of acting must be interpreted by Christian women as befitting those who belong to God.

In summary, the Pastoral Epistles both continue the ancient tradition of reading meaning into existing conditions and manifest a different approach of making regulations for an organized society of Christians. When the passages, such as 1Tm 2:8-15, seek to interpret the meaning of the customs, they go back to the Genesis account of the curious relationship that exists between men and women as interdependent images of God. Titus 2:3 probably hints of the same thing by saying that "older women must behave in ways that befit those who belong to God" though there are Christian overtones of redemption in this. At any rate, it is the connection with God which is the basis of the insight. On the other hand, the regulations about widows and deaconesses or deacon's wives simply state administrative decisions which arose out of hard experience. They have no deep theological meaning.

Note on the Pastoral Epistles

Full length commentaries on the Pastoral Epistles are

somewhat rare. The work of Martin Dibelius and Hans
~~~~~~~ *The Pastoral Epistles* (Philadelphia: Fortress,

villain of some feminists. ~~~~~~~~
enemies. It is not fair to quote him out of context, either the
context of what he wrote or the context of his own times. It is
especially unfair to quote him in disregard of the point he
was making.

That Paul accepted the social customs of his times and
that these customs were sometimes anti-feminist in our
present understanding (or in the understanding of some of
us) is beyond doubt. To say that they were stated by Paul to
make the point that women are inferior is to do violence to
his sayings. Societies have existed for a long time with
women in various positions from chattels to matriarchs.
They all seem to work to a certain extent. Women's rights do
not seem to be inalienably granted either by a natural law or
by a divine mandate. Neither do men's. The Bible in general
and Paul in particular are not really concerned about human
rights. However we dislike the fact, Christianity did not set
out to change social conditions. Slavery, war, some rather
despicable governments, unjust taxes, etc. were accepted
simply as facts. Christianity concentrated first on the
changed status of the individual in the light of the redeeming
death and resurrection of Christ. Resurrection was important as the clearest example of what life could be like.
Customs were interpreted to bring out the new potential
which could be discerned. This was the real value of the
Biblical approach.

We live in a changing society. The changes in women's
rights cannot be validated nor condemned by citing isolated

Biblical texts. The rights extend from substantial things such as equal pay for equal work to the abacadabra of "chairperson" and "Ms," etc. They will need to be gained from other persons who now claim whatever rights may be at stake. The essential question is: what is the motivation behind such seeking of rights? If it is resentment, a desire to have what others possess, a determination to be considered capable of anything, then the potential revealed in the quest is frightening and degrading. Only if the movement reveals hitherto unsuspected glories can it lift us all higher. Paul at least sought that kind of insight.

7. The Legal Status of Women

It would be helpful if the Bible had left us a brief statement on the legal rights and restrictions of women. Unfortunately, it does not do so. The New Testament has little by way of legal enactments about women and the Old Testament, whose Mosaic Code is full of laws, has only some few disconnected and often obscure regulations. For the sake of convenience I shall deal with these under the general titles of property rights, divorce and social customs.

The property rights seem central to such laws as do concern women. In the tribal society from which Israel sprang the property belonged to the tribe and always returned within it during the jubilee year. Although there are no explicit laws regulating inheritance, in fact the control of property was handed on from father to son. Daughters rarely inherited anything. Nb 27:8-11 has a stray law in which daughters can inherit where there is no son, but it is late and even then the property had to remain within the tribe; cf. Nb 36:6-9. Widows did not inherit their husband's property and were dependent on their own fathers or eldest sons. Women might, it seems, have property in their own name from a marriage gift (dowry as such is never mentioned). There were no laws relating to their making of contracts, such as appear in the Mesopotamian codes or in the post-exilic community of heretical Jews at Elephantine

then has a few regulations which limit the man's freedom in divorcing. Dt 24:1-4, the most famous passage, begins, "When a man after marrying a woman and having relations with her, is later displeased with her because he finds in her something indecent, and therefore he writes out a bill of divorce and hands it to her, thus dismissing her from his house: if on leaving his house she goes and becomes the wife of another man and the second husband, too, comes to dislike her and dismisses her from his house by handing her a written bill of divorce; or if this second man who has married her, dies; then her former husband, who dismissed her, may not again take her as his wife after she has become defiled." The phrase "finds in her something indecent" is so vague as to be almost inapplicable and indeed was a great cause of dispute in later Judaism. Why this law was established is not known; the following verse simply says: "That would be an abomination before the Lord, and you shall not bring such guilt upon the land which the Lord, your God, is giving you as a heritage." Apparently, the law is based not on sexual taboos but on something pertaining to respect for the land which the Lord is giving; perhaps it has something to do with paying indemnity for the woman and decreasing the husband's property.

Other regulations are also phrased as limiting conditions upon the man. Dt 22:13-19 prohibits him from divorcing his wife at all if he has falsely accused her of having had intercourse with another before the marriage; Dt 22:28-29 forbids his divorcing his wife if he raped her before the marriage. No reasons are given for these laws.

It is sometimes said that women were considered as mere property since the last "word" of the Decalog lumps them with property: "You shall not covet your neighbor's wife, nor his male or female slave, nor his ox or ass, nor anything that belongs to him" (Ex 20:17). The later version in Dt 5:21, however, reads: "You shall not covet your neighbor's wife. You shall not desire your neighbor's house, or field, etc. . . ." Even the earlier version cannot be construed as making wives the same as property. Legal language, even among ourselves, has its own ways. The fourth article of our Bill of Rights reads: "The rights of the people to be secure in their persons, houses, papers and effects against unreasonable searches and seizures, shall not be violated." No lawyer would claim that persons are property simply because they are listed together with houses and papers.

The point I am making here is not that women had equal rights before the law; they didn't. Ex 30:4-16 deals with pledges or vows made by women; these are valid unless the father or husband revokes them. Other inferiorities of women before the law can probably be read by implication into other regulations, but not as clearly as in this one. In all the ancient Semitic law codes, women were legally the inferiors of men and the only difference is how far inferior. In Israel and much more in later Judaism they seem to have been near the bottom of the scale. However, this impression may be based on lack of information; the laws which do exist are few and obscure. There is no evidence that they were based on a general principle that women are inferior human beings and certainly not on any religious statement that women were created inferior to men.

Later Judaism at the time of Christ became exceedingly narrow in its attitude toward women. Josephus wrote: "The woman, says the Law, is in all things inferior to the man." A famous rabbinic prayer thanks God that the man was not created a woman or a slave. Although Judaism had a unique system of universal education, it was only for boys. Only one woman, Beruria, is ever quoted in the rabbinic writings.

on the scene.

However, to pursue our usual approach, it is not the laws or customs themselves which are so important, but the interpretation. As noted under the most famous passage about divorce, the civil law was connected with some understanding that God's holiness was involved in remarrying a divorced wife. Behind this must be an awareness of the key insight which governs the Law: "you shall make and keep yourselves holy, because I am holy" (Lv 11:44; 19:2; 20:7, 26; Mt 5:48; 1P 1:16). The Tenth Word of the Decalog prohibiting a man from desiring his neighbor's wife or property is governed, as are all the other Words, by the preliminary insight that everyone must be like the God who has delivered Israel from slavery (i.e., Ex 20:17 must be read in the light of Ex 20:1-6). Without this religious awareness there is no reason for secular laws to be in the Bible. The insight may be clearly stated or one may need to search for it; but it is the insight which is the objective of the Biblical teaching.

For example, women in the Jewish society of the first century A.D. wore veils. The rabbis interpreted this as a sign that a woman is like one who has done wrong and is ashamed of the people. Paul observed the same custom and interpreted the headdress as a sign of a Christian woman's authority and dignity before God. The custom was the same in both cases; the difference was between the inspired and the non-inspired interpretation.

In conclusion, we can say that on the basis of the few

laws which are recorded, on parallels from the non-biblical codes and on some of the narrative materials, it appears reasonable to judge that women were legally an inferior class during Biblical times. We do not know the extent of such laws nor do we know clearly the secular reasons for the laws. We can suspect that most of them are tied to the property laws of a patriarchial system. The Biblical texts never say that these laws or customs are based on a religious conviction that women were created inferior to men. Whenever such laws are connected with motivations, they are connected with the insight that God is holy and that all people must strive to become like him. Rabbinic Judaism has many harsh statements about women which certainly consigned them to an inferior position within marriage. Jesus protested against this. It is significant that whenever the New Testament discusses marriage at any length it always brings the subject back to the ancient comment in Gn 2:24: "the two of them become one body" (cf. Mt 19:5; Mk 10:7; 1 Cor 7:10; Ep 5:31). The significant theological insight is always that of the unity of man and woman, not of inferiority.

Note on the Legal Status of Women

Leonard Swidler, *Women in Judaism* (Metuchen, N.J.: Scarecrow Press, 1976) treats of the rabbinic material and reaches an extremely negative conclusion. George Tavard, *Women in Christian Tradition* (Notre Dame, Ind.: Notre Dame U Press, 1973) also struggles with the critical opinions, but he has difficulty with the Biblical interpretations.

---

8. Summary of the Biblical Essays on Women

The passages treated in this chapter cover practically all the major statements on women in general which are found in the Bible. The Book of Wisdom might be brought in; it has some touching things to say about the heroism of

languages it is also a generic term for men and women. Unless the context makes it clear that the male gender is crucial, the sayings apply to both men and women. Sex does not make a decisive difference in our relationship with God.

Secondly, the passages which concern women are not aimed at establishing social regulations for them. The customs and regulations existed before the passages were written. In only a few cases, such as 1Tm 5:3-16, is the opposite true. The glaring difference in these exceptional cases illustrates that the purpose of the writers was almost entirely to interpret what was being done, not to set a new course of action. Of course, we must recognize that the Bible acted as a screen to filter out the unacceptable; it is impossible to see a religious significance in a custom which is totally immoral. No sacred author ever used sacred prostitution or polygamy as a topic for religious insights into the potential of human beings. So the practices which were subjected to interpretation were approved, at least as a partial expression of the glory of men and women.

Central to the best insights is the often unexpressed conviction that women are made in the image of God. The most obvious image is that of life-giver. The picture runs far beyond that of the simple child-begetter. Women bring life not only to children but to men. The power extends to giving instruction, at least by example; ultimately, it extends to a sanctifying power that gives the life of faith to husbands. As we shall see in the next chapter, the initial insight was stated in Gn 2-3. Man is incomplete without woman; he needs her to find some sort of answer to the riddle of who he himself is. Woman may also be a mystery, but she is Lady Wisdom. As the later Christian tradition expressed it, Mary became the Mother of God. Woman becomes the life-giver, not just the Child-bearer but the Christ-bearer and that reveals to us all that we are truly God's sons and daughters.

We cannot trace any sudden changes in social conditions brought about by the Biblical teaching on women. In 1Tm 5 widows receive a social apostolate which was new. It is, after all, a small thing. The changes in society which undoubtedly resulted from the practice of Christianity over the centuries are much more due to the symbolic pictures of women than to any legislation. That must be our next topic of concern.

SYMBOLS

1. Preliminary Remarks

We live by symbols. The advertising industry uses symbols and concrete images to attract attention, beguile, persuade, and most often to create an image of what we would like to be. Our history abounds in sayings such as "Remember the Alamo" which mean more than the words. True symbols are more than clever uses of words. In the Christian tradition the "body of Christ" is far more than a clever comparison of all Christians to a human body.

The first problem in understanding Biblical symbols of the sort we shall be using is to ask which comes first, the abstract thought or the seen reality? Is God diagnosed as First Cause and then expressed by saying "father," or is "father" first experienced and then the insight applied however inadequately to God? To our point, is wisdom first diagnosed in God as the omniscient and then personified by speaking of Lady Wisdom? Is the power of God to develop all human capabilities first reasoned to and then expressed in the feminine image of a city as "she?" Is God first seen as life-giver and then as mother? Or is the process of Biblical thought (and much popular thinking) just the other way around? Is it the visible realities, father, mother city, wise woman, which are the starting point?

It is the supposition of this chapter that the latter is the case. It is not an unimportant point. Granted that all understanding must begin with the things that are seen, there is a very great deal of difference between beginning with an abstraction made from that experience and a beginning from seen realities with the purpose of expressing an insight into the hidden realities.

2. The Woman in the Garden—Gn 2-3

The story of the Garden of Eden in Gn 2-3 is well enough known not to need retelling. It should be noted, however, that the story is told in two scenes. Once the serpent appears, the whole action changes.

What are we dealing with here? A record of facts? A made up story? A fable? Professionally put, the choice would be between historical narrative and cultic myth. Or are we dealing with a piece of writing which was unique when it was written and is probably unique today? The majority of scholarly opinion would fall toward the yes side of that last question.

The Gn 2-3 account was probably written in the era circa 1000-900 B.C.; i.e. just after David and Solomon firmed up the united kingdom of Judah and Israel. The evidence is mostly from literary style as compared to other literary styles in the Bible, but the dating is fairly firm. The account is a magnificently fashioned piece of writing which appears full-blown at its first telling. The lack of a prior literary tradition behind the story needs some comment. Creation myths are fairly common and usually develop over long periods of time. Israel's unique story of its own origins shows something of this sort of development. The earliest stories relate to tribal memories, particularly the stories of Abraham and the God who appeared to him. The next great outburst of story telling concerned itself with the deliverance from Egypt. It was such stories which gave the Israelites a name and a cohesive memory; they also gave them a distinctive religion. However much these stories were later redacted and modified, they all had a nucleus of historical

happened to man

presently observed to be. In those basically agricultural societies man was observed to be governed by cycles of birth and death in himself and in nature around him. The cycles were unpredictable and uncontrollable. Good or bad for man had not much rime or reason. The pagan could only say that there were more powerful beings behind it all and that these gods were simply irrational or capricious. The stories or myths were slowly hammered into shape over the centuries to explain this and to give some way of gaining control over the gods by offering due homage. So the stories were acted out in cultic rituals and were written down.

The pagan, of course, had no factual reports of what had happened at the beginning of time. His historical memories were more circumscribed than those of the Israelites. He was aware that his stories of the beginning were religious interpretations of present facts, and so he never presumed to date the time when the world began. The only date was the timeless now. Such is the naure of myth.

As noted above, Israel's religion was not based on such myths or theories of what was behind observed human actions; it was based directly on the known facts that God had appeared to the Patriarchs (circa 1800 B.C. as a round figure) and to Moses (circa 1300 B.C., to use another round figure). The tribal memories did not actually say a lot about the kind of God who had appeared, but what they did say was decisive. God ("El" first and then "Yahweh") was a definite person. By the time of Moses the tradition defined him as the

the only God who was out there. It was part of the experience
of God that he was a powerful being; Warrior was a better
name for him than Father in the early stages. Being so
powerful, he did exactly what he wanted to do. He was not
irrational but he was not to be judged by human reason. The
world as it existed was that way precisely because God
wanted it to be. After the Mosaic experience the Israelite
learned that a good deal of the irrationality of life was due to
his own aptitude for freely doing something other than what
his God had freely willed. But despite all the complications
and failures, he forever remembered that God had promised
him good things during his life and had rescued him from
perils which were quite beyond his own power to overcome.

Such in rough approximation were the relevant features
of Israelite faith when David reigned. A kingdom had been
established and it was a very respectable kingdom among the
empires of the time. It sparkled with its new Temple and
official liturgy. New prosperity led to new culture and in one
of those inexplicable bursts of creativity literature blossomed. History and cultic poetry were improved. New techniques of story-telling were invented which rank among
literature's greater achievements. The Joseph story, the
Succession Narratives, Ruth and many other shorter pieces
date from this era. The authors are unknown, but are
grouped under the type name "Yahwist" since that was the
name of God which was consistently used. This Yahwist
tradition is often judged to have had substantial connection
with the wisdom tradition which I have mentioned
frequently in this book. The Garden of Eden story belongs to
the Yahwist tradition.

Such being the preliminaries, what do we know about
the actual writing of the account in Gn 2-3? Let us begin
with the second scene in Gn 3. Basically, this is a
sophisticated reflection and faith understanding of the
psychology of human life as the author saw it being lived in
his time. To begin at the end, men and women are conscious
of living outside of paradise—to borrow a word, as they
themselves did. Men sweat and slave to tame nature and
make it fruithful, yet it always fights back and eventually

buries them. Women are always drawn inevitably toward
[text obscured] children and yet they find in it pain

to satisfy. Especially, the understanding
securely and permanently escaped them.

To express these ideas the Yahwist stole bits and pieces
of symbols and story lines from the pagans, invented a few of
his own, but gave the story as a whole a radically different
twist. The tree of life was a common enough symbol; trees of
knowledge of good or evil were more dificult to come by, but
he put one in his garden. He understood that human beings
wanted a tree of knowledge which would lead to a tree of life.
He understood that when they tried to make a tree of
knowledge on their own, they not only failed; they failed in
ironic ways by half succeeding. Adam and Eve ate of the tree
and they did learn how to keep life going; they learned that
they were naked and what their nakedness was for.

The role of the woman should be noted in this part of
the story. The author is aware that the flood of human evils
and frustrations is far too great to be simply man-made. He
could not accept the pagan account that such frustration was
due to the capriciousness of gods. He stated his faith that the
human couple were caught up in a cosmic struggle between
the all-mighty Yahweh and a force of evil which he
personified as a serpent. The serpent was the cleverest of all
the animals in his zoology. It was the woman to whom the
clever serpent spoke. As the story tells, the man simply went
along with the woman. The story plot does say something
about the social conditions; men may excercise the power in
society, but women are the clever ones. On the other hand,
the story places the climax in the condemnation of the

serpent and the final conquest over it by the seed of the woman. Only then is the man Adam brought back into the picture. This, of course, is a part of the story which could only rely on Israel's faith in an all-mighty God who finally restores the order he wants.

If we now turn back to the prior part of the story in Gn 2, we get a picture of God creating the man first of all and installing him as a king in paradise. But the story of his sway over all things ends in an ironic conclusion; he is so superior that he is lonely. Dominion over the lesser things cannot satisfy him; he is incomplete without a mate. And so God creates the woman Eve. In an anticipation of what is to come in the next chapter, an ancient rime is recalled:

> *This one, at last, is bone of my bones*
>   *and flesh of my flesh;*
> *This one shall be called "woman" (in Hebrew,* ishsha*)*
>   *for out of "her man" (in Hebrew,* ish*) this one has*
> *been taken. Gn 2:23*

The most observable fact of human birth is that the child is taken out of the woman. The insight of faith also saw that the origin of life ran in both directions. Neither male nor female were able to be alone or self-sufficient. One need only reflect upon the endless struggle of teen-agers to be independent of their parents and then surprisingly tie themselves down by falling in love with their boy or girl. The pattern of life does not change in that essential. And so the author added a wise aside to all who would reflect:

> *That is why a man leaves his father and mother and clings to his wife, and the two of them become one body (in Hebrew, one* self*). Gn 2:24*

This is the text which is at the basis of every major statement of the New Testament concerning marriage. It is an insight

into life as it is lived, as it can be lived at its best, and of the
creative hand of God who made it so. Faith and human

who supported Adonias lost out; the victory went to a
woman, Bathsheba, and to a prophet, Nathan. It was not a
very orderly process; some commentators believe that one of
the purposes of writing the Garden of Eden story was to
reassert the power of the men over the harem. Whether this
be true or not, the new kingdom did recognize the power of
women to control the throne and when it happened in the
later history of the kingdom, it was usually with baneful
results. Within that context of history it is understandable
enough that the Garden story begins with the creation of the
man as the master of all he surveys. Yet the importance of the
woman to complete the man, and indeed, the recognition
that she was the clever one, forced its way into the truth of the
story-telling. It is difficult to consider Gn 2 an anti-feminist
tract if one considers the whole plot. Man is incomplete
without the woman; she is the one the subtle devil tempts,
and it is in her that the final victory is foreseen:

> *I will put enmity between you and the woman,*
> *between your offspring and hers;*
> *He will strike at your head,*
> *while you strike at his heel. Gn 3:15*

Note on the Woman in the Garden

John L. McKenzie is one of the most perspicacious commentators on myth in general; cf. Jerome Biblical Commentary, 77:23-31, or *A Theology of the Old Testament* (New York: Doubleday, 1974). A very good but brief overview can be found in Bruce Vawter, *On Genesis* (New York: Doubleday, 1977) and less satisfactorily in E.A. Speiser, *Genesis* (Anchor Bible, New York: Doubleday, 1964).

---

3. The Girl at the Dawn of Creation — Pr 8

In Pr 8 a little girl appears at the dawn of creation, playing before God, delighting to be with the sons of men. How she got there and how the author knew she was there is the first bit of detective work we must do; then we can ask what this says about the place of women in Hebrew society.

Back in the chapter on Women in Proverbs I noted that Pr 5-9, broadly speaking, is a collection of wisdom instructions on adultery. The admonition is made up of traditional bits of extremely pragmatic parental advice. That part can be paralleled in the international proverbs. What is unique is a counterpointing of a picture of the rewards of chaste fidelity (Pr 5:15-20), and a poetic picture of Lady Wisdom and the Woman Folly in Prov. 9. Although "the wife of your youth" (Pr 5:19) and the "strange woman" (Pr 5:3) are now called "Wisdom" (Pr 9:1) and the "Woman Folly" (Pr 9:13), it is evident from the context as it now lies before us that Prov 9 was a development in some way from Prov 5-7. The Woman Folly in Pr 9:13-18 still seduces the young man in the streets as the strange woman did in Pr 7. The allure of secret evil with its promise of otherwise unattainable knowledge is the same. The early instruction says:

The lips of an adultress drip with honey,
           .... is smoother than oil;

Stolen water is sweet,
    and bread gotten secretly is pleasing!
Little he knows that the shades are there,
    that in the depths of the nether world are her guests.
                                              Pr 9:17-18

So also "Wisdom" in Prov 9 is like the "wife of your youth" in Prov 5 and her blessings are exactly the opposite of the death and foolishness of folly.

Forsake foolishness that you may live;
    advance in the way of understanding,
For by me your days will be multiplied
    and the years of your life increased. Pr 9:6 and 11

The "wife of one's youth" has become "Wisdom," as was already indicated in Pr 7.

Say to Wisdom, "You are my sister!"
    call Understanding, "Friend!" Pr 7:4

That stands at the beginning of the very real-life description of adultery, as I have previously noted. Of course, long before this a connection between lovemaking and wisdom had been made in the perceptive use of "know" to describe sexual "intercourse"—which is our interpretative way of saying that something more than a physical action is involved. So, however abstract the word "wisdom" may be, it is tied down in this context of Pr 5-9 to a real woman. Nor is it just happenstance that the word is feminine (*hokmah* in Hebrew); it is so in all the ancient Semitic languages and even in Greek (*sophia* in the New Testament) and Latin. Somehow Wisdom is a woman because to perceive the life-giving reality one must go in to a chaste wife.

To reapply the detective story analogy, we have now set the scene of the crime. Before and after Pr 8 we have pictures of a chaste wife who is called "sister Wisdom" or simply "Wisdom" and an adulteress who is called "the strange woman" or "the Woman Folly." But the Wise Man must search for the origin of the plot. How did woman come to have such knowledge? Or at least, pretend to it? How do we explain her Mona Lisa smile? What secret does she know which men can attain only by going in to her? Child-bearing was a mystery to them in its medical aspects, but they saw also the larger mystery of life. Who can explain it? Who can explain the sudden life-fulfilling joy of becoming a parent? How can such a revelation of achievement and power come from a woman? What is in woman after all?

To the Wise Man it seemed that there must be something in the loving smile of a mother which was there from the beginning. Wisdom must be sought in all the affairs of life, which is where he begins in Pr 8:1-5. It is always the guide of the intelligent man (Pr 8:6-11); it directs those who rule (Pr 8:12-16); it is better than riches and honor (Pr 8:17-21). "Sister Wisdom," however, is the beginning of all prudent action and somehow she must have been at the beginning with the wise Creator.

> Does not Wisdom call,
>   and Understanding raise her voice?
> On the top of the heights along the road,
>   at the crossroads she takes her stand;

By the gates at the approaches of the city,
  in the entryways she cries aloud:

When there were no depths I was brought forth,
  when there were no fountains or springs of water;
Before the mountains were settled into place,
  before the hills I was brought forth;
While as yet the earth and the fields were not made,
  nor the first clods of the world.
"When he established the heavens I was there,
  when he marked out the vault over the face of the
deep;
When he made firm the skies above,
  when he fixed fast the foundations of the earth;
When he set for the sea its limit,
  so that the waters should not transgress his com-
mand;
Then was I beside him as his craftsman,
  and I was his delight day by day,
Playing before him all the while,
  playing on the surface of his earth;
  and I found delight in the sons of men.
"So now, O children, listen to me;
  instruction and wisdom do not reject!
Happy the man who obeys me,
  and happy those who keep my ways.
Happy the man watching daily at my gates,
  waiting at my doorposts;
For he who finds me finds life,
  and wins favor from the Lord;

But he who misses me harms himself;
all who hate me love death." Pr 8:22-36

If we go back now to the questions at the beginning of this chapter, we may get some clues as to how the Wise Man knew that there was a little girl present at the creation. It was a picture, of course, projected back from married life as men understood it at its best to a necessary embodiment in the original order.

It is the method which the Wise Man used in all of his best insights. The Garden of Eden story, as we have seen, was made up essentially out of a shrewd understanding of human psychology and the faith of Israel in a God who disposes all things for good in the long run. The story spoke of the potential which was in men and women. Images for the story were taken to a great degree from preexisting pagan myths. But the final story was not a myth in the pagan sense; it was not even used as a cultic myth. As far as we know, it was never acted out as the pagans always seem to have acted out their myths in religious ceremonies. At a later date an even more drastic revision of the pagan creation myths was written by the Priestly authors of Gn 1, the story of the seven days of creation. In that story the male and female figures are equally and specifically revealed as images of God.

God created man in his image;
in the divine image he created him;
male and female he created them. Gn 1:27

We do not know what needs in society that composition from later times met. It has something to say about the place of men and women at the top of creation; it says something about the power of faith, not of politics. We know not much more than this. Pr 8 was written later. It obviously met some need in society to assert the dignity of women in chaste marriage. We know no more than that. But it did arise out of ɔ consideration of life as people lived it when they

get the ....

experience of some sort; the evidence

conveniently and consistently at hand is Israel's and its interpretation of experience is unique, or as we say "divinely inspired."

Consequently, Pr 8 tells us a great deal about how the men of faith looked on their womanfolk. The Wise Men were with few exceptions men. But they had the wisdom to see God in a woman's eyes for she was an image of God the Wise. In later Christian times "Lady Wisdom" was experienced as the Logos, the Word of God. But he had a mother and of her it was said that she pondered all these things in her heart. Thus was the reality of God and of woman enhanced.

Note to the Little Girl Craftsman

Since the approach to Pr 8 used here is unusual, there is no source which can be listed as further exemplifying the matter. William McKane, *Proverbs* (Philadelphia: Westminister, 1970) is a fairly good commentary on the book in general. O.S. Rankin, *Israel's Wisdom Literature* (New York: Schocken, 1936), 222-264 is an example of a search for the explanation of the female figure in Pr by examining other literatures and tracing ideas rather than lived experiences.

4. The Jerusalem Connection—Isaiah

We must now venture into a stream of thought which is so pervasive and overpowering in the Old Testament that it challenges all reduction to simple formulae. Simply put, it is this: God cannot be confined anywhere; and yet he manifests his presence in specific places. Eventually, Jerusalem was by choice—his and mens'—the place of his dwelling. From it all blessings went out to mankind, but not easily. Jerusalem was a queen, a virgin, a mother, but only in her best moments. She was also a harlot. Such was the experience.

For our purposes, however, a preliminary remark must be made on why a city should be called "she" in the first place. As far back as the documentation goes in the West Semitic cultures cities were always "she." A capital city was a "queen." "She" was a "virgin," but also a mother. This bears looking into.

We can only theorize as to how this came to pass. Urbanization was one of mankind's larger inventions. A city represented all kinds of power which the countryside did not have. Out of the city came goods and learning, plans and cooperative efforts, city walls, better water, law courts, etc. What better image for a life-giving source than a mother? There was more to it than that. The supreme god was always male. But if he was going to be the lord of life, he had to have a woman. So the royal city became a woman-consort of the god. The "virgin" represented the idea of youth, incipient fertility, beauty—perhaps. At least, the word was used.

Now all of this is rather heady, but it represents the way things really were. The Israelite and his pagan neighbor of 1000 B.C. looking at the somewhat grubby streets of Jebus, or Jerusalem as it was renamed, made the mental image come true. They saw something which the eye could not see. As a matter of fact, they all seemed to use a sort of double vision. They saw a quite real city and they saw another city in the heavens. Cities and temples were said to be built according to some celestial blueprint. Both the pagans and the Israelites said so. What is notable about the Israelite is that he took all

of this in and used it without ever compromising the oneness
of his God. He never made Jerusalem a consort goddess, but

had left behind. Jerusalem as the "daughter of Zion," the
virgin, the life-giving mother became more important. Let
us look at some of the passages.

Standing in the dusty street of some forgotten
Mesopotamian village, a great poet to whom we can only
give the code name "Deutero-Isaiah" (or Second Isaiah)
looked across the desert to the west and saw a return to
Jerusalem. His reinterpretation of Israel's history goes far
behind the usual story of Moses and the Exodus to the times
when Abraham first set out from this same direction and
indeed from the time when God first made man in the
Garden of Eden. Unlike Abraham who did not know where
he was going this captive people knew their destination
precisely—Jerusalem. That city dominates the whole series
of poems from Is 49 to 55, except for the counterpoint in the
Songs of the Servant (Is 49:1-6; 50:4-11; 52:13-53;12).
Moreover, there is a shift in the picture of God as Israel's
experience of him accumulated. To Abraham he was simply
the vague El; to Moses he was mostly the Warrior God who
defended the people from all those Egyptian troops. But to
Deutero-Isaiah he was the Creator. Not only that, he was the
odd sort of Creator who had intended all this catastrophe so
that it might become abundantly clear that he was a Savior-
Creator from the beginning and was delighting again in a
new creation.

The concentration of the images on the city of Zion can
be sampled in one great poem, though it is repeated

elsewhere in such songs as are found in 49:14-50; 3; 50:1-3; 51:1-52:12, and echoed in a later collection called "Trito-Isaiah," e.g.: 60:1-22; 62:1-12; 66:5-17.

> *"Raise a glad cry, you barren one who did not bear,*
> > *break forth in jubilant song, you who were not in* labor."
> *"For more numerous are the children of the deserted wife*
> > *than the children of her who has a husband,"*
> > *says the Lord . . . .*

> *Fear not, you shall not be put to shame;*
> > *you need not blush, for you shall not be disgraced.*
> *The shame of your youth you shall forget,*
> > *the reproach of your widowhood no longer* remember.
> *For he who has become your husband is your Maker;*
> > *his name is the Lord of hosts;*
> *Your redeemer is the Holy One of Israel,*
> > *called God of all the earth.*
> *"The Lord calls you back,*
> > *like a wife forsaken and grieved in spirit,*
> *A wife married in youth and then cast off,"*
> > *says your God.*
> *"For a brief moment I abandoned you,*
> > *but with great tenderness I will take you back,*
> *In an outburst of wrath, for a moment*
> > *I hid my face from you;*
> *But with enduring love I take pity on you,"*
> > *says the Lord, your redeemer . . . .*

> *"My love shall never leave you*
> > *nor my covenant of people be shaken,"*
> > *says the Lord, who has mercy on you . . .*
> > > > *Is 54:1, 4-8, 10.*

The picture of the wayward wife who is taken back is

from the older prophecy of Hosea. The in-gathering of the
⸻ ⸻ from the old Abrahamitic promise and later

briefly does the older masculine idea of a ⸻
come into the picture (e.g. Is 55). Although the establishment of the Davidic monarchy had spawned an amazing
literary progeny and among its unique achievements in
world literature had created a picture of creation, the Isaian
poems go far beyond them. Something in the ancient
wisdom of all that culture had coalesced to picture God, the
Creator, as a mother. The pagan worshipped a fertility
goddess who represented both love and war. Israel grasped
the true understanding of a city which represented God as
the begetter and the bringer of peace.

Yet it was essential that the picture should be of a
woman. The picture somehow emerged from experience, as
did the pagan rites of fertility. The stern soldier or the
lawgiver could not contain God, as society could not put all
its values in the male society. The way in which this people's
deepest thoughts ran says far more about the status of women
than any legal enactments. It remained the dominant picture
of Yahweh the Savior through the rest of Israel's history.

In Christ's time a new and magnificent Temple had
been built. The new Temple did not have much effect; it was
the vision of the heavenly Temple which was the core of the
reactor which powered Judaism. Yet all Jewish life
throughout the world centered in this spot; without the
visible temple and the invisible Throne of God, Judaism
would have been inconceivable as a society expressing its
beliefs. It had tremendous difficulty in adjusting when
Jerusalem was finally destroyed.

One of the most startling things that Christ said was that the messengers of the Gospel should go out to the ends of the earth. It took them quite a while to understand how far out. It absolutely startled early Christians when they found that Antioch on the Orontes was becoming more important to their infant church than Jerusalem. Although all would have admitted that God is a Spirit and is not confined to a place, still the traditions of Jerusalem and the core message of Judaism said that there had to be a place where He acted in a special way and that place had to be Jerusalem. Much is said in the Acts of the Apostles and Epistles of Paul about the problem of circumcision. That is, of course, just a symbol word for the whole problem that plagued early Christianity. How could there be a new Chosen People without a place to identify with?

The Christian understanding finally shaped itself around a new concept of a people who were so closely identified with Christ that they could be called "the body of Christ." Other expressions are used such as Temple, vine, net, rock, but they are more clearly metaphors. This one, this "body of Christ," seems to have been more than just a comparison. At any rate, it offered a satisfying explanation of how a diverse group of people could be held together in a religious society without an actual capital city called a queen. This reality was also called a "church" on some occasions. "Church" is a feminine word and the proper pronoun for it is "she." But there was much more behind it than simple grammar. "She" was essential to the "body of Christ." The double vision saw the Christian assemblies as a Temple, as a City of God, as a heavenly reality.

Note on Mother Jerusalem

The article on Jerusalem in Xavier Leon Dufour, *Dictionary of Biblical Theology* (New York: Seabury, 1973) is a good place to begin sampling the immense amount of material on this subject. John McKenzie, *Dictionary of the*

early life of Jesus. Both are additions to the basic preaching of the Gospel; nothing of this sort is found in Mark or John or anywhere else in the New Testament proclamation. Matthew's account centers around Joseph; Mary is mentioned by name only three times (Mt 1:16, the genealogy; Mt 1:18, the engagement of Mary; Mt 2:11, the shepherds' visit to Mary and the child), and only incidentally as Joseph's wife (Mt 1:20, 20) or as Jesus' mother (Mt 2:11, 13, 14, 20, 21). For our purposes we may omit Matthew in favor of Luke who says more about Mary.

The Lukan story is easy to remember since it is so well planned.

Announcements of the births	*Births*
Of John the Baptist to Zachary	Of John the Baptist Zachary's Canticle Growth of John
Of Jesus to Mary Mary's visit to Elizabeth Mary's Canticle	Of Jesus Shepherd's visit and Canticle The Presentation Simeon's Canticle Anna's prophecy Growth of Jesus

The pattern is not perfect in its symmetry, but there is more than enough to show that somebody arranged the story in this way. We say: the facts prove the point. In reality, facts prove very little until someone arranges them in a pattern which interprets. The Lukan arrangement of the Infancy Story clearly bespeaks an intention to interpret. Our problem is to grasp what the interpretation is.

A look at the history of the development of the stories, insofar as we can reconstruct them, helps. The basic data seems to have existed in the Jerusalem church from a very early date. We do not know how extensive this information was; the quite disparate accounts in Matthew and Luke would suggest that it was very extensive and that only a selected portion of it was used in the Gospel accounts. We do not know how early or on what insights the material first began to be shaped into interpretative stories. We can detect parallels to the traditional method of Jewish midrash in some of the treatment; Matthew is strong on interpreting the infancy events on the basis of Old Testament themes. But the absence of the material in the Pauline writing and the Gospel of Mark would imply that in the early stages of development of the Infancy Narratives no clear theological meaning was perceived.

Luke, however, arranged his story of the public life of Jesus and the story of the early church (Luke 3-24 and Acts) according to a grand design which illustrated that the ancient prophecies of salvation through Jerusalem and so to the nations were being fulfilled in the working of the Spirit within the church (cf. Lk 24:44-49 and Ac 1:1-9 as examples). He seems to have perceived that the infancy stories could also be used to illustrate this theme. Luke's writing in the Infancy Narrative is not greatly different from his style in the rest of the Gospel, so we can presume that Luke had a certain freedom to shape the material. However, he put most of his interpretative sections in the form of Canticles. Thus the story is divided off by the Magnificat (Lk 1:46-55); the Benedictus (Lk 1:68-79), the Gloria in Excelsis (Lk 2:14) and the Nunc Dimittis (Lk 2:29-32), to use the traditional

Catholic names for the Canticles of Mary, Zachary, the

from an understanding of the literal meaning
texts but then it always applies it to contemporary needs. So
the Magnificat is apparently made up from a pre-Christian
Jewish hymn to "the daughter of Zion," a summation of the
themes found in the Psalms and Isaiah which saw "mother
Jerusalem" as symbolic of God's life-giving salvation. The
final verse recalls the ancient Abrahamitic promise to save
all nations. By putting this on the lips of Mary, Luke gave it
a new interpretation. The Benedictus is made up of the same
Abrahamitic promise which is slanted in the direction of a
promise of freedom for all men. The final stanzas apply this
to John the Baptist as the messenger of freedom. The Gloria
is also a traditional hymn of praise to God the peace-giver.
The angel voices a conventional way of portraying the
communication of God to man, make it apply to Jesus. The
most distinctive hymn is the Nunc Dimittis and it gives the
crux of Luke's interpretation. The hymn is addressed to
"Master" (in Greek, *despota*, a title for God). The servant
who is dismissed is Israel. Luke has reinterpreted the role of
Israel as the servant who brings salvation to the nations.
Luke does not say directly who the new servant is; but the
theme of his two-volume work is that the Spirit is now
working through the church. Significantly, Luke made
Simeon relate the words in the presence of Mary, who seems
to have been already a symbol of the church.

The author of the Epistle to the Hebrews reminded his
Christian brethren: "You have drawn near to Mount Zion
and the city of the living God, the heavenly Jerusalem" (Heb

12:22). As noted in the previous chapter on Mother Jerusalem, the need for the early Christian community to maintain its ties with the Israel of God and its traditions was enormous. The author of Hebrews didn't say where the heavenly Jerusalem was, but it was certainly a present reality which existed somewhere. Luke made the same point in a much more concrete manner by the way in which he told the infancy stories. The center of the piece was a woman.

Luke is well aware in his writing that he is describing mysteries, not the cause and effect of secular historians. The mystery, as he saw it, was in the working of God in the career of Jesus and in the church. The Spirit was mysterious both in his power to change men's lives and in his impalpability. He was near and yet untouchable and uncontrollable. The Old Testament had recognized the same thing about God. He dwelt in light inaccessible, and yet he acted in definite times and places. Zion or the Temple was his preferred dwelling place. Yet the Jew never believed that God could be confined to Jerusalem. His very imagery about "her" as daughter, virgin or mother also recognized a localization in women. A similar thing had happened with the localization of God's power in the king, though after all the sad history of that institution it was somewhat obscure for centuries just what that meant.

When we ask our usual question as to what the Lukan Infancy Narrative tells us of the status of women in the New Testament times, we must answer "both very much and very little." It certainly was not Luke's concern to define a new social status for women by using Mary and Elizabeth and Anna. One cannot say, for example, that since Mary journeyed through Palestine by herself, therefore Mary asserted a new independence for women. We do not know that much about the social conditions and such a conclusion certainly ignores what the story is all about. Nor—more importantly—can we argue from later theological precisions about the Mother of God, the Immaculate Conception, the Mediatrix of all graces, etc., that Christianity circa 80 A.D. had changed the fundamental social status of women. But neither can we argue that the stories had no impact. Luke ... from the data he had received;

But perhaps ...

8. The author of that proverbial insight had ...

boggling realization of the mystery of life which was known to a certain extent by chaste mothers. He had concluded that the knowledge of such a power and wisdom had to be in women from the beginning. So he had placed a little girl at the dawn of creation who watched as God created in his own exuberant and wise way. Luke, following largely the creation-redemption theology of Isaiah, seems to have understood that the Jesus event had begun as a new creative act and that there was a secret understanding of it in the church. This is a view which Paul also espouses in his doctrine of the great mystery. Placing another little girl at the beginning of this new creation story, giving that interpretation to the facts and emphasizing that she treasured all these things and reflected on them in her heart (Lk 2:19) made of her another little girl of wisdom. Nobody seems to have been surprised. That these stories in later centuries did become central in winning for women a new social status is clear in the historical record. That they also at times restricted women to the mother role is also a fact. The interpretation of the facts was once again the decisive thing for good or ill. But there was a new beginning in these real people which was brought out by seeing them also as symbols.

Note on the Infancy Account

Fortunately, the best thing written on the Lukan Infancy Narrative is readily available in Carroll Stuhlmueller's article at the beginning of the commentary on the Gospel of Luke in the *Jerome Biblical Commentary*, 44:20-44. A vast body of more technical data exists, most of which is noteworthy because of its divergence. I have drawn to a certain extent on Paul Minear, "Luke's Use of the Birth Stories" in Leander E Keck and J. Louis Martyn, *Studies in Luke-Acts* (Nasville: Abingdon, 1966), 111-130; Stephen Benko, "The Magnificat", JBL 86 (1967), 263-275; H.H. Oliver, "The Lucan Birth Stories and the Purpose of Luke-Acts," Nov. Test. Stud. 10; 202-226; W. Barnes Tatum, "The Epoch of Israel: Luke I—II and the Theological Plan of Luke-Acts Nov. Test. Stud. 13; 184-195. The classical commentators such as Bultmann, Dibelius and Conselmann, are noteworthy mostly for their confusion on the Infancy Accounts.

---

6. The Woman in the Sky

This is what we proclaim to you;
what was from the beginning,
what we have heard,
what we have seen with our eyes,
what we have looked upon
and our hands have touched. 1Jn 1:1

This brief declaration at the beginning of the first letter of John states very clearly the source from which all the writings produced by the band of missionaries associated with the Apostle John came. Always it came from what they had heard, seen, touched.

If we look into that most mysterious book called

Revelations or Apocalypse, we are tempted to abandon this
⸻ writer says he saw these

The basic message of apocalyptic is always. God
overcome. As an abstract principle, it is clear and rather dull.
As an experience of life, it is not all that simple. Not only
does God seem to take his own time getting around to
conquering; it is difficult at any point to tell who is winning.
The drama is being played out with a great deal of deception
or at least of subtilty.

The Apocalypse was written to Christians in Asia
Minor around the seaport of Ephesus during the reign of
Domitian (81-96 A.D.), who was the first Roman Emperor to
persecute Christians systematically. Earlier admonitions in
Paul clearly indicate that Christians had been brought up to
respect Roman authority and to see God behind the order
which the State provided. It was no simple matter, therefore,
for Christians to decide what to do when Rome began
nibbling away slowly at freedom of religion, which had
always been an accepted policy in Rome. Apparently, there
were sincere Christians who arose in the assemblies and
preached, or "prophesied" as the commonly used term put
it, that Christians must accomodate themselves to the new
regulations. Others were not so sincere; they urged
Christians to save their necks by abandoning their accepted
beliefs or starting a new religion which would be accepted in
Rome. Somebody had to draw a line.

The Apocalypse does. It draws a line precisely between
those who are within the Temple of God and those who are
in the exterior court (Rv 11:2). The image is drawn from the
Jewish Temple and interprets the Jewish experience of

trying to be God's people. There had always been those
within the Jewish community who had tried to compromise
and manipulate. The scene had become extremely confusing
at times. "False prophets" vied with "true prophets." The
problem always was to distinguish the true from the false
adherents within the Chosen People. The need to do so is
expressed in the image of separating those who come to the
Temple between those who are truly in the Temple and
those who are in the exterior court. It was also observed that
those who truly served God were usually the persecuted. So
the first major section of the Apocalypse ends with the true
witnesses of the Old Testament slain in the streets. But at the
very last a trumpet blast announces the surprising truth:
"The kingdom of the world now belongs to our Lord and to
his Anointed One, and he shall reign forever and ever" (Rv
11:15).

Using this experience of the past, the author turns to the
contemporary scene. The quiet days in Jerusalem when all
the believers were of one heart and one mind were long gone.
The Risen Christ had seemed so decisive at one time; now
among Christians he was divisive. Christians had not
conquered Rome; Rome was just getting its teeth sharpened
to conquer Christians. Christians were not all of one mind;
false prophets had arisen among them. With an ancient
consciousness of the power of evil, all the New Testament
writers had pointed out that wickedness was more than a
human invention or imperfection. Behind the day to day
bickering and compromising, behind the police round-ups
and the diverse "ways" in which Christians reacted, was a
truly demonic power. Since this demonic power was
extremely deceptive, one might find a devil within oneself.
How does one describe in compelling terms this understanding of life?

The story of Esther illustrates one way of saying it. The
story is well-known. Esther, a Jewish girl in Susa, became
queen to King Ahasuerus. With political aid from another
Jew, Mordecai, she prevented a slaughter of Jews by getting a
royal edict that Jews could resist persecution by force of

arms. They did so with royal glee and effectiveness. The story

story had been told, the Greek and explanation of the dream:

> *Then Mordecai said: "This is the work of God. I recall the dream I had about these very things, and not a single detail has been left unfulfilled—the tiny spring that grew into a river, the light of the sun, the many waters. The river is Esther, whom the king married and made queen. The two dragons are myself and Haman" (Est 10:1-4 in the Greek as translated in NAB).*

Now this is extremely ironic. Mordecai, who prevented the slaughter of the Jews but bloodied his own hands, sees himself as a dragon. At least, the Greeek translator saw that. He created a dream scene to express the idea that the world of evil beyond human sight works not only in the obvious enemies of Judaism but also sometimes within the heroes of Judaism. The theme was a popular one in apocalyptic; the devil is a clever rascal who looks just like an angel, and the idea has perdured in our popular speech.

So the group of Johannine preachers apparently adapted an apocalyptic sermon, which they had been using for a long time, to the contemporary situation. The basic warning was against the false Christians. The struggle at the top is described in rapid strokes; the Victor Christ is born as a child and snatched up into heaven. That left the chief protagonists in the battle on earth the rank and file

Christians. How would they be pictured? Paul had called them the "body of Christ," the "Temple"; John in his Gospel had called them the "Vine" and the "Sheepfold." The Johannine band called them "the Woman." In the Garden of Eden story the chief actors had been the Woman and the serpent; the hopeful climax would come when the seed of the Woman crushed the head of the serpent. The Christian experience of the first century had added insights and symbols to this. All men were born of a woman; the church was born of a Woman also. As the Infancy Narratives had begun to interpret Mary's symbolic role, so the Woman symbol was appropriate to indicate that the Victor was a real man. It was appropriate also since the Jerusalem theology had identified "her" as the mother of Israel, the instructress of all nations, the very life-giving symbol of God himself. Since the city was a queen, this woman had a crown of twelve stars on her head. The Woman, who remained on earth, had a continuing work in God's plan. First, she had to flee into the desert to escape the dragon. The ancient serpent had changed into a dragon, huge and red and with seven heads and ten horns. Then the vision is interrupted and after an interval (Rv 12:7-12) it begins a second time with the Woman giving birth to the boy. Now the woman is given eagle's wings to fly off to her place in the desert. To turn the Esther imagery around, the serpent spews out a torrent of water to drown her, but this time the tactic fails and the earth swallows up the river. So the dragon goes off to devour the offspring of the Woman and finally to sit by the seashore and await another dragon from the sea.

It is useless to try to identify precisely all the symbols; they are taken from the whole range of human experience. If we say that the sea beast is the Roman power across the Mediterranean, one wonders why the red dragon is waiting since Rome was already in Asia with military power. The Christian experience was that one bit of trouble was hardly over when another appeared. Beast after beast comes on the scene. The Woman is always fleeing to the desert. That is a true picture of the Church's experience.

For our purposes, we may well ask why the Church—[illegible] commentator agrees that we are looking at the [illegible] Babylon who [illegible] woman's world. That is simply a conclusion from the way people experience life.

Note on Apocalypse

Andre Feuillet, *The Apocalypse* (Staten Island: Alba House, 1964) is a good place to begin since it has a careful outline of the history of the exegesis of Revelations. Paul S. Minear, *I Saw a New Earth* (Washington: Corpus Books, 1968) is an extremely interesting treatment which sees Christians almost exclusively as the enemies of the church. The latest commentary is J. Massyngberde Ford, *Revelation* (Anchor Bible, New York: Doubleday, 1975). The book relies on the unconventional theory that the author is John the Baptist. In any survey of commentators the frequency of Roman Catholic authors is notable; for them the Woman is almost always identified with Mary, the mother of Jesus.

---

7. Summary

In looking back over these symbols, one must be impressed by the number and profundity of the female images. Male symbols were, of course, used. But by the time of the New Testament the old figure of God as the Warrior or even the Great King had begun to fade. There was little of concrete reality to point to. What held the Jewish communities together on an everyday basis were the figures of Mother Jerusalem and Wisdom. People could see the city and the teacher was an ordinary part of life.

In fact, what seemed to have made these Jewish symbols different from the "personifications" of other peoples was the grounding in the visible reality. The pagans never seemed to have known exactly what to make of women. They were chattels in much of daily life and goddesses in the poets' imaginations. But the Jew and later the Christian seems to have looked first at real life-women or feminine things and to have seen straight through them to some nobler vision which appeared in diaphaneus fashion behind the woman. The Jerusalem theology certainly shaped both Judaism and early Christianity in powerful ways. Had it been merely an airy abstraction, it would be impossible to understand the crisis in Judaism when the city of Jerusalem was destroyed. Had women been unimportant to early Christianity precisely as women, it would be impossible to understand why Luke shaped his Infancy Narrative as he did, or why the Woman of the Apocalypse was such an important element of the vision, or why the insights into the dignity of women in marriage were so important to the Pauline and Petrine tradition. Somehow God was always seen to be emerging from real women as they lived lives of faith and holiness.

Moreover, it should be noted that these symbols in some way tend to congeal around life and wisdom. There is certainly no way of tracing a straight line of historical development between the various pictures. They are pictures of people, as complex and as variegated as real people. Yet in a way they define the people who lived by the tradition. The symbols ran both ways, defining the God in whom they believed and defining the people who believed in the God. These feminine symbols proclaimed that this Chosen People, Jewish and then Christian, were people who listened. The Gospel had to be listened to and taken into one's heart. As one learned more, life became more abundant. The ancient understanding of God as the life-

giver and the bestower of all understanding was renewed in
the preaching of the Gospel, especially in John and Paul.

should also be understood here.

logical conclusion. However, the female symbols said it
much better.

CONCLUSIONS

The conclusions of this study, insofar as I am able to make conclusions, will be stated first negatively and then positively. Negatively, there are prejudices and faulty methodologies which we can set aside or at least seriously question. Positively, there is much to be learned about looking at what is going on in our world with the eyes of faith and penetrating into the reality of God which is mirrored in women.

1. The Negative Conclusions

First of all, it is simple enough to perceive how many of the crasser prejudices arise from quoting texts out of context, often in faulty translations, or simply veiling personal dislikes in Biblical language. That women are seductresses, that women are made for men, that married women are forever incapable of perfection because they must serve their husbands or because they are not virgins, that they have no official role in the church, that they must have as many children as possible and that their proper place is entirely in the home are self-serving conclusions reached from other premises than the Bible presents. I presume that there are many more.

Neither is the dominant approach of contemporary scholars—the "time-conditioned conclusions"—particularly convincing or helpful to me. The approach seems to be based on our own time-conditioned patterns of thinking in terms of principles and conclusions. As this study has pointed out, perhaps too often, the customs of the times were certainly the raw material from which the observations were drawn. But the objective was not to draw conclusions about required ways of acting from immutable principles; it was to arrive at insights into what the customs which already existed said in a faith context. If the "conclusions" are thrown out because we cannot accept them today, we had better clip out of our Bibles the total passages in which they occur.

Another broad area of negative conclusions is that we cannot find immediate answers to our own time-conditioned problems. The Bible will not help us to answer directly the question of whether women should get equal pay for equal work. For such matters, we must use our own best judgment. The Bible will help us, however, to test our conclusions.

One question of this sort is of special concern to the Roman Catholic community; namely, whether women can be ordained priests. For this the Bible has no answer. The evidence for an order of "priests" in the New Testament is exceedingly small, if we take "priests" in the rather restricted sense of one who is commissioned for sacramental ministry. No such exclusive group is described in the New Testament. No specific person is ever named as celebrating the Eucharist, apart from Christ himself. The "presbyters" of Jm 5:14-15 who anoint with oil and utter the prayer of forgiveness may or may not be priests in our sense of the word, and if they are, little can be made from the use of the masculine gender. In the lists of qualifications for "Bishops" and deacons, short shrift is given to priests (only Titus 1:5-6 mentions them). And in the midst of the deacon list of 1Tm 3:11 occurs that obscure reference to "the women likewise. . . ." 1Tm 2:12 does exclude women from being "teachers" and indeed "in any way to have authority over a

man." But that was nothing new and the concern of the
~~passage was not to legislate~~ but to see the irony in the

silence may be attributed to the most ~~...~~
suppositions. Perhaps priests were a rarity among all those
apostles, prophets, teachers, administrators, assistants, etc.
who are clearly noted (cf. 1Cor 13:4-11; Rm 12:6-8). On the
other hand, considering the Jewish antecedants and the
subsequent practice, priests may well have been exclusively
males. But then we are faced with the extremely odd fact that
practically nothing is said about the significance of an office
which seems to us to be so important in the church. That is
really the missing ingredient in the present discussion, the
perception of what priests, irrespective of whether they must
be male or can be female, really say about the living image of
God.

3. The Positive Findings

It is discouraging to ask questions for which the Bible
has no answer, either for the time in which it was written or
for our time. However, there is more to it than that if we are
willing to face the challenge of observing our own times
with wisdom and to seek meanings. Then the Bible does
point a way.

In the stories which we studied we noted how women as
well as men must seek for an understanding of life, the
beauty in human reactions and the use of power. Power is a
beautiful thing. Natural functions and societal conditions
connected women closely with the life-giving power of God.
But it was not only in child-bearing that women imaged

God. Judith acted for the Warrior God in a military confrontation; Mary the mother guaranteed the social probity of her son. There were no laws which said that women could or should do such things, but when they did them or when stories were told about them doing so, the community accepted them as proper womanly deeds reflecting a divine power.

What they learned about power is the same as the men learned. It is to be used, but to be used only as a gift. Sometimes the women fought against God. Naomi denounced Yahweh bitterly and the Samaritan woman tried to use Christ for her own amusement. They finally surrendered. Jezabel did not and ended in dire tragedy. But people learned from these stories. They could praise God who was behind Judith's boldness or Mary's free acceptance of motherhood.

The essays concerning women from Proverbs to Paul tell us little of how women ought to act today or any day. That was not their first intention. The Wise Men looked at the way women did act in their society and then tried to discover what that said about women's potential for good or bad. Sometimes the Wise Man got no farther than a chuckle, as in his remark about a nagging wife being like a roof dripping through. Sometimes he was a filter for straining out the bad. He looked at temple prostitution and concluded that it was a very bad thing indeed. It was a very pragmatic view. Temple prostitution might be justified by the pagan on what we could call a theory of a fertility cult, but when the irate pagan husband found out about his wife's pandering, there might be trouble, cultic myth or not. The Wise Man carried his insight much further. He understood the lure of the secret affair, but he knew that it held no secret except a path that led to Sheol where there was darkness of mind as well as body.

By the time he had reached that conclusion, the Wise Man had stated his faith in Sheol as a terrible revelation of what man might become. He saw the other side of the coin as well. A young man who pursued Wisdom by clinging to the

wife of his youth found not a successful way of life, but an
~~i~~ ~~~~ ~~himself~~ in the eyes of his wife. She was the

know. Jerusalem was a real city before ~~~~ ~~~~
saving God. Mary was a real mother before she was a symbol
for the new Jerusalem. Any city was a place before it was a
"she," a symbol of fruitful power, whether for good, as
Jerusalem at its best, or for evil, as Babylon or Nineveh. The
symbolism began in concrete realities, not in abstract ideas.
Interpretation of women's role, if it is to follow the Biblical
approach, must begin in observing women as they are. God
acts in them or they act on their own. They become symbols
by what they are.

The most powerful of these symbols, apart from the
body of Christ sayings, were feminine. The feminine
symbols often say that God is very like the woman whom we
popularly describe as feminine—loving, peaceful, instructing, contemplative, life-giving. Thus we have Israel as the
bride, Jerusalem as the city of peace, or as the mountain from
which instruction flows, Mary as the mother who ponders
all these things in her heart, the Woman of the Apocalypse as
the one who gave birth to the male child. Sometimes, too, the
harsher experiences entered in as a self-learned lesson—the
wayward wife who must learn that she cannot escape true
love (for "stern as death is love; relentless as the nether world
is devotion," Cant 8:6), or that a sword of sorrow must lay
bare the way of salvation (Luke 2:19), or that the Woman
clothed in the sun and the stars must be persecuted (Rv 12:3
ff.). But sometimes the feminine images are very unlike the
popular picture (true or false) of femininity. Jerusalem is a
conquering city, the Woman clothed in the sun and the stars

is also described as an army set in battle array, Eve does crush the head of the serpent in some way. This, too, is part of the reality in human experience.

The insight always began from an observation of facts, not from some abstract theory or principle. It interpreted the facts by a most immediate awareness of the presence of God in the affairs of this planet. We have a problem with such thinking because of our instinctive rections bogotten by a scientific age. We surround the God of nature with so many physical laws that he almost vanishes; we look for the Lord of history only after we have exhausted the study of sociology. Jeremiah said:

> *Among the nations' idols is there any that gives rain?*
> *Or can the mere heavens send down showers?*
> *Is it not you alone, O Lord, our God, to whom we look?*
> *You alone have done all these things.   Jr 14:22*

It may sound extremely naive as we watch our nightly weather report on TV, but it contains the essential question. Who ultimately, by little or far, controls the natural phenomena and for what purpose? Is he free to do as he wills? And what of us and our freedom?

Much of the Biblical data is reflection of men and women acting freely within the necessities of life. We are more inclined to interpret life from its freedoms; the necessities are also there. Rm 1 is a commentary on the implacable "wrath" which was destroying Roman society. 1Cor 7 is largely an admonition against inflexible ways of acting which the Corinthians were in danger of imposing on themselves.

In Rm 8:20-21 Paul says: "Creation was made subject to futility, not of its own accord, but by him who once subjected it; yet not without hope, because the world itself will be freed from its slavery to corruption and share in the glorious freedom of the children of God." Human beings can interpret life in this flexible way, once they accept the faith

wife of his youth found not a successful way of life, but an image of himself in the eyes of his wife. She was the mysterious life-giver, to himself as well as to his children; he could share in her wisdom and eventually find the Wise God within himself. He saw these things in an image, but without the mirror he would never have seen them at all.

Finally, the feminine symbols reveal the deepest ... of women. It should be noted ... Eve was

symbolism began.
Interpretation of women's role, if it is to ...
approach, must begin in observing women as they are. God acts in them or they act on their own. They become symbols by what they are.

The most powerful of these symbols, apart from the body of Christ sayings, were feminine. The feminine symbols often say that God is very like the woman whom we popularly describe as feminine—loving, peaceful, instructing, contemplative, life-giving. Thus we have Israel as the bride, Jerusalem as the city of peace, or as the mountain from which instruction flows, Mary as the mother who ponders all these things in her heart, the Woman of the Apocalypse as the one who gave birth to the male child. Sometimes, too, the harsher experiences entered in as a self-learned lesson—the wayward wife who must learn that she cannot escape true love (for "stern as death is love; relentless as the nether world is devotion," Cant 8:6), or that a sword of sorrow must lay bare the way of salvation (Luke 2:19), or that the Woman clothed in the sun and the stars must be persecuted (Rv 12:3 ff.). But sometimes the feminine images are very unlike the popular picture (true or false) of femininity. Jerusalem is a conquering city, the Woman clothed in the sun and the stars is also described as an army set in battle array, Eve does crush the head of the serpent in some way. This, too, is part of the reality in human experience.

The insight always began from an observation of facts, not from some abstract theory or principle. It interpreted the facts by a most immediate awareness of the presence of God in the affairs of this planet. We have a problem with such thinking because of our instinctive rections bogotten by a scientific age. We surround the God of nature with so many physical laws that he almost vanishes; we look for the Lord of history only after we have exhausted the study of sociology. Jeremiah said:

> *Among the nations' idols is there any that gives rain?*
> *Or can the mere heavens send down showers?*
> *Is it not you alone, O Lord, our God, to whom we look?*
> *You alone have done all these things.   Jr 14:22*

It may sound extremely naive as we watch our nightly weather report on TV, but it contains the essential question. Who ultimately, by little or far, controls the natural phenomena and for what purpose? Is he free to do as he wills? And what of us and our freedom?

Much of the Biblical data is reflection of men and women acting freely within the necessities of life. We are more inclined to interpret life from its freedoms; the necessities are also there. Rm 1 is a commentary on the implacable "wrath" which was destroying Roman society. 1Cor 7 is largely an admonition against inflexible ways of acting which the Corinthians were in danger of imposing on themselves.

In Rm 8:20-21 Paul says: "Creation was made subject to futility, not of its own accord, but by him who once subjected it; yet not without hope, because the world itself will be freed from its slavery to corruption and share in the glorious freedom of the children of God." Human beings can interpret life in this flexible way, once they accept the faith and the hope which goes with it. Being submissive does not mean bowing before an implacable necessity, even divine. It means seeing the free choice of God in the events of life. ~~~~~ ~~~~ ~~~~ an acceptance of existing conditions or a ~~~~ ~~~

revealer? If we ask: what are her rights? help much. It did not think in those terms. We cannot cite Paul on woman's rights: "There does not exist among you Jew or Greek, slave or freeman, male or female" (Gal 3:28). It is not an abstract statement of rights, but an observation of facts. It first arose not from a crusade, but from an incident in which the Holy Spirit came upon Gentiles. It was repeated frequently in Paul's experience as he saw people of all sorts embracing the faith. His statement is an insight into the freedom of God to call whom he chooses and the freedom of individuals to respond.

The word which still grates most on women is "submissive." It seems to speak of an immutable order of inferiority and is interpreted rigidly as conformism to a static role in society. I have tried to explain this word since it is so unusual in the Greek vocabulary that it obviously says something else. Christ submitted himself to his Father (1Cor 15:28); ordinary Christians should submit themselves to the civil authorities (Rm 13:1); young men should submit to their elders (1P 5:5). The only common element in these sayings is a freedom to accept something in concrete circumstances which conforms us to the free will of God. In an off-hand exhortation in 1Cor 16:16 Paul says: "You know that the house-hold of Stephanas is the first fruits of Achaia and is devoted to the service of the saints. I urge you to serve (our odd word "submit") such men and under everyone who cooperates and toils with them." Cooperation is here clearly seen to be necessary for the church which gathered around Stephanas; yet there is a free choice to cooperate.

If we ask how this helps us solve any of the problems of women in our present society, we must answer that it gives few definite answers. It negates some ways of acting which it observes in society; for example, adultery or shrewishness. But we should probably have concluded the same on our own. What it does is to force us back into evaluating our past or future actions on the basis of faith. If we ask what does the Bible say about abortion, we must confess that it says nothing directly. No specific text solves the modern problem with the precision which we need. Nevertheless we must give an answer and indeed an answer which is firmly based on our faith. The cutting edge of that faith is an acceptance of God as a life-giving God and of ourselves as his images. On that point the Bible has much to say.

Oddly enough, most proposed solutions depend on a faith statement at the end. If zero population growth is adduced as a justification for abortion, then we are making a faith statement that the human race will be improved by zero population growth. Nobody knows if this is true. The argument may be dressed up in truly dramatic visions of a planet smothering in its own juices. That is as much an apocalyptic vision as the ancient literature of faith ever produced. If we argue that women alone have the right to decide whether they shall have a baby, then we are making a faith statement that such unlimited power has been placed in women's hands by someone or some force. That is a faith statement. Such being the case, one need not apologize for a Biblical statement of faith in God the life-giver and men and women as free cooperators in the use of such power. How this faith statement shall operate positively is a mystery we seek to penetrate. Any solution which does not take it into consideration is simply scratching the surface with pragmatic solutions, and as our recent experience shows, tends to impose on us another set of rigidities of social attitudes and governmental regulations.

Freedom for women can come only from within. What is in women (or men) can only be learned by a slow growth of understanding from experience aided by faith. True liberation for women cannot grow from imposed societal patterns, either the prevailing ones or the ones we champion. It must begin with a penetration into the mystery of woman

and happy those who keep my ways,
Happy the man watching daily at my gates,
waiting at my doorposts.
For he who finds me finds life,
and wins favor from the Lord;
But he who misses me harms himself;
all who hate me love death. Pr 8:32-36

is arguably the most colorful and exciting part of the continent. It comprises what we call the Top End and the Red Center—two extreme climatic and geographical divisions, which is what makes the Territory so fascinating. It has the tropical, World Heritage–listed Kakadu National Park, with crocodiles and water buffalo to the Top, and in the Center the desert, the "Dead Heart"—not actually dead at all, only lying dormant until the rains transform it into the greatest garden on earth.

The pervading theme of the series is family. Family offers endless opportunities for its members to hurt and be hurt, to love and support, or bitterly condemn. What sort of family we grew up in reverberates for the rest of our lives. One thing is certain: at the end of the day, *blood* binds.

I invite you, dear reader, to explore the lives of my families. My warmest best wishes to you all.

Margaret Way

Men of the Outback
THE CATTLEMAN, Superromance
THE CATTLE BARON'S BRIDE, Harlequin Romance
HER OUTBACK PROTECTOR, Harlequin Romance

Look out for Cecile's story, coming in August from Harlequin Superromance: THE HORSEMAN

She was full of surprises, Daniel thought in some amazement.

So much for the immature girl without a scrap of make-up! What he saw in front of him was a dead-sexy little buttercup blonde. She was wearing a swishy blue dress that doubled the impact of her violet eyes. He hadn't expected this transformation. He was so astounded he had trouble hiding it.

"Have a problem with the way I look, Daniel?" she asked sweetly, pleased at his readable reaction.

"No, ma'am." He half shrugged. "You look different, that's all." Daniel studied her face. "What's the problem?"

"I'm sick with nerves, if you must know."

"I promise I'll lay down my life for you." He said it lightly. Then it struck him. He had just said something that he actually *meant*.

Margaret Way

Men of the Outback

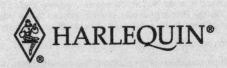

HARLEQUIN®

TORONTO • NEW YORK • LONDON
AMSTERDAM • PARIS • SYDNEY • HAMBURG
STOCKHOLM • ATHENS • TOKYO • MILAN • MADRID
PRAGUE • WARSAW • BUDAPEST • AUCKLAND

ISBN 0-373-18241-4

HER OUTBACK PROTECTOR

First North American Publication 2006.

Copyright © 2006 by Margaret Way, Pty., Ltd.

This edition published by arrangement with Harlequin Books S.A.

® and TM are trademarks of the publisher. Trademarks indicated with
® are registered in the United States Patent and Trademark Office, the
Canadian Trade Marks Office and in other countries.

www.eHarlequin.com

Printed in U.S.A.

French champagne for every possible joyous occasion." She was born and educated in the river city of Brisbane, Australia, and now lives within sight and sound of beautiful Moreton Bay.

Books by Margaret Way:

HARLEQUIN ROMANCE®
705—THE OUTBACK ENGAGEMENT†
709—MARRIAGE AT MURRAREE†
737—THE CATTLE BARON'S BRIDE††

†*The McIvor Sisters*
††*Men of the Outback*

Don't miss any of our special offers. Write to us at the following address for information on our newest releases.

Harlequin Reader Service
U.S.: 3010 Walden Ave., P.O. Box 1325, Buffalo, NY 14269
Canadian: P.O. Box 609, Fort Erie, Ont. L2A 5X3

CHAPTER ONE

Darwin Airport
The Northern Territory
Australia

INSIDE the domestic terminal Daniel surveyed the swirling crowd. A full head and shoulders over most people he had an excellent view over the sea of bobbing heads. He was confident he'd spot the girl, technically his boss. There were tourists galore. Most were probably headed for the World Heritage listed great national park, Kakadu, but many of the faces in the crowd were familiar; Territorians returning from a stint in the big coastal cities of the eastern seaboard; business, pleasure, maybe both. Striding along to the check-in counter, where his charge had agreed to be, a booklet on the Northern Territory in hand, he constantly exchanged waves and friendly calls. He was a familiar figure himself after nearly six years of working for Rigby Kingston, a pioneer cattleman recently deceased. His allotted chore for the day was picking up Kingston's long estranged granddaughter, Alexandra, and ferrying her back to the station.

She could have flown to Alice Springs. That would have been a lot closer to Moondai. It was a bit of a haul from Darwin in the tropical Top End of the Territory to Moondai in the Red Centre but he'd managed to kill two birds with the one stone, dropping his leading hand off at RDH, the Royal Darwin Hospital, for a deferred minor op and picking up the girl who had made the long trip from Brisbane. But surely even a city girl would appreciate the magnificent spectacle of great stretches of the Top End under water? That was what she was going to see. Vast swathes of floodplains teeming with nomadic water birds; chains of billabongs floating armadas of exquisite multicoloured waterlilies; the western fringe of Kakadu, the North, East and West Alligator Rivers snaking through the jungle. That stupendous panorama, especially the endless vistas of waterlilies and the thundering waterfalls of the Wet were to him as much an enduring image of the Top End as were the crocodiles.

They were into March now. The Wet, the *Gunemeleng* as the aboriginals called it, was all but over. Two cyclones had threatened the tropical North, one extremely dangerous. It had put Darwin, destroyed in Cyclone Tracy in 1974, on high alert. Mercifully cyclone Ingrid had taken herself off into

Finke, the oldest river on earth, ninety-nine per cent of the time dry, was now flowing bank to bank. These days it thrilled him to fly over it rejoicing in all the waterfalls that ran off the ochre coloured rock faces into serene green gullies.

Born in tropical North Queensland not far from the mighty Daintree rain forest he had become used to the desert environment. It was very, very special. Maybe the girl would think so, too. After all she had been born on Moondai and spent enough years there to remember it.

"Dan!" A voice boomed.

A passenger off the Brisbane-Darwin flight, a big affable looking man, pushing sixty with keen blue eyes threw out an arm. It was Bill Morrissey, a well respected member of the Northern Territory Administration.

"How are you, sir?" Respect and liking showed in Daniel's face.

They shook hands. "Hot and tired." Morrissey wiped his forehead with a spotless white handkerchief. "What brings you into Darwin?"

No harm in telling him. "I'm here to pick up Alexandra Kingston and deliver her to her family."

"Lordy!" Morrissey put a hand to his fast thinning

hair as though to check it was still there. "Wouldn't like to be that poor child! Not with those relatives. Rigby's will would have totally alienated his son and grandson and let's not forget the second wife, Elsa. I have to see it as an angry man's last response. Rigby cut his family out of the main game even when it's a fact of life dynasties die out without sons to take over. Daughters tend to walk off with some guy out of the family field."

"True," Daniel acknowledged, having witnessed that scenario first-hand. "But in all fairness to Mr. Kingston, Lloyd and Berne aren't cut out to be cattlemen. Maybe Mr. Kingston made demands on them they simply couldn't cope with, but they have no taste for the job on their own admission."

"Well, they could never be carbon copies of him," Morrissey replied. "A lot of rich families produce at least a couple of offspring who have no head for big business. Now the girl's father, Trevor, *was* shaping up to be a chip off the old block. Tragedy he was killed. It happens in our way of life. You're still going to be around, though, aren't you, Dan? Can't see how they could possibly do without you. You might be young, but you're up there with the best."

Daniel heard the sincerity in the older man's voice. "Thanks for the vote of confidence, sir. I'm committed to one year at least under the terms of Mr. Kingston's will."

Morrissey clamped a hand on his shoulder. "Trust

"Twenty-eight." Sometimes it seemed to Daniel he had to be at least double that age, he had seen so much of life.

"Do you have any idea how well regarded you are?"

Daniel gave his very appealing, crooked grin. "If I am I'm very glad. I've worked hard."

"That you have!" Morrissey agreed, knowing the full story. "Rigby certainly thought so and we all know how demanding he was."

"He wasn't loved, that's for sure!" Daniel agreed wryly, "but I always found him fair enough and willing to *listen*. One of the things that made him so successful I guess. He never had a closed mind, even for a relative newcomer to the game like me. Besides I've learned to love the Territory. It's my home now."

"And the Territory needs young men like you," Morrissey said, comfortable with the mantle of mentor. "Young men of brains and vision. You've got both." He thrust out his hand for a final shake. "Best go now. Can't keep the chauffeur waiting. When you're next in Darwin come and see me. When your twelve months are up I guarantee I'll find you something to suit your talents."

"Might hold you to that, sir." Daniel grinned.

Morrissey began to move away, then paused, looking back. "By the way, Joel Moreland has expressed a desire to meet you. Not for the first time I might add. The Big Man's heard about you. Now he wants to take a good *look* at you. You could be in luck, there, my boy. Moreland is a Territory icon. I'll set it up for lunch. Just the three of us."

"That's great!" Daniel was surprised and deeply flattered. It never hurt to have friends in high places he thought as he strode off. Joel Moreland was known in the Territory as the man with the Midas touch. Not one of his many ventures stretching back forty years and more had failed. Not that the man with the Midas touch hadn't known his own tragedy. Moreland's son and heir, Jared, had been killed in a freak accident at an Alice Springs rodeo well over twenty years before. Apparently he had put his own life on the line to save a cavorting teenager from a maddened bullock. The Grim Reaper no more spared the lives of those rolling in money than he did the poor.

Well *he* knew all about being poor but strangely he'd never developed any lasting complexes about it. He was a fighter. He'd spent much of his childhood fighting for the honour of his pretty little mother and the good name some callous guy had stripped from her without looking back. People didn't label the illegitimate *bastards* any more. It was politically incorrect. When he was a kid grow-

little help. Even the strongest couldn't do it on their own. A Channel Country cattleman called Harry Cunningham had given him and his mother that helping hand when they were so down on their luck he'd been filled with fear his vulnerable mother would resort to taking her own life. Harry Cunningham had been their saviour, the man behind his education.

"You've got to have an education, Dan. You're smart as they come, but education is everything. Get it. Then you can pay me back."

Well he had paid Harry back, reviving the fortunes of Harry's run-down station only to have Harry's daughter, his only child, sell the valuable property within a month. Some sons-in-law proved themselves to be eminently capable as substitute sons but as Bill Morrissey had pointed out this particular daughter had married a city slicker who had shied away violently from the prospect of taking on a cattle station. Far easier to take the money and run.

It was Harry's glowing recommendations that had come to the ears of his late employer, Rigby Kingston. That's what had gained him a job on Moondai, rising to the rank of overseer. It was *he* Rigby Kingston had looked to. Not his remaining son, Lloyd, or Lloyd's son, Bernard. It wasn't often a man bypassed the males of his family to leave the bulk of his estate to a granddaughter, moreover one who had been banished. What was his reasoning? Did Kingston secretly want his heirs to *fail?* Having been robbed of his favourite son, Trevor, the girl's father, the rest could go to hell? Rigby Kingston had been a very *curious* man. Yet tyrannical old Kingston had left him, Daniel Carson, a nobody, however dramatically he had risen, a handy little nest egg of $250,000, on top of his salary, on the proviso he remain on Moondai as overseer for a period of twelve months after Kingston's demise.

It was all so damned *bizarre!*

It didn't take him a minute more to spot the Kingston heiress. All five feet two of her. Her slight figure, standing brolga-like on one leg, was a few feet from the check-in counter, booklet on the Territory in hand. He didn't know what he had been expecting. An ultra smooth city girl in expensive designer gear. There were plenty of them about. It surely wasn't *this!* A cute little teenager—okay she was twenty, nearly twenty-one, but what the heck, she didn't look a day over sixteen and she was showing at least five or six inches of baby smooth skin between the end of her T-shirt and the top of her tight jeans. He took in the delicate coltish limbs, jeans sinking on nonexistent hips, the T-shirt blue with a silver logo on the front of her delicate breasts, gen-

What the hell! He wasn't such a dangerous looking character, *was* he? Maybe his hair was overly long. It was very thick and it grew at a helluva rate and there weren't too many hairdressers around Moondai. He had lived with his image so long he couldn't really tell how he presented. Perhaps seen through those saucer eyes staring at him he looked a touch wild; eyes that were so big and radiant a blue they dwarfed her other small features. Except maybe the mouth. Not a trace of lipstick so far as he could see, but then makeup was a mystery to him, but beautifully shaped. He had a notion he was staring back, but she was *such* a surprise packet.

Obviously she didn't agree with the notion that a woman's hair was her crowning glory, either. Hers was cut to within an inch of its life. Buttercup-yellow, curling in the humid heat into a cap of pretty petals. A few escaped onto her forehead. What was the definition of sexy for God's sake? Against all the odds Miss Alexandra Kingston, looking like she wasn't all that long out of school, fell into that category.

He collected himself enough to tip a jaunty forefinger to the brim of his black akubra. It felt like he *towered* over her all the more so because he was wearing high heeled riding boots. He scrutinised her shoes, soft moccasin kind of thing. "Ms Kingston?" he asked, trying to keep all trace of dryness out of his voice and not succeeding all that well.

"Sandra, please." She cleared a husky throat. "No one calls me Ms Kingston." Her hand rose defensively to her neat little skull as though to check on an unfamiliar hair style.

Probably just cut it, he thought. Unceremoniously with a pair of nail scissors like an expression of rebellion.

"I *am* an employee," he pointed out.

"Hey." She shrugged. "I said you can call me Sandra."

"How very egalitarian. Dan Carson." He introduced himself. "I'm your overseer on Moondai and your chauffeur for the day. I'm here to transport you to the station."

"Transport?"

He saw her gulp. "Now why make it sound like you're going on a road train?" he chided gently. Road trains that transported anything from great numbers of cattle to petrol were an awesome sight on Outback roads.

"I was worried about the word, *transport*," she said smartly.

Her voice all of a sudden had an unexpected *bite* to it, an *adultness* that had him re-evaluating her. "Set your mind at rest. We go by helicopter," he told her. Could there be a trace of *hostility* in those bluer

acid. "Only Moondai's no home of mine, Mr. Carson."

"Please—Daniel." He dipped his head. "I'm not in *my* element with Mr. Carson."

"Great! I'm glad we've got that sorted out."

So it *was* antagonism.

"Actually I thought Christian names might be beneath you." She was desperate to cover up the fact she felt as if she'd been struck by lightning. Daniel Carson, her overseer, was a marvellous looking guy with Action and Adventure emblazoned all over him. He'd make the perfect hero in some epic movie, she thought. Dark, swashbuckling good looks, splendid body, commanding height. The aura was *mesmerising*, but his manner was definitely nonthreatening.

"Nothing so old-fashioned," he mocked gently, looking towards the luggage carousel. It was ringed by passengers all staring fixedly towards the chute as though willpower alone would cause the luggage to start tumbling through. Every last one appeared to be in a desperate hurry to be somewhere else. "The baggage hasn't started to arrive as yet," he commented, unnecessarily, just making conversation. "How many pieces do you have?"

"Just the one," she murmured, so overloaded by

his presence, she transferred her attention to the milling crowd. Multiracial. Multilingual. English predominated; a variety of accents, Aussie, Pommie, New Zealander, American. Lots of backpackers. A group of handsome Germans, speaking their own language, which she had studied for four years at high school; Italian, Greek, Scandinavian, ethnic groups from all over the South-East Asia region.

As the gateway into Australia, Darwin, named in honour of Charles Darwin, the famous British naturalist, was a real melting pot; a far more cosmopolitan city than her home base, Brisbane. In fact it had the *feel* and even the smell of Asia. Hot, my God, how hot and such *humid* air! Almost equatorial but somehow vibrant, the scent of jasmine, joss sticks, spices; beautiful golden skinned Asian girls, dead straight shining hair sliding down their backs, strolling by in little bra tops with tiny shorts, a trio of older Asian women wearing gorgeous silk tunics over trousers.

She saw her overseer, Dan Carson, pause to smile at an attractive flight attendant who came over all giggly and flushing. Who could blame her, Sandra thought, wanting to put an instant stop to it. "Hi, Dan!"

"Hi, Abby!" His eyes eventually moved back to Sandra's small censorious face. Mentally he began to rearrange his first impressions. Young she might be, but she was as sharp as a tack. "You believe in travelling light?"

mouth. "Not especially in women. They generally travel with mountains of luggage."

"You'd know, would you?" Another haughty look as like a replay, two more attendants smiled and wiggled their fingers at him while he grinned back, saluting them with a forefinger to the broad brim of his hat already tipped rakishly over his eyes. Not only her overseer but a playboy of sorts though there was something almost mischievous in those grins.

"I'd say so." He turned back to her.

He used that flashing, faintly crooked white smile like a sex aid she thought looking on him sternly. "Well I'm not staying long."

"How totally unexpected." He couldn't keep the mockery out of a baritone that flowed like molasses. "Seeing you've inherited the station and all."

Sandra's eyes glowed the blue of a gas flame. "So what are you saying, that's *amazing?*"

He shrugged. "No more than if you said you'd climbed the Matterhorn on your own. Still, I'm sure your grandfather had his reasons."

She gave a cracked laugh. "He did. He hated me. Now he's gone he wants Moondai to go to wrack and ruin. Then again, my grandfather never could miss an opportunity to cheat the family out of their expectations. How did he come to hire *you?*" She met his eyes squarely, not bothering to conceal the challenge. "Surely there's Uncle Lloyd and cousin Bernie to take charge?"

"Both of whom prefer a different lifestyle," he returned blandly. "No, actually the job got dumped on me."

"You don't sound as though you expect to lose it any time soon?" she cut in.

Pretty perceptive! "Now this is the tricky bit," he explained. "Under the terms of your grandfather's will I can't check out for at least twelve months."

"What?" She rammed both hands into her jeans pockets. Her waist was so tiny he knew he could span it with his two hands.

"You didn't know about it?" The way she tossed her head reminded him of a high stepping filly.

"My mind went blank after the first few minutes of hearing the will read."

"Pays to listen," he commented briefly. "Ah, the baggage is starting to come through. Let's go." He grabbed hold of her soft leather hold-all and slung it over his shoulder. "You can point out which suit-case is yours when it arrives. Or is it a backpack?"

"It's a designer case," she said flatly.

"Sweet Lord!" Try as he might he couldn't prevent a laugh.

"Envious?"

"Not at all."

She was a *tiny* little thing. He could fit her into his back pocket.

"He *loves* me." She stared straight ahead, almost trotting to keep up with him and his long, long legs.

"Loves you?" he repeated, as though amazed she was ready for romantic love. "Would this friend be your fiancé?"

"He's gay," she said quite patiently, considering how she felt. Outside, all mock toughness and tart banter. Inside, a throbbing bundle of nerves.

Daniel took up a position beside the carousel as the throng miraculously parted for him like the Red Sea for Moses.

"He's nearly eighty," she continued, trying to keep her attention on the circling luggage when she felt like flopping in a heap. It had been a long, long trip from Brisbane. Another one faced her. She was terrified of light aircraft and helicopters. With good reason. "He has his Abyssinian cat, Sheba, and he has me. We're neighbours and good friends."

"So where do you live?" he asked mock politely, lifting a hand to acknowledge yet another enthusiastic wave from the far side of the luggage carousel.

All these women trying to communicate with *her* overseer, instead of getting on with their business.

Sandra fumed. She didn't feel in the least good humoured about it. An attractive redhead this time, who seemed to have peeled off most of her clothes in favour of coolness. It was irritating all this outrageous flirtation.

"You don't need to know," she told him severely. "But I'm desperately missing my flat already."

"Like the older man do you?" he asked, rather amused by her huffiness. It was fair to say she didn't *look* like a considerable heiress. She didn't dress like one, either. She was definitely *not* friendly when he was long used to easy smiles from women.

"The older the better," she said with emphasis. "You seem awfully young to be overseer of a big station?" She eyed him critically. He radiated such *energy* it needed to be channelled.

"I grew up *fast*," he answered bluntly. "I had a very rough childhood."

"That's hard to believe." He really was absurdly good-looking. Hunk was the word. Stunning if you liked the cocky macho male always ready for the next conquest. "You look like you were born to the sound of hundreds of champagne corks popping… already astride your own pony by the time you were two."

He smiled grimly. "You're way off." He watched the expensive suitcase tumble out onto the conveyor belt, getting exactly the same treatment as the most humble label.

Haven't I just." There was a forlornness in her eyes before the covers came down.

He hefted her heavy suitcase like it was a bundle of goose down. "Listen, how are you feeling?" he asked, noticing she had suddenly lost colour.

"Quite awful since you ask!"

Such a tart response but he didn't hold it against her. "Did you have anything to eat on the plane?"

Dammit if he didn't have a dimple in one cheek. "A big steak," she answered in the same sarcastic vein. "Actually I had an orange juice. Plane food lacks subtlety don't you think? Besides, I hate planes. I thought I might throw up. I didn't really want to precipitate a crisis."

He pondered for half a second. "Why don't we grab something to eat now?" he suggested. "There are a couple of places to grab coffee and a sandwich. Come to think of it I'm hungry, too."

She didn't bother to argue. He was used to taking charge as well. He didn't even consult her about what she wanted but saw her seated then walked over to the counter to order.

Two waitresses, one with a terrible hair day, sped towards him so quickly, the younger one, scowling darkly, was forced to fall back to avoid being muscled aside. No matter where you were good-looking guys managed to get served first, Sandra thought disgustedly.

Macho Man returned a few minutes later with a laden tray. "This might help you feel better," he said, obviously trying to jolly her up.

"Thank you." She tried to fix a smile on her face, but she was feeling too grim.

He placed a frothy cappuccino with a good crema in front of her, a plate of sandwiches and a couple of tempting little pastries. "We can share. There's ham and whole grain mustard or chicken and avocado."

"I don't really care."

He rolled his eyes. "Eat up," he scolded, exactly like a big brother. "You're not anorexic are you?" He surveyed her with glinting eyes. "Not as I understand it, anorexics admit to it."

"I eat plenty," she said coolly, beginning to tuck away.

"Pleased to hear it." He pushed the plate of sandwiches closer to her. "What did you do to your hair, if it's not a rude question? Obviously it's by your own hand, not a day at the hairdressers?"

To his consternation her huge beautiful eyes turned into overflowing blue lagoons.

It made him feel really bad. "Look, I'm sorry," he apologised hastily, remorse written all across his strongly hewn features. "You have a right to wear

so contrite she had an urge to t[...]
moment thing when she'd barely [...]
of it. "A little friend of mine died rec[...]
mia," she said, her expression a mix of g[...]
derness. "She was only seven. When she [...]
beautiful curly hair, I cut mine off to be supp[...]
Afterwards the two of us laughed and cried [...]
selves silly at how we looked."

He glanced away, his throat tight. "Now that's the saddest story in the world, Alexandra."

"You just want to die yourself."

"I know."

The sympathy and understanding in his voice soothed her.

"But your little friend wouldn't want that," he continued. "She'd want you to go on and make something of your life. Maybe you even owe it to her. What was her name?"

"Nicole." She swallowed hard, determined not to break down. She could never ever go through something so heartbreaking again. "Everyone called her Nikki."

"I'm sorry." He sounded sad and respectful.

She liked him for that. It was oddly comforting considering he was a perfect stranger. "The death of

life," he
beloved

nodded,
into his
ere was.
g, thick,
et-black
ed up in
leaming
y struc-
leam of
ld *rasp*.

you choose. It actually looks
t be cool?"
f her hand across her eyes
big macho guy looked
ll him. A spur of the
een able to speak
ntly of leukae-
rief and ten-
ost all her
ortive.
our-

She could almost *feel* it, unable to control the little shudder that ran down her spine. He was the sort of guy who looked like he could handle himself anywhere, which she supposed would add to his attractiveness to women. A real plus for her, however, was that he could be *kind*. Kindness was much more important than drop dead good looks.

"I know what loss is all about," he said, after a moment of silence, absently stirring three teaspoons of raw sugar into his coffee. "There are stages one after the other. You have to learn to slam down barriers."

"Is that what you did?" Her voice quickened with interest, even as she removed the sugar. Obviously he had a sweet tooth and too much sugar wasn't good for his health.

thought was about sixteen," he said, not altogether joking.

"Try again." She bit into another sandwich. They were *good*. Plenty of filling on fresh multigrain bread.

"Okay I know you're twenty." He concentrated on her intriguing face with her hair now all fluffed up.

"Nearly twenty-one." She picked up another sandwich. "Or I will be in six months time when I inherit. If I'm still alive, that is. Once I'm on Moondai and at the mercy of my relatives who knows?"

He set his cup down so sharply, a few heads turned to see if he'd cracked the saucer. "You can't be serious?"

"Dead serious," she confirmed. "My mother and I left Moondai when I was ten, nearly eleven. She was a basket case. I went into a frenzy of bad behaviour that lasted for years. I was chucked out of two schools but that's another story. We left not long after my dad, Trevor, was killed. Do you know how he was killed?"

"I'd like you to tell me." Obviously she had to talk to someone about it. Like him, she appeared to have much bottled up.

"He crashed in the Cessna."

He sat staring at her. "I know. I'm sorry."

Her great eyes glittered. "Did your informant tell you the Cessna was sabotaged?"

"Dear oh dear!" He shook his head in sad disbelief.

"Don't dear oh dear me!" she cried emotionally.

Clearly her beliefs were tearing her to pieces. "Sandra, let it go," he advised quietly. "There was an inquiry. The wreckage would have been gone over by experts. There was no question of foul play. Who would want to do such a thing anyway?"

She took a deep gulp of her coffee. It was too hot. It burnt her mouth. She swore softly. "You may think you're smart—you may even *be* smart—I'm sure you have to be to run Moondai, but that was a damned silly question, Daniel Carson. Who was the person with the most to gain?"

He looked at her sharply. "God, you don't think very highly of your uncle, do you?"

"Do you?"

"My job is to run the station, not criticise your family."

Tension was all over her. "So we're on different sides?"

"Do we have to be?" He looked into her eyes. A man could dive into those sparkling blue lagoons and come out refreshed.

"I don't *want* Moondai," she said, shaking her shorn head.

"That includes cousin Berne?"

She put both elbows on the table. "He was a dreadful kid," she announced, her eyes darkening with bad memories. "He was always giving me Chinese burns but I never did let him see me cry. Worse, he used to kick my cat, Olly. We had to leave her behind which was terrible. As for me, I could look after myself and I could run fast. I bet he's no better now than I remember?"

"You'll have to see for yourself, Alexandra." He kept his tone deliberately neutral.

"I won't have one single friend inside that house," she said then shut up abruptly, biting her lip.

He didn't like that idea. "I work for you, Sandra," he told her, underscoring *work*. "If you need someone you can trust you should consider me."

She continued to nibble on her full bottom lip, something he found *very* distracting. "I certainly won't have anyone else. I wasn't going to offload my troubles onto you, not this early anyway, but I'm a mite scared of my folks."

He was shocked. "But, Sandra, no one is going to harm you." Even as he said it, his mind stirred with anxiety. The Kingstons were a weird lot, but surely not homicidal. Then again Rigby Kingston had left an estate worth roughly sixty million. The girl stood between it and them. Not a comfortable position to be in.

Frustrated by his attitude, Sandra dredged up an old Outback expression. "What would you know, you big galah!"

He choked back a laugh. "Hey, mind who you're calling names!"

"Sorry. Galah is not the word for you. You're more an eagle. But surely you realise they must have been shocked out of their minds by the will. Uncle Lloyd would have fully expected to inherit. He wouldn't want to work the place. He'd sell it. Bernie would go along with that. Bernie disliked anything to do with station work. You must know that, too. Where do you live?" she asked abruptly.

"I have the overseer's bungalow."

"Roy Sommerville, what happened to him? He was the overseer when we left."

"Died a couple of years back of lung cancer. He was of the generation that chain smoked from dawn to dark."

"Poor old Roy! He was nice to me."

"Anyone would be nice to you." His response was involuntary.

She grimaced. "I don't recall Uncle Lloyd ever bouncing me on his knee. His ex-wife, Aunty Jilly, used to dodge me and my mother all the time. No wonder that marriage didn't work out. Bernie was

know. "Any fond memories?"

"Hello, we're talking Rigby Kingston here!" she chortled. "The most rambunctious old son of a bitch to ride out of the Red Centre."

He shook his head. "When you'd melt any man's heart." A major paradox here when Kingston had left her his fortune.

"I don't *want* to melt men's hearts," she exploded, the blood flowing into her cheeks. "It's all smiles and kisses one day. Rude shocks the next. I don't like men at all. They don't bring out the best in me."

He held back a sigh. "I think you must have had some bad experiences."

"You can say that again! But to get back to my dear old grandpop who remembered me at the end, I do recall a few pats on the head. A tweak of the curls before he was out the front door. I didn't bother him anyway. He was happy enough when my dad was alive. After that, he turned into the Grandad from Hell. He seemed to put the blame for what happened to my dad on my mother."

"How could *she* have been responsible?" he asked, puzzled.

"Uncle Lloyd blew the whistle on a little affair

she had in Sydney," she told him bleakly. "Mum used to go away a lot and leave Dad and me at Moondai. Uncle Lloyd said she was really *wild,* but then he was a great one for airing everyone else's dirty linen." She broke off, staring at him accusingly. "You must have heard all this?"

Why pretend he hadn't when an unbelievable number of people had made it their business to fill him in on Pamela Kingston's alleged exploits? Lloyd Kingston wasn't the only one who liked airing the world's dirty linen. Apparently Sandra's mother had been famous for being not only radiantly beautiful but something of a two-timing Jezebel. There had even been gossip about who Alexandra's father really was. Alexandra didn't look a bit like a Kingston which now that he had seen her Dan had to concede. The Kingstons were dark haired, dark eyed, *tall* people with no sense of humour. Pamela had routinely been labelled as an absentee wife and mother who spent half her time in Sydney and Melbourne living it up and getting her photo in all the glossy magazines. Dan knew she had remarried eighteen months after her first husband's death. Wedding number two was no fairy tale, either. It too had gone on the rocks. Pamela was currently married to her third husband, a merchant banker with whom she had a young son. It seemed Sandra had moved out fairly early. He wondered exactly *when?* Not yet twenty-one the combative lit-

ious forms it took as the illustrious Dr. Freud.

"All right, what are you thinking about?" Sandra cut into Dan's pondering.

"I was wondering when you left home?"

At the question put so probingly she began to move the salt and pepper shakers around like chess pieces. "To be perfectly honest, from which you might deduce I'm given to telling lies—I'm *not*—I've never really had a home."

"You and me both," he confessed, laconically.

Instantly she was diverted from her own sombre thoughts. "So there's more?" She leaned forward, elbows on the table, all attention.

"If you think I'm about to share my life story with you, Ms Kingston, I'm not!"

She shook her head. "Is that a hint *I'm* communicating too much?" she asked tartly, slumping back in her chair.

"Not at all. It strikes me you've spent a lot of time alone?"

She sighed theatrically, then stole one of his sandwiches. "That's what happens when your mother has had three husbands."

"One of them was your dad," he pointed out.

She nearly choked she was so quick to retort.

"That son of a bitch Lloyd challenged that at least a dozen times before I was ten.'"

The muscles along his jaw tightened. He knew all about labels. "He's not a very nice person," he said shortly.

"He's a bully," she said. "And I'm going to prove that. He really *really* upset my mother. I know she wasn't the woman to exercise caution but don't you think she would have been completely insane to try to put one across my dad let alone my fearsome old grandpop. My dad always knew I was his little girl. He used to call me 'my little possum.' He told me every day he loved me. I think he was the only person in the entire world who did. Then he went off and left me. I was so sad and so angry. My mum and I *needed* him. It's awful to be on your own." She dug her pretty white teeth into her nether lip again, dragging them across the cushiony surface, colouring it rosy.

"So a man does come in handy?" he asked.

She looked into his eyes and he saw the sorrow behind the prickly front. "A dad is really important."

Hadn't he faced that all his life? Even a bastard of a dad.

"Getting killed was the very last thing your dad *wanted*, Sandra. Unfortunately death is the *one* appointment none of us can break. I'm sure your mother loves you. Your grandfather too in his own way."

"God that's corny!" Now she fixed him with a contemptuous glare. "In his *own* way. What a cop-out!"

who is older than you by three years."

"I can count," she said shortly, hungrily polishing off another one of his sandwiches. "I actually got to go to university. I was a famous swot."

"Head never out of a book?"

"Something like that." She shrugged, picking away a piece of rocket. "In a locked room. My stepfather, Jeremy Linklatter, IV, developed a few little unlawful ideas about me."

He who thought himself unshockable was shocked to the core.

"You can't trust anyone these days," she said in a world-weary fashion. "Certainly not men. There should be a Protection Scheme for female stepchildren."

"Hell!" he breathed, hoping it wasn't going to get worse. "He didn't touch you?"

Her expression showed her detestation of stepfather Jeremy. "Not the bad stuff." How was she confiding all this to a stranger when she had never spoken about it at all? There was just something about this Daniel Carson.

"Thank God for that!" He released a pent-up sigh. "The guy must have crawled out from under a rock. So when did you leave home?"

She shrugged, licking a little bit of avocado off her fingertip. "I went to boarding school. Then I went on to uni and had on campus accommodation. It proved a lot safer than being at home."

"Did your mother know what was going on?" Surely not. That would have been criminal.

She sighed. "My mother only sees what she wants to see. She can't help it. It's the way she's made. Besides, Jem was pretty adept at picking his moments. I was always on high alert. Occasionally he got in an awful messy kiss or a grope. Once I pinched his face so hard he cried out. Then I took to carrying a weapon on my person."

He could picture it. "Don't tell me. A stun gun?"

"Close. A needle with a tranquillizer in it."

"You're joking!" That was totally unexpected. And dangerous.

"All right, I am. But I was desperate. I took to carrying my dad's Swiss Army knife. You know what that is?"

"Of course I know what it is," he said, frowning hard at the very idea of her needing to carry such a thing as a weapon. "I have one, like millions of other guys. It's a miniature tool box."

"You don't have one like mine. It's a collector's item," she boasted. "An original 1891 version."

"Really? I'd like to see it."

She laughed. "And I'd enjoy showing it to you only I couldn't bring it on the plane."

got. He just had all these urges. Men are like that."

"Indeed they're not," he rapped back. "Evil men give the rest of us ordinary decent guys a bad name. It's utterly unfair. There's something utterly disgusting about a predator."

"That's why I like my gay friends," she announced, wiping her hands daintily on a paper napkin before brushing back the damp curls at her temple.

"How long was your hair?" he asked, his eyes following the movement of her small, pretty hands.

"That's a funny question, Daniel Carson."

He gave his dimpled, lopsided smile. "Oh, I dunno. I'm trying to visualise you as the girl you were."

"If you *must* know, I had a great mop of hair. A lot of people thought it was lovely. Say, those sandwiches were good. I think I must have been starving. I might even have another one of those little pastries. Oh, it's yours!" she observed belatedly.

"Take it," he urged. "You're the one paying."

"What?"

"Just a little joke," he said. "My shout this time."

"Which reminds me," she said in quite a different voice. "I want you up at the house."

His eyebrows shot up. "You can't mean living there?"

"I can mean and I do mean." She sat back, fiddling with her thumbs.

"Just forget about it," he answered flatly.

"Might I remind you, Daniel, I'm the boss. I want you about two steps up the hallway from me. I don't know you very well, but I'd find having a great big guy like you around—especially one with a Swiss Army knife—reassuring."

He frowned direly. "Sandra, your fears are groundless."

"Sez you!" she responded hotly, sitting up straight. "Do you know how many people get killed over money?"

"There could only be one in a million who don't finish up in jail," he told her in a stern voice.

"A few more than that filter through," she struck back.

He studied the flare-up of colour in her cheeks. "Listen, Ms Kingston, if you're under the impression your family would agree to that, you're very much mistaken. Both your uncle and your cousin would see me gone only neither of them can do my job. It was your *grandfather* who hired me. It was your grandfather who gave me so much authority. As you can imagine your uncle and your cousin bitterly resented that fact, even if they didn't want to take over the reins. After twelve months I'll have no alternative but to quit."

"You *won't* quit while I need you," she told him

"Just leave it for the time being, won't you?" he asked in his most reasonable voice. "See how the family reacts."

"In that case, Daniel, you better be present," she said. "So where did you come from anyway? Are you a Territorian?"

"I am now, but I come from all over."

"You're worse than I am," she sighed. "Could you be a bit more specific?"

"Maybe not today."

She looked at him searchingly. "So what about a compromise? Where *precisely* did you learn to manage a cattle station. You're what?" Her blue eyes ranged over him.

"You want me to produce a birth certificate? I'm twenty-eight, okay?"

"Most overseers aren't off the ground by then," she observed, impressed.

"Then I must be the eighth wonder of the world. As it happened, I learned from the best. My mother and I lived like gypsies moving around Outback Queensland until we came to rest in the Channel Country when I was about eleven. A station owner there, a Harry Cunningham, offered her the job of housekeeper after his wife died and there we stayed until he died some years back. His daughter sold the station almost immediately after. Something that must have the old man still swivelling in his grave. But such is life!"

There were a hundred questions she wanted to ask, but the first was easy. "So where is your mother now?"

His handsome face instantly turned to granite. "I'm like you, Alexandra. I'm an orphan."

"I'm sorry." She saw clearly he had no more dealt with the loss of his mother than she had the loss of her father. *Orphans*. Hadn't her mother been lost to her the day she married that rich, worthless scumbag, Jem?

"Not as sorry as I am," he said.

"What happened to her?" She spoke as gently as she could, fearing she was about to be rebuffed.

"I think we'll just leave it," he said.

CHAPTER TWO

HE TOOK her on a journey that filled her with fascination. The landscape beneath them was so vast, so timeless in character Sandra found herself awestruck. The first hellish minutes, just as she expected, had been taken up with fighting down her fears. She would never be cured of them. Not just of helicopters. In a chopper one couldn't look out on a fixed wing, causing not only in her, but in many people the sickening sensation the aircraft might simply drop out of the sky. She feared *all* aircraft. She'd been battling that particular phobia since she was a child and the family Cessna had taken a nosedive into the McDonnell ranges, not far from Moondai, with her father strapped into the pilot's seat. That was the start of it.

He did it, Sandy. Your uncle Lloyd. He caused it to happen. He'd know how. He was always jealous of your father. He couldn't let him inherit.

Some words are scorched into the memory as were some scenes, like her mother sobbing out accusations...

He did it, Sandy. He couldn't let your father inherit.

So where did that leave her, her grandfather's heir-ess, all these years later? No way was she sitting pretty. Just like her father she was a target. But un-like her trusting father she had learned the hard way to always be on red alert. It helped too to have backup. Small wonder she'd decided, very sensibly, to shift her overseer into the homestead for a time. Daniel Carson had an aura that made a woman feel safe. She suspected there was more than a hint of Sir Galahad about him. She even liked the way he stared down at her from his towering height, though occa-sionally it had made her feel like toppling backwards.

He was an excellent pilot. He was handling the helicopter with such confidence and skill she was actually approaching a state of euphoria, where she believed nothing bad could possibly happen. Pho-bias were only there to be licked! The ride was so *smooth!* She gave herself up fully to the pleasure and excitement of the flight.

The immensity, the primeval nature and the re-moteness of the landscape, lit by the brilliance of a tropical sun left an indelible imprint on the mind. This was a land unchanged in aeons. It appeared far more splendid than she remembered as a child. Of course there was no better way to see it than from a helicopter with its three-dimensional visual ef-fects. She felt as free as a bird, wheeling, skim-ming, darting across the glorious cobalt sky.

she was seeing them, from the air. A foaming white waterfall was coming up on the right. It crashed over the towering stone escarpment, throwing up a white haze like a great curtain. In contrast, the walls of the canyon glowed like a furnace, a throbbing orange-red streaked with bands of iridescent yellow and pink. Millions of litres of water were being delivered into the turbulent stream below, although the rains had abated some weeks back.

Gradually as the inundated land began to settle there would be an abundant harvest. The animals and the birds would begin to breed. Wildflowers would open out, going to work to form a prolific ground cover over the warm, receptive earth. All the varieties of palms and pandanus would put out new fronds. The golden and crimson grevilleas would bloom, the hibiscus and gardenia would spread their scent and colour across a background of lush greens. Mere words couldn't prepare a visitor to the Top End for the sight. Suddenly after years in the city, Sandra felt the tremendous pull of the great living Outback. The Outback had fashioned her. She had been happily content as a child. Maybe she could be again?

Beneath her mile after mile of lagoons filled to

the brim with beautiful waterlilies swept by. She knew the species: the sacred lily of Buddha, the red lotus, the pink and the white and the cream, and the giant blue waterlily with flowers that grew a foot across. The master of the waterways was down there, too. One could never forget that. The powerful salt water crocodile. She shuddered at the very thought. Moondai in the Red Centre was a long way from the crocs though according to the magnificent aboriginal rock drawings on the station they had inhabited the fabled inland sea of prehistory.

Daniel turned his handsome head to smile at her with a real depth of pleasure in his eyes. She smiled back, both of them in perfect accord; both captive to the space, the vast distances, the sunlight and the colours, the incomparable beauty of nature. Here was the very spirit of the bush. The air was so *clear,* it was like liquid crystal. By now, Sandra was so enthralled she'd completely forgotten how initially she had wanted to turn back. She felt happily content to fly with Daniel, an almost telepathic communication between them. It struck her he was really her kind of person. One knew these things right away.

It dawned on her very gradually their air speed was slowing. Steamy heat was rising from the waterlogged soil.

"Everything okay?" She turned to him, an alarmed croak in her voice.

from her lungs. All illusions of safety were abruptly shattered. Her worst nightmares appeared to be coming true. They were in trouble. Didn't trouble follow her around? The helicopter was losing power *and* altitude. She craned her head. Beneath them lay a forest of paperbarks with their slender trunks standing in who knows how many feet of water. At least she could swim. She thought of the crocs. Their bodies would provide a nice feed. Troubled though her life had been she felt a sharp nostalgia for it. She wanted a *future!*

Okay, time to pray. What was the point, a dissenting little voice said. Her most fervent prayers hadn't saved Nikki from a tragically early death. She would pray all the same. She couldn't afford to get on the wrong side of God. Maybe *her* time was up? Hers and Daniel Carson's. Maybe that was why he didn't feel like a stranger? They were going to die together.

She was suddenly indignant. There had been *enough* trouble in her life. She deserved a break. She couldn't submit to her fate without paying strict attention to their plight. Not that she could do anything, basically, but try to help Daniel spot a place to set the chopper down.

Sandra stared fixedly at the magnificent landscape beneath them that had abruptly turned hostile. Daniel would have no other option but to force land.

Tell him something he doesn't know.

But where? The vast terrain was covered in glittering swamps with a canopy of trees growing so close together if they were monkeys they could scamper across it. She even had a fevered thought if the worst came to the worst, they could bail out, land in the water then if they were lucky spring up a tree with a prehistoric monster snapping at their heels.

If there was one thing Daniel had learned it was to stay cool under pressure. Even immense pressure like this. They were a few kilometres into a big, flooded paperbark swamp. The manifold pressure had dropped off and he was losing power and RPM. Air speed was declining as well. He knew the girl was only too aware of it and the consequent danger, though he was so focused on what he was doing he dared not turn his head to look at her or even speak.

Seventy knots to sixty and bleeding off fast. No matter how he wished otherwise he had Alexandra Kingston with him. A girl whose father had been killed in a plane crash.

He couldn't lose another second. He used his radio to report a mayday, giving his bearings. What could be causing this failure? He scanned the control panel which was going haywire. Something was screwing the system. The helicopter was regu-

on the outer perimeter by pandanus.

Fifty knots.

God almighty! Was this the way it was going to end? A life span limited to a few decades? What a bloody mess. Adrenaline kicked in, flushing through his system. He was a good pilot, wasn't he? A very good pilot. Now was not the time to be modest. He was *lucky* as well, which was almost as good. He had the girl with him and she deserved a life. They had to survive. He had to land the chopper safely even if he clipped the rotors which was a strong probability. He could sense the girl beside him was sitting rigid with fear, but she wasn't screaming. Thank God for that! Many would be yelling their heads off at this point, when they were on the brink of a crash. She was, in fact, pointing frantically to a pocket handkerchief-sized clearing at the same time he spotted it coming up.

He lined the chopper up. The clearing was shaped like a playing field with its boundaries set at one end by a stand of pandanus, at the other by four paperbarks, their foliage iridescent in the sunlight.

Hell he almost loved her. She was far from stupid and she had kept her head. He had to applaud that.

Okay. It was now or never!

The swamp was rising to meet them with crocs in it for sure. Didn't you just love them? He had to judge the tips of the branches of the trees by centimetres. He could feel the tremendous rush of adrenaline through his body, even the thrill of extreme danger. Paradoxically it gave him a weird feeling of excitement as well as fear; a buoyancy he had experienced before in tight situations.

Ten metres above the water, the surface was quivering and shimmering like a sea of sequins, then it churned into waves by the strong down draught. He couldn't run the chopper on in case the skids got hooked onto the arched root system of the trees. If that happened, the chopper would flip over. A rotor tip only had to clip those trees. He could hear a hissing sound clearly. The clearing seemed to be lit up, preternaturally brilliant. It could signal the end but he took it as a good omen. He hovered, shutting everything out of his mind but the need to set the machine down safely. The will to survive transcended fear…all the blades were at the same pitch…

That's it. Hold it still. Praise the Lord!

At the last moment, Sandra shut her eyes, her small hands clenched into fists. Death was always waiting in the wings. She didn't want to see it coming. If she was going to die she was going to die. There was not much anyone could do about fate. But if anyone could save the situation this guy might. Sweat was pouring off her yet her blood was

Though she waited in limbo for the moment of impact and probable annihilation, the chopper seemed to come down in ultra slow motion as the rotor blades set up a whirlwind. The machine didn't *hit* the water, rather it seemed to Sandra's bemused mind it came down as lightly as a brolga on its tippy toes. She felt the skids sink and held her breath in case the probing skids got caught up in the trees' root systems and tossed the fragile aircraft around like a child's toy. Dread paralysed her limbs. This was a nightmare!

Only slowly, so slowly, the skids settled on the swamp bed.

She couldn't believe it!

Sandra's eyes flew open. The chopper was bobbing on the surface of the swamp, the body surrounded by streams of bubbles. There was a gurgle of water somewhere but they were stable.

Eureka!

The aircraft gave a groan that was almost human. Daniel killed the engine. The beating rotors, main and tail, gradually stopped their thundering.

All was still.

Sandra couldn't even turn to face him. Whole moments passed while her racing heartbeats slowed

to normal. Then she turned to him whooping trium-
phantly, unaware her face was milk-white with
shock. "Carson, you have to be the coolest cat on
the planet!"

"Supernatural!" he agreed wryly, tasting blood on
his bottom lip.

They hit an exultant high-five.

"Which reminds me, you idiot! You could have
killed us."

"I look on it more as a truly great save." Daniel
stared at the control panel. "The person I should really kill is whoever's been tinkering with the chopper."

"What are you saying?" She heard the shrill note
in her voice.

"Nothing. Absolutely nothing." Daniel backed off,
removing his earphones and unbuckling his seat belt.
"I have to get out and take a look. You stay here."

The very idea made her break out in a sweat. "You
didn't think I was just going to jump in? There must
be crocs in there."

He shook his head almost casually. "The water
around us isn't deep. It's already begun to subside.
Nevertheless we could become waterlogged even supposing I can fix whatever problem we have. The good
thing is we're not far out of Darwin. Air Rescue will
scramble another chopper in no time. I'll send you
back with them. You'll have to be winched up. I'll stay
with the chopper until we can get it airborne."

"So who's going to pinch it around here?" She re-

remember?"

"The *desert*, sweetheart," he jeered, not even aware in the stress of the moment he had called her that. "The Red Centre is completely different to the Top End. Desert and tropics, both in the Territory. Moondai might as well be a million miles away from the crocs."

"And I couldn't be happier about that," she retorted. "But shouldn't you stay put? You could come to a grim and gruesome end. I think I'd hate that."

He merely shrugged. "You don't happen to know how to handle a rifle?" He sounded extremely doubtful.

Sandra snorted. "Do I ever! My dad taught me how to handle a gun. I'm sure I remember. It's like learning to ride a horse."

Daniel studied her in amazement. "He must have started you off early?"

"Because I wanted to *learn*," she replied tartly. "Bernie could shoot. I had to be able to shoot too in case he planned a little accident. Grandpop used to think becoming a good shot was character building. So what do you want me to do?'

He frowned. "I'm going to make a full circuit of the chopper. It's a miracle we didn't sustain any damage to the main rotor. We're centimetres from the trees. What I want you to do, if you feel up to it, is cover me just in case we have a nosey visitor. Just don't shoot *me*, okay? Want to have a run through first?'

She unbuckled her belt and stood up though her legs were still wobbly. "Might be an idea. Where's the rifle?"

He moved to collect it from where it was stashed, broke it open to load it, snapped the action shut, then passed it to her. "Think you know what you're doing?"

"I'd prefer a dirty great cannon," she muttered, making her own checks and feeling it all coming back. "But I do know which end of this thing shoots." She swung up the rifle and took aim through the chopper's reinforced forward windshield. "If there really is a croc out there where do I shoot him? Right between the eyes? They've got tiny brains haven't they?"

"I've never had the pleasure of finding out. Just don't miss or it will come right after me."

"Then me." She slicked stray tendrils off her forehead. "I'm ready if you are."

"Then let's *do* it!' he said.

He plunged straight down into the water which only a week before would have been over his head. "Fuselage appears to be unscathed," he called to her eventually, his eyes scanning the waxed, glinting sides. "I want to check the shafts of the tail rotor. Keep your eyes peeled for ripples in the water."

moved about near soundlessly in the swamp stirring up the mud on the bed so the shining water turned dark and murky. Sandra followed him from one side of the helicopter to the other, her keen young eyes focused on the surface.

"Skids are in a web of roots and vegetation," he yelled to her. "That's the danger. They'll have to be cleared."

"I bet there are leeches in there?" Her voice was level, her face pale but resolute.

"Too right. The little buggers are stuck to my legs."

"Oh how vile! You can't *do* anything, can you?" she called.

His voice came back to her sounding perfectly in control. "I'm going to use my old faithful Swiss Army knife. I have to clear that vegetation. Just cover me."

She watched him plunge beneath the muddied waters coming up with coils of vines and gnarled roots that he tossed away across the swamp.

Only now could she smell the stomach-turning odour of mud and rotting vegetation. "Finish soon, Daniel," she begged him. Her whole body was vibrating with tension and the rifle felt very heavy.

"Doing my best!" he grunted and plunged again.

A brilliant sun burned down on the small clearing, the paperbarks and pandanus standing all around like sentinels. Sandra had never felt so exposed in her life.

Hurry, hurry, Daniel.

She saw his sodden dark head decorated with trails of luminescent green slime emerge at the very moment she spotted thirty feet beyond him an arrowhead of ripples across the stagnant surface of the swamp. Then at the apex of the triangle nostrils and behind that twin blackish bulges about twenty-two to twenty-three centimetres apart.

Eyes, that glinted gold!

She was so panicked for a moment she felt she might pass out. It was coming at surprising speed for such a great cumbersome creature. It was *surging* towards the challenger in its territory ready to dismember it limb from limb and stash the feast for a week later.

Horror was as sharp as a drill. "Get out!" she yelled. "Daniel, get out. It's a croc."

His lean, muscular body shot out of the water, his strong arms lunging at the body of the helicopter towards the open cockpit, hauling himself up.

Sandra took aim down the sights of the handsome bolt action rifle which had been fitted with a small telescope to make distant targets appear closer. Her whole face was pinched tight with control while she waited for the *precise* moment the

she held her nerve. Her finger that had been holding steady on the trigger, squeezed… The butt plate kicked back into her shoulder as the firing pin struck the rear end of the cartridge.

The noise was deafening in the torrid, preternatural quiet of the swamp.

"I've killed it. I think I've killed it." Her voice was ragged. There were runnels of sweat running down her face. "Did I?" she called to him for confirmation, "or did I just nick it?" Now the crisis was over she was shivering. "I should have had an M16."

"Sorry, they belong to the armed forces." Swamp water was streaming off him, as he stood within the chopper, his boots oozing mud. Leeches were feasting off him. "No worries, you got him all right," he assured her. "Didn't you see his yellow belly as he rolled?"

"Hell I'm good!" she congratulated herself. "I hope he's not just playing dead? Maybe he wants both of us to think so until it's time to make a leap into the cabin."

He shook his head. "What do you want, a tooth for a trophy? You got him, Sandra. Good and proper. I would never have guessed you could shoot so well. You turned into Annie Oakley right before my eyes."

She staggered away to sit down. "Who's Annie Oakley anyway? One of your girlfriends?"

He moved to the edge of the doorway, beginning to remove the brown and black leeches with the help of his Swiss Army knife. "Hell, Ms Kingston, none of my girlfriends can shoot like you. You could give a lot of guys lessons. Annie Oakley, for your information, was a famous American markswoman. Supposedly Buffalo Bill's girlfriend though I believe she married someone else."

"Maybe it was a sore point she could shoot better. Uugh!" she shuddered, watching him remove the bloodsuckers with no show of revulsion. "How's this for adventure? What are you going to do to top it?"

A lock of wet raven hair flopped over one eye. He tossed his head to dislodge it. "I could carry you on my shoulders across the swamp?"

"No thanks."

"Changed your mind about going back with me?"

She hugged herself, rocking back and forth. "What do you reckon went wrong?"

"Too early to say." One leg was clear.

"You seemed pretty sure it was tinkering before?"

He kept silent, concentrating on the sickening task to hand.

"Do you mind answering?"

"Maybe I was a little too quick off the mark back there. The chopper will be checked out. Accidents happen all the time."

CHAPTER THREE

SANDRA awoke with a start. She ached all over. That's what happened when you had to be winched into a helicopter. She rolled over onto her back, throwing an arm across her eyes. She was in a hotel room back in Darwin, waiting for Daniel to make a reappearance. He had remained with Moondai's downed chopper while Air Rescue had ferried her back to Darwin. She really ought to get up, take a shower, tidy herself up. Everyone had been very kind to her, smoothing her way. She knew people would have been just the same had she not been Rigby Kingston's heiress.

It was night outside. Darwin throbbed with life but inside the hotel room all was quiet save for the hum of the airconditioning. It was a very nice room; thickly carpeted, nicely furnished, the decor suited to the tropical environment, softly lit, a beautiful big waterlily print behind the bed. She slid her bare feet to the floor, sat a moment, then walked over to the

ans crossed at the lights.

Where was Daniel? He seemed to stand alone as an ally. Their shared ordeal had established quite a bond, as such hair-raising incidents tend to do, although she'd been feeling quite kindly disposed towards him even before that. She knew he viewed her as a young person who needed looking after. A loner. An orphan. He seemed to identify with that. Her lack of height—she was five-two—had never helped. Actually she was very good at fending for herself. A result of having a mother like Pam who really loved her but somehow had never been able to demonstrate it as a parent should. Not that her mother hadn't had her own harrowing time. Losing her husband the way she had, then being thrown out of Moondai had caused huge psychological trauma.

Her ever present memories began flashing through her brain again. She let them roll like a video clip. There was her mother lying on a bed, an arm thrown across her swollen, tear-streaked face. There was she, a bewildered, grief-stricken child, standing beside the bed, her hand on her mother's shaking shoulder, trying to make sense of a world that had been turned violently upside down.

I loved your father, Sandy. Our marriage would have survived if only he'd come away with me from Moondai. Moondai killed him. Moondai and your uncle Lloyd.

Uncle Lloyd said I'm not Daddy's. Is it true?

Would our marriage have survived if you weren't? Of course you're Daddy's little girl. Your uncle would say anything—anything at all—to try to discredit me.

Then how come Grandad threw us out? How could he do that if I'm his granddaughter?

Her mother's answer was always the same. *His grief was too powerful, Sandy. In a way he started to believe your uncle. But never, never doubt. You are Daddy's daughter. I swear to you on my life and his memory.*

Well, her doubts had persisted. It was only years later she had learned to thrust them aside. That was after her mother had married Jem—the second guy didn't count. Then she was truly on her own. She had never let her mother know what a sicko Jem really was. Her mother seemed happy with a man who liked to impose his will on everyone else, and now they had their son, her stepbrother, Michael, whom they both adored. Didn't she love Michael herself? Spoilt rotten Michael, despite the bad parenting was a nice little kid. And she was now an heiress who could have anything she liked. That's if she managed to survive the next six months. She would officially inherit on her twenty-first birthday

Twenty minutes later she was showered, shampooed and dressed to descend to the hotel restaurant. She had scrubbed up rather nicely she thought, splashing out on makeup, a pretty dress, and a couple of squirts of perfume to give Daniel Carson a bit of a jolt. She was a *woman,* not the coltish youngster he thought he had taken under his wing. That attitude had set her a challenge and she liked challenges. She liked Daniel. He had saved her life. How could she not?

So where was he? Surely he'd be back by now, whether they'd been able to restart the helicopter or not. One thing was certain, a team of sharpshooters couldn't stick around in that swamp at night. It was crawling with crocs. A mechanic with the rescue team had been winched down to him. Maybe together they could get the chopper back in the air as they hadn't run out of fuel. It had to be some mechanical defect.

The digital clock said 7:23 p.m. She was hungry. All she'd really had all day was hers and Daniel's sandwiches and a cup of coffee. She was starting to worry about him. She didn't want to go ahead and eat without him. Even as she thought it, the phone rang. She reached it at speed.

"Ms Kingston?"

Mysteriously her heart leapt. Was that significant? "Daniel, where are you?" She hoped she didn't sound too needy. She wanted to project the weight of maturity.

"Keep calm. I'm down the hallway. Isn't that what you wanted? Your overseer close by."

"You bet. What happened about the chopper? Did you get it out?"

"It took a lot longer than expected. It's grounded for a complete inspection."

"So what was the problem?" She caught her reflection in the mirror, all pink cheeked and bright-eyed as if they were having a cosy chat.

"You wouldn't know if I told you."

"Just tell me this. Should we contact the police?"

"No way," he said.

He had such a sexy voice on the phone. It was sort of like being *caressed*. She took a deep breath. "Listen, we can't talk on the phone. I'm hungry."

"Aaah, yes, I remember your appetite. Give me ten minutes okay?"

She'd probably have given him an hour.

She was *full* of surprises Daniel thought in some amazement. So much for the immature, just-out-of-school girl without a scrap of makeup! What he saw in front of him was a dead sexy little buttercup blonde of at least twenty. She was wearing a swishy

pected this transformation. Even her delicate breasts had perked up an inch or two. He was so astounded he had trouble hiding it, which didn't gel with his usual cool.

"Well good evening." He tried to smile his way out of it.

"Have a problem with the way I look, Daniel?" she asked sweetly, pleased at his readable reaction. Maybe she wouldn't take her little blue dress off.

"No, ma'am." He half shrugged. "You look different that's all.'

"*You* don't." She surrendered to the impish urge to put him in his place.

He winced. "So, you don't want to be seen with me?"

"I was only being a smart alec," she confessed, kindly.

He glanced down at himself. "I did try to order a dinner suit but they didn't have one in stock. I had to make do with what I've got on."

She made a business of looking him up and down as a prospective employer might the new chauffeur. What, she wondered, wouldn't he look good in? He was wearing what was obviously a new open necked shirt, white with fine beige and blue stripes and new denim jeans. "And those ridiculous boots?" she said, staring down at his feet. "You're towering over me."

"Yeah, well, most guys would. What was I supposed to do, buy a pair of loafers? This lot cost enough. My gear was ruined by the time we were finished in the swamp."

"Lose no sleep," she said loftily. "You'll be properly reimbursed."

"Thank you, ma'am." He bowed slightly.

"And you needn't be cheeky."

"I didn't know I was. I thought I was being respectful as befitting my position."

"Now that sounded sarcastic, Daniel," she warned, looking back over her shoulder for her clutch. "Where are we going?"

"Somewhere cheap," he said.

"*I'm* paying."

"That's different," he smiled, the dimple deep in his cheek. "I hope it suits but I've already made a booking at a little Vietnamese restaurant a short walk from here. I know the owners. The food's great."

"It's not noisy is it?"

"Not so it'll damage your ears." He studied the small face that had within a few short hours blossomed from a furled bud into full flower. "What's the problem, a headache?"

"I'm sick with nerves, Daniel, if you must know." She walked back to pick up her purse.

"I promise I'll lay down my life for you." He said

much as tweak a hair of your head," he said, trying to fight out of a daze.

"My hero!"

If he weren't shocked enough, she upped the ante by going on tiptoes and landing a kiss on the point of his jaw.

The food was as good as he had promised and more. The restaurant was small but fully booked. Only Daniel was clearly a favourite they would regrettably have been turned away.

"How come everyone likes you?" Sandra asked, tucking into prawns in a delicious spicy sauce.

"It's my sunny nature," Daniel explained. "*Not* everyone likes me, however. My boyish charm doesn't work on your uncle Lloyd or Berne. Berne and I often have words."

"What about?" she asked with interest.

He shrugged. "Just about anything sets Berne off."

"So he hasn't changed," she said dryly.

"I never had the great pleasure of knowing him when he was a kid."

"He was the biggest pain in the arse in all the world. Pardon the language." She glanced around hoping no one had heard her. Mercifully they were all too busy eating.

"You obviously feel strongly," he remarked, underlining the *strongly*.

"I apologised, didn't I? So, did you find anything suspicious? You can tell me now."

"Nothing we could pin on anyone." He shrugged. "If you really want to know it was like this." He launched into a detailed account of their preliminary findings until she held up her hand.

"Sorry. Like they say, that's way over my head. The real question is, are you game to charter another chopper and fly back to Moondai? More to the point, am I game to go with you?"

"It's the only way I know to get there, unless we walk." He forked another sea scallop.

"Do I need to remind you I'm an heiress?"

"No, ma'am."

"You're not going to keep calling me ma'am are you?" she asked crossly.

"I thought as you're my boss, I should. You don't seem to like Ms Kingston."

"What if dear old Uncle Lloyd is right and I'm *not* a Kingston?" she asked waspishly, then resumed eating.

"You must be. You remind me of your grandfather."

That set her beautiful eyes asparkle. "Do you want to hold on to your job, Daniel?"

ing voice at will. *"Please."*

"You really want to know?"

"Would I have asked if I didn't? To be honest, after surviving today's little mishap I feel we're meant to be friends." To prove it she solemnly took a scallop from his plate.

"Then I wouldn't lay it on you."

"That bad?"

Relaxed and smiling a minute before, he suddenly looked grim. "Absolutely awful. Your own childhood couldn't have been a dream?"

"It was okay until we lost Dad. Then everything changed. He used to call out from the front verandah, "Hi, my little darlin', I'm home." It wasn't my mother he was talking to. It was me. Sometimes I think both my parents needed their heads examined getting hitched."

He nodded. "Another case of if only I knew then what I know now. It makes me very wary of having a passionate affair."

"Now that I can't swallow." She threw him a look of disbelief.

"Meaning what?"

She shrugged a delicate shoulder. "I imagine

there's no end of women willing to go orgasmic—
is there such a word?—over you."

"Sandra, for that you need a good spanking."

"Please," she moaned. "Don't you dare talk
down to me."

"I didn't mean to." Frankly he was at a complete
loss how to treat her. It was easier before when she
looked like a little damsel in distress, but now? Just
looking at her made him gulp for air.

"That's okay then." She nodded briskly. "I'm
twenty, soon to be twenty-one. I've led an adven-
turous life. Some might say *seedy.* I think *I* would
in my place."

His tongue got the better of him. "So why am
I convinced you're a virgin?" As soon as he said
it he could have bitten his tongue out because
street smart as she claimed to be she coloured up
furiously.

"Daniel Carson our relationship does *not* extend
to discussing subjects like that." She tilted her head,
looking down her small perfect nose. "What do you
mean anyway? When I had all my hair and I was six
kilos heavier I was *hot!*"

He couldn't help himself. He laughed aloud.
"You'd set off a few smoke alarms right now." He
hadn't missed the appreciative glances coming her
way especially from one guy who might need sort-
ing out. "Better get cracking then and put back those

"Would I dare?" He raised his black brows. "There's actually nothing I like better than to see a girl with a healthy appetite."

She shrugged. "Maybe dining with you wasn't a good idea. All I've had all day was those sandwiches at the airport. Besides I can afford it remember? I'm an heiress. Except I don't want to be and I don't want Moondai."

"I think you can be persuaded to change your mind. Moondai is a wonderful place."

"Well it makes *your* eyes light up," she commented. "*You're* not hoping to marry me, are you?" She cocked her head to one side. "Because I have to tell you I'm not an easy target. Being an heiress attracts scores of guys."

"I wouldn't be a bit surprised if you finished up with several hundred suitors," he retorted, watching the waiter approach with their main course, chilli baked reef fish.

"Daniel Carson, you're *priceless!*"

"No, I'm one of those guys who like to make their own way in life, Alexandra."

"You'd better point out another if you see one," she returned breezily. "Oh goody, here comes the waiter! What about dessert?"

"You can have dessert if you want," he replied. "They do a delicious coconut dish with gula melaka syrup and another ginger one that's very good. I'm going to have one."

"How could they ever fill you?" She was in awe of his height and superb physique.

"My sweet little mother used to say that to me nearly every day of the week. *How am I going to fill you, Danny?*"

Some tender note in his voice, the poignant expression on his dynamic face tugged on her heart strings and made her close her eyes.

"Hey what are you doing?" he asked in alarm as a teardrop ran from beneath her thick lashes and down her cheek. "Sandra?"

She opened her eyes and choked back a cough. "Something went down the wrong way," she lied.

"Here, have a glass of water." He began to pour one.

"Thanks." She drank a little, looking up brightly as the Vietnamese waiter arrived at their table. "Ah, this looks sensational!" She smiled.

He was out of it—after all it had been quite a day—when the insistent ring of the phone ripped him out of the enveloping clouds.

"Daniel? Get down here fast," a voice hissed.

Instantly he was on red alert. "Sandra?"

"Someone else you know?" she asked sharply.

tive blond women of this world had to put up with, he thought wrathfully. He shouldered into his shirt, not bothering to button it. Sandra was several rooms along from him down the corridor. He was at the very end of the hallway.

Outside in the passageway, he caught the back of a heavily built guy, not tall, striding purposefully towards the lift. At that hour—it was 2:30 a.m.—there was no one else about. Daniel recognised him immediately as the guy in the restaurant who'd been giving Sandra looks Daniel hadn't cared for. "Hey," he called, lengthening his own stride. "Hold it there, fella!"

"You talkin' to me?" The man swung round, on his face an expression of challenge.

"You see anyone else nipping around at this hour?" Daniel closed the distance between them. "You staying at this hotel?"

"Sure I am," the guy blustered.

"Name and room number, please?"

"You security or somethin'?"

Daniel was reminded of a cornered bull. "Right on," he clipped off, daring the other man to question him further. "I've just had a phone call from a hotel guest saying some idiot was tapping on her door, wanting an invite in. Could that possibly be you?"

The guy swore. "Look I'm lost, okay? Had a bit too much to drink with a couple of my mates. Probably on the wrong floor."

"So what's your room number, Mr.?" Daniel pressed his body forward slightly so the other guy had to back up.

"Three Fourteen and it's Rick Bryce."

"Well I agree with you when you say you've had too much to drink and you *are* on the wrong floor."

"Listen, mate." The guy started his appeal. "I don't want any trouble."

"Then you won't mind if I escort you to your room? Management might have a couple of quick questions."

Minutes later when Daniel tapped on Sandra's door, softly calling her name, she opened it a fraction peering at him with huge eyes.

"Come in." She made a grab for his shirt, trying ineffectually to pull him through the door.

"We're going to have a conversation then?" He made it easy by stepping inside. She was wearing what looked like a flirty mini but was probably the latest in nightwear. Her small face was distressed. He knew distress on a woman's face when he saw it.

"Was *he* the guy?" she asked. "I peeped out and saw you talking to him. You had him backed right

Daniel nodded. "Several floors down. His name is Rick Bryce. He claims he had a bit too much to drink and got mixed up with the floor."

"Rubbish!" she said fiercely, shaking her head. "Why does this stuff happen to me?" she moaned, crossing her arms over her delicate breasts.

"What stuff?" He watched her suddenly take off on a rage around the room.

"Men knocking on my door." She threw her arms wide. "Men trying to get in. Stop asking me questions."

"Sandra, settle down," he said soothingly. "You don't have anything to worry about. I promise."

She exhaled noisily. "I felt like he could break in. I knew he couldn't, but I felt he could." Her eyes were swallowing up her face.

"You should have rung management immediately." He looked back at her intently. Suddenly remembering the things she had told him, the little pieces started to fall into place.

"I rang *you* didn't I?" she cried. "I knew you'd be here in a few seconds. I trust you, Daniel. I don't trust anyone else."

"Gee that's sad," he said quietly, running a hand

through his sleep-tousled hair. "So, are you going to go back to bed? We have a big day tomorrow."

"Sure." She looked sheepish all of a sudden and a tad ashamed. "Thanks a lot, Daniel. Sorry I had to wake you up."

"That's absolutely no problem at all. You're certain you're okay?" She looked very pale and agitated.

"He gave me a fright, that's all. Don't you ever get a fright?" She turned roundly on him.

"So what's this really about?" he asked, his voice quiet and reassuring. "The odious stepfather?"

Colour swept her pale cheeks. "Don't be so stupid, Daniel," she raged. "I've been over that for years." She swung away from him, her exposed nape, her delicate shoulders and the fine bones of her shoulder blades like little wings so vulnerable to his eyes. The fabric of her nightdress was gossamer light. For a little space of time he could see through it as she moved into the glow of the bedside lamps. The outline of her young body was incredibly erotic. Emotions assailed him, very real and very deep but he thrust them vigorously away. He was her knight in shining armour wasn't he?

"That's a *yes,* Daniel," she burst out, turning back to him. There was a little vein beating frantically at the delta of her throat. "I hated...I *hated*..."

Images sprang to Daniel's mind that gave him a chill. "He must have been a real sick, sad bastard,

"Some best!" Daniel threw himself down into an armchair. "Do you want me to wait here until you fall off to sleep?"

Her beautiful eyes quieted. A passing ripple of expression told him she liked the sound of that, but she looked at him coolly, the twenty-year-old with attitude. "Kinda kooky isn't it, Carson?" she challenged.

"Not at all." He shrugged, lifting his arms and locking them behind his head. "You're not all grown-up until you're twenty-one. Why don't you just hop into bed and close your eyes. I promise I won't leave until you're fast asleep."

"Can we talk for a bit?" She slipped beneath the coverlet, her body so ethereal a man would have to shake the sheets to find her.

"No," he said firmly. "Plenty of time to talk tomorrow. Close your eyes now."

She sat up briefly. "Will you tell me something, Daniel?"

"If I can." Sometimes she sounded so darn endearing.

"Wouldn't you have liked a younger sister?"

He thought of his early life the way it was. No place for a little sister. "There was only room for me and my mum."

"You'd have made a lovely brother, too." She sank back again, sounding young and wistful.

"*Good night*, Sandra," he said pointedly.

"All right, all right." She plumped up the pillow, irritable again, then punched it. "By the way, thanks. Did I say thanks?"

"Yes, you did."

"One more request. Do you think I can have a glass of water?"

"Okay." He stood up, wondering briefly and wildly what it might be like to join her. "After that, you promise to be good?"

"I promise." She gave him an utterly beautiful smile.

He walked into the ensuite, filled one of the glasses with water, then returned to the bedside. "Here." He put the glass into her hand.

She took a couple of quick gulps then passed the glass back to him. "I'm so glad you were here to-night. You're really dedicated to your work, aren't you, Daniel?" She stared up at him as though he just might give her a brotherly peck on the forehead.

Instead he gave her a quick glance with silver eyes cool. "Yes, ma'am." He put the glass down on the bedside table, then turned off the lamps, leaving one burning in the ensuite. He moved well away from the bed, resuming his seat in the armchair. Once there, he threw back his head and started to snore.

CHAPTER FOUR

IN THE end Daniel was able to get them aboard a nine seater charter flight bound for the Alice. The station helicopter remained grounded in Darwin undergoing a more thorough inspection than the one hurriedly carried out at the swamp site. All Sandra knew was it had something to do with mechanical components in the tail rotor that had worked their way loose.

It was almost noon before the twin engine Cessna landed on Moondai, depositing them on the station strip before taking off on the last leg of the flight into Alice Springs. The Alice as it is affectionately known is located almost in the very centre of the continent and the town that most symbolises the legendary Red Centre. Sandra had memories of going with the family to the annual fun carnivals the town put on. There was the annual Henley-on-Todd regatta when teams raced in leg-propelled, bottomless boats across the dry bed of the ancient river. Everyone, locals and tourists alike, delighted in the ridiculousness of it all. Then there was the Alice Springs annual rodeo with big prize money. Her father had often competed in that. But the festival she had most loved as a child was the riotous Camel Cup Carnival also raced in the dry bed of the Todd River. Those memories, mostly fond, reassured her if only slightly. She was extremely nervous of meeting up with her dysfunctional family again. Why wouldn't she be? Her grandfather's will had left her immeasurably better off than them.

She looked around this remote world that was now hers. She had almost forgotten the size of the place, the primal *stillness* like a great beast sleeping. The fiery colours of the earth contrasted wonderfully with the deep cloudless blue of the sky. "What, no welcoming party?" she quipped.

"Amazingly, no." Daniel picked up her luggage and piled it into the back of a station Jeep that was parked with the keys in it. "Did you want one?"

"It's all too late for that, Daniel," she sighed with resignation. "You know and I know they hate me."

"Win them over," he advised.

"Don't joke, I'm *serious*."

"So am I. Just give yourself *and* them a chance."

"Right!" She pulled a face. "I'll have them eating out of my hand."

"Like me," he said, dryly.

She felt a flush of heat run right through her body. That had sounded so *nice!* "So what do you suppose

cropped hair. "What's the worst they can do to me, do you reckon? Carry on bitterly resenting me, or move right on to hatching *more* plans to get rid of me? And *you,* for that matter. I can't wait until we get the final report on the chopper. It seemed very convenient to get downed in a crocodile infested swamp. I mean tiny ole me mightn't have made much of a meal, but *you* surely would have."

"Well it didn't happen. You turned into Annie Oakley right before my eyes. Anyway, you can bet your life there'll be nothing to *prove.* The chopper held up for the flight from Moondai to Darwin. Anyway there's no point in speculating. Let's wait and see. Don't be afraid."

"It takes courage to act unafraid," she said quietly.

"You've got it," he said. She had proved that at the swamp.

"How can you say that after what happened last night?" She frowned into the shimmering distance. The desert mirage was at play creating its fascinating illusions. Today it was long ribbons of lakes with vigorous little stick people having a corroboree around the shores.

"Hey, don't look so worried." His tone was light. "*What* happened exactly? I stayed with you until you fell asleep which was almost immediately. I'm not so insensitive that I can't understand what living with that stepfather of yours did to you. Besides you're not alone in your fears of being on your own in a hotel room with some drunken oaf pestering you. It would upset most women."

"You think he'll do it to someone else?"

Daniel opened the passenger door for her. "I've had a word with a couple of people and they in turn will have a word with others connected to the hotel business. They'll be on the lookout for him."

"He kept calling me *blondie!*" Sandra took her seat in the station vehicle.

"Forget it. It's over." Daniel climbed behind the wheel beside her, turning the ignition.

"Stay by me, Daniel," she urged.

The drive up to the homestead seemed to go on forever. She'd forgotten about all the *space!* They passed numerous outbuildings which all looked solid and cared for, painted a pristine white. Colourful desert gardens thrived around the married staff's bungalows and the bunk houses for the single men. It all presented with so much character and appeal it could have been the setting for some Western movie.

"Someone is doing a good job around here," Sandra said with approval as they approached the walled home compound.

He gave her an ironic glance. "Don't take it personally. I'll call you Sandra when we're on our own. In front of your family and the staff I'd like to leave it as ma'am or Ms Kingston. Take your pick. Think about it, Sandra. It's more respectful and it will make for fewer waves. I couldn't imagine taking liberties with your grandfather and calling him Rigby. He was always Mr. Kingston."

"He was more than seventy!" Sandra pointed out scornfully.

"Well until you're approaching seventy I think I'd better stick to calling you Ms Kingston."

"How would you like it if I called you *Mr. Carson?* For that matter are you sure Daniel mightn't be considered too familiar?"

He shook his head. "No, Daniel's okay. Your grandfather called me Dan. I should tell you now what you would have learned had you paid attention to the reading of the will. Your grandfather left me $250,000 on top of my normal salary providing I stayed on for a period of twelve months."

Her mouth fell open in astonishment. "Was that the *only* way he could get you to stay?"

"You don't think I might have earned it?" He glanced at her with glinting eyes.

"Now that's a stupid question. I'm *sure* he made you earn it. It's just so unexpected. Did Grandpop find his heart at the last minute or was he counting on *you* to prop *me* up?"

"Absolutely!" His voice sounded amused. "That's until you make a decision, Ms Kingston."

She swung her head. "I don't see anyone in the back seat."

"A little practice will make Ms Kingston come easier," he told her reasonably. "I might have been in your grandfather's good books, but that's where it stopped. Lloyd and Berne bitterly resented my influence with him. Berne went ballistic when he heard about my legacy."

"When it had nothing to do with him," Sandra said crisply. "They got plenty. They can stay in the house for as long as they like."

"That will make it hard all round."

"You bet!" she said drolly.

They were driving through an avenue of venerable old date palms with massive trunks. It was all coming back to her. Beyond the eight foot high wall smothered in a bright orange bougainvillea she would get her first glimpse of the homestead from which she and her mother had been banished. At least the tall iron gates were wide open in some sort of welcome, launching them into the home gardens.

The light dazzled. The wind caught boldly coloured blossom and sent it whirling to the ground.

ing everywhere scenting the air.

This is all mine!

She spoke aloud in wonderment. "Can you believe it? I own all this."

"Lucky you!" Daniel said, giving her a sardonic look. From apprehension she had gone to excitement. The big question would be, did this place speak to her? Had she really come home or would she stay a while then put it on the market? He'd had experience of that. He knew had he been born to a splendid inheritance he would have used every skill he possessed to build it up further and hold it for his heirs. But fate was a fickle thing. Rigby Kingston had amassed wealth and a pivotal role serving his country as a big beef producer. He had lost the one son who might have been able to assume his father's mantle but neither his remaining son nor his grandson had what it took to be a cattleman or to even play a significant role in the running of the station. How could Moondai fare better with a young woman at the helm? The cattle business had always been a male-orientated concern for obvious reasons. It was a hard life, too tough for a lone woman. Had Rigby Kingston mapped out a plan he hoped might work?

The Kingston heiress was addressing a question to him, bringing him out of his speculations. "Just what do Uncle Lloyd and Berne do with themselves all day? They surely can't sit around the homestead?"

"Your uncle has his all consuming interest, botany."

"Still at it, is he?"

"I understand his knowledge of the native flora is encyclopaedic. No small thing. Berne works around the station. Nothing too stressful."

"That must make it difficult for both of you as you're not friends?"

"Not even remotely," he assured her, "but I try to give him space. Your uncle involves himself in the business side of things from time to time, though Andy Fallon—he's an accountant and a good one— runs the office. Do you remember him?"

Sandra shook her head. "He must have arrived after we left. What about Elsa? She might have been Grandad's second wife, but Mum always called her *The Ghost!*"

"Well she does move around the place very quietly," Daniel said, thinking that was pretty well the way he too pictured Elsa. "She bothers no one." Daniel was still wondering how Rigby Kingston had ever married such a socially inept woman, especially after the idolized first wife, Catherine, who had died fairly early of cancer. "Lloyd and Berne hardly acknowledge her, which is pretty sad. Meg is still the housekeeper. You must remember Meg?"

Is that what Pamela had called them, Daniel thought cynically. City *jaunts?* He had heard so much about Pamela he now felt a lot of the bad stuff had to be true.

"We're almost here," he said, casting her another quick glance. In the baking heat she looked as fresh as a daisy, her skin as smooth and poreless as a baby's. She wore a neat little top almost the same colour as her hair and navy cotton jeans that were chopped off midcalf. The feisty look on her face, the angle of her small, delicately determined chin, were only self protection. He knew she was thrumming with nerves.

And he was right. Sandra stood out on the broad paved circular driveway looking up at the house that had figured so frequently in her dreams. Now she was the *owner,* about to inspect the premises and renew her troubled relationship with her family. Not that she had ever considered Elsa, *family,* which was really odd given Elsa's status. But Elsa had never involved herself, standing curiously aloof from them all. Her mother was right. Elsa had acted more like a visitor than mistress of Moondai. Strange behaviour from a woman who at one stage had run an Outback charter company with her first husband, a confirmed womaniser. Pamela always said divorce from that first philandering husband had dealt a blow to Elsa's psyche from which she had never recovered.

"So what do we do now?" Daniel looked to her for further instructions.

"You come up with me," Sandra said. "Every girl needs a Daniel when she's walking into the lion's den."

Moondai homestead was built of beautiful golden limestone, arcaded on both levels, the ground floor open, the upper level bordered by white wrought-iron balustrading. Tall, graceful vertical French doors set off the horizontal mass of the impressive façade. The shutters to the French doors were and always had been painted a subtle ochre to complement the golden limestone. The entrance hall was guarded by beautifully carved tall double doors with brass fittings that gleamed from many years of frequent polishing.

As Sandra peered into the cool interior a tallish, thin figure suddenly appeared, ankle-length skirt flapping, as if caught in a draught.

"It's Elsa, Sandra," Daniel prompted, in case there was any confusion. Elsa Kingston had aged a great deal even in the time he had been on Moondai.

"Gawd!" Sandra breathed irreverently. This wasn't the Elsa she remembered. Elsa had been a

dra! Welcome home, my dear."

Sandra responded at once. "Forgive me, Elsa, I didn't recognize you for a moment."

"I dare say I've changed a lot." Elsa not only hugged her, but she kissed Sandra on both cheeks.

"I suppose *I* have, too," Sandra answered tactfully, dismayed by Elsa's appearance and trying hard not to show it. "Thank you for the welcome." As a child Elsa had never ever so much as patted her on the head. Why now the affectionate greeting, even if she was grateful for it?

"Let me look at you!" Elsa stood back, staring at Sandra with eyes that had faded from their clear, striking light blue to almost colourless. Her once fine-grained skin was a maze of wrinkles. Clearly she hadn't cared for it in the Outback sun. Her long thick blonde hair, once her best feature, she had allowed to turn a yellowish-grey. Today it was bundled into a thick knot with stray locks flying loose. She wore no makeup to brighten her appearance. Her clothes could have been bought at a Thai street stall. The whole effect was one of eccentricity. Sandra felt a deep stirring of pity. This shouldn't *be!* Elsa looked as if the life had been drained out of her.

"You're still the image of your mother," Elsa was

saying, "though you're so thin. I can't catch even a glimpse of your poor father."

"Nevertheless his blood runs through my veins," Sandra said, determined not to become upset. "Daniel will be staying in the house for a while, Elsa. I intend to learn as much as I can about the operation of Moondai in the shortest possible time. I want my manager on hand."

Elsa didn't look like she was about to argue. "Just as you say, dear." She nodded. "It's a very big house. There's plenty of room. What about the west wing?"

"I'll look around first," Sandra said, softening it with a smile. The west wing was about as far away from the main bedrooms as one could get. She endeavoured to move forward, but Elsa seemed oblivious to the fact she was blocking the way. "Where's the rest of the family?" Sandra couldn't prevent the touch of sarcasm.

"They're waiting for you in the library," Elsa said in a voice that conveyed disapproval. "I should have asked immediately, forgive me, but how are you feeling after your scare? Lloyd told me about the mishap to the helicopter. Such dangerous things, helicopters. *All* light aircraft!"

"We survived, Elsa," Sandra answered dryly.

"Thank God," Elsa responded with what sounded like genuine fervour. "Do you *want* to stay at the house, Dan?" She turned to Daniel uncertainly.

Daniel looked unsurprised by the question or the bleakness of Elsa's tone. "I didn't see anything to *be* afraid of, Mrs. Kingston."

Elsa's gaze went beyond him, as if looking into the past. "He was a hard, *hard,* man. No heart, no compassion."

"He did live through a terrible tragedy," Daniel offered quietly.

"Where's Meg?" Sandra sought to break up the sombreness of the exchange. She looked about her. The black and white marble tiles of the entrance hall gleamed, the woodwork shone. A beautiful antique rosewood library table stood in the centre of the spacious hall, adorned by a large bronze urn filled with an arrangement of open and budded blue lotus with their seed pods and open and furled jade coloured leaves. Everything with the exception of Elsa looked *cared* for.

"She has a few more jobs to do, Alexandra," Elsa said. "You'll see her soon."

"Good. I'm looking forward to it. Probably at lunch. You want lunch don't you, Daniel?"

"A sandwich will do me fine." Daniel shrugged off lunch with the warring Kingstons. "Like Meg I have plenty of work to do."

"Shall we go through to the library?" Elsa asked, long thin hands fluttering like birds on the wing.

"Actually, Elsa, I'd like to freshen up first." Sandra lifted her head to the first floor gallery that was hung with pictures. "Which room have you given me?"

Elsa's gaze dropped as if to consult the marble tiles. "I thought your old room…perhaps you might want another…Meg said you should choose…I wasn't sure…"

"Thank you," Sandra said. "I'll look around before I decide." Her family had kept her waiting. Now they could wait for her. "You can bring up my luggage now, Daniel." She gave the order, mock lady of the manor.

"Yes, ma'am." There was an answering wicked light in Daniel's eyes but Elsa, still fixating on the tiles, didn't notice.

"So what have you in mind?" Daniel asked, after they had negotiated the divided staircase and were several feet along the east wing.

"Not the master suite that's for sure," Sandra said. "I bet Uncle Lloyd has moved in there already."

"I wouldn't know."

"Let's check it out!" Sandra rushed ahead. The hallway was still carpeted with the same valuable Persian runner.

She threw open her late grandfather's bedroom door, gasping a little to see it was indeed occupied

Lloyd in residence. I doubt very much if it's Bernie. I don't want it anyway. I'll have my parents' suite. *You* can have my old room, Daniel. That way you'll be near me."

"Does it have a dear little bed?" Daniel asked sarcastically, wondering how he could be remotely comfortable living up at the house let alone in what had been a small girl's bedroom.

She turned her head over her shoulder. "I trust you. You trust me. You can have any furniture you want, Daniel. Just don't interfere with my plans."

"Yes, ma'am."

"We're alone, aren't we?"

"Your ancestors are on the wall." He cast a glance at them.

"Arrogant looking bunch aren't they?"

"Don't mistake arrogance for iron determination," he said. "The Kingstons and others like them pioneered an industry. They pioneered what is still in many ways wild frontier country."

"I stand corrected, Daniel," she said, mock repentant. "Are you sure your dad wasn't a cattleman?"

His gaze had the cool intensity of a big cat's. "Ms Kingston, I'm not sure *who* my dad was," he said bluntly.

The colour in her cheeks went from soft pink to crimson. She put out a tentative hand. "Daniel, I didn't mean to hurt you."

"You haven't," he assured her crisply. "Let's get you settled."

"Right." She surged forward. "It's along here." She pointed and Daniel followed with her case. "You're over there."

"God, Sandra. It's opposite yours."

She raised haughty brows. "So what's so disturbing about that? It's not as though we intend playing little seduction games."

"Indeed no!" he said sternly.

"Oh come off it, Daniel. I couldn't care less where you sleep as long as it's close by. You can get someone to help bring up your things."

"I'm not happy about this," Daniel said, shaking his head.

"And I understand. But, Daniel, I *need* you. I'm not asking you to move in with me so quit pulling those anxious faces. I'm like a soldier who needs backup in a combat zone. Think of it like that."

They found Lloyd Kingston and his son Bernard, sitting in splendour in the library—an *enormous* room—which housed thousands of books and maps which no one to Sandra's knowledge had ever read, or even attempted to read outside herself. As a child she had loved climbing up and down the moveable

library. For one thing her grandfather, if he hadn't exactly ridiculed his son's consuming interest in plants, was extremely irritated and disappointed by Uncle Lloyd's lack of interest in the cattle business, or indeed business in general. Bernie too barely tolerated his father's passion for wildflowers, herbs, native plants and the like but he, no more than his father, had enjoyed station life. What they both enjoyed was reaping the benefit of Rigby Kingston's success. Finding "enlightenment" her grandfather had called it when her uncle Lloyd took off on his field trips.

So far it didn't look like he had found it. Though Rigby Kingston's will had left them both rich, neither Lloyd nor Bernie had made the slightest attempt to vacate the family home. Likewise Elsa who was still nipping at Sandra's heels wearing the long-suffering expression of an early Christian martyr.

"Sandra, my dear." Lloyd Kingston rose to his impressive feet, with quite an air of bonhomie. He came towards his niece as though he too, like Elsa, meant to catch her into a bear hug.

"Uncle Lloyd! You haven't changed a bit." Sandra suffered the hug which was mercifully brief. "You're as handsome as ever." As indeed he was.

Tall, dark haired, eyes so dark they were almost black. He hadn't gained weight in midlife though his upper torso had thickened somewhat lending him more substance. Lloyd turned his head. "Berne, come greet your cousin." Narrowed eyes swept over the silent Daniel. "You may go now, Daniel." The politeness of the tone didn't conceal the order. "That was a terrible business with the helicopter. And so awful for Sandra! What exactly happened again? You did tell me when you called."

Daniel gave him a direct look. "It's being thoroughly checked over, Mr. Kingston. I prefer we wait on the full report. It might take time."

"You're the only guy I know who could have landed it." Berne Kingston moved to join the group, giving off an aura of aggression plain for all to see.

"Maybe someone wasn't counting on it," Sandra said. "How are you, Bernie?"

His mouth twisted but he made no attempt to touch her nor she him. "Long time no see." He examined Sandra carefully from head to head. "You're so like Aunty Pam it hurts," he said finally. "Except Pam would have made two of you. You've scarcely grown. And what's with the hair?"

"Nothing terminal," she answered, "so don't get your hopes up. I didn't expect to see you here, Bernie. Were you waiting around especially to welcome me home?"

"You can't honestly believe that?" he asked flatly.

ways was devious, but Moondai should have gone to Dad, not you, and me, before you. You were last in line."

"The last shall be first."

"Oh, funny!" Berne sneered.

"Bernard, do you think you could stop," Lloyd Kingston appealed to his son, before directing a sharp glance at Daniel. "Daniel, I said you could go."

Daniel didn't move, but there was a coolness in his eyes. "No offence, Mr. Kingston, but I work for *Ms* Kingston."

"I prefer Daniel to stay for the moment, Uncle Lloyd," Sandra broke in. "I mightn't have been here today only for him."

"Quite so, quite so." Lloyd Kingston gained control of himself quickly. "But this *is* family business, after all. Please, come and sit down. Elsa, you'll join us?"

"Thank you," Elsa said in a stilted voice.

Berne followed suit. "So what are your plans?" he fired off at Sandra. "You're going to sell the place?"

"What does it matter to you, Bernie?" Sandra asked, sinking into a deep leather armchair.

"It matters a lot. You seem to have forgotten

Grandad gave Dad and me the right to remain here for as long as we want."

"Elsa, too," Sandra reminded him, turning her head to smile at the other woman. "I didn't think you'd want to stay, Bernie. Unless you've changed a good deal you hate station life?"

Berne's face so much like his father's darkened. "Don't tell us you intend to keep the place going? As if you could!" he added scornfully.

"Maybe *I* couldn't on my own, but Daniel can until such time I put a professional manager in place. That's if Daniel doesn't want to stay."

Berne gazed from one to the other. "You're pretty cosy aren't you? Daniel this, Daniel that."

"Oh, do get a grip on yourself, Bernard," his father implored. "You can't waste your life like I have. Sandra is right. You're no more suited to station work than I am. Dad knew that."

"That is no reason why he should have left Moondai to Sandra," Berne responded hotly, his thin cheeks flushed. "What the hell does *she* know? Less than either of us. It's all so unfair. We can't even contest it. Dad's lawyer told us it'd be a waste of time."

"Have you ever known your grandfather to get legal matters wrong?" Lloyd asked very dryly. It appeared, unlike his son, he was in a conciliatory mood. "Dad spent a lot of time in Brisbane in the months before he died. He meant then to cut us out.

dad's will was as big a ...

"I bet it wasn't a shock to Daniel here," Berne's handsome face was twitching with pent-up anger.

"Meaning?" Daniel's powerful, lean body stirred restlessly.

"You know exactly what I mean," Berne exploded. "You, after all, were in my grandfather's confidence. He had such faith in you. You were damn near the grandson he never had. Was he hatching some plan, do you suppose? The cogs and wheels never stopped turning. Sandra was his heiress. *You* were the sort of guy who could take over the reins. You've proved to be very successful running Moondai and while you were at it, running rings around me, deliberately showing me up. Dad's an old dinosaur. All he wants to do is study his stupid plants."

"So what *are* you saying, Berne?" Lloyd Kingston broke in testily.

"I'm not a fool, Dad," he exploded, showing no respect for his father at all. "I've gone over and over this. Either Grandad expected that without him the whole place would go to wrack and ruin or he could fit Sandra up with a suitable husband. A lot of people in the know seem to think Daniel here is outstanding. He's a real go-getter. He never stops working to impress. Yet he's a nothing and a no-one. Dirt poor until Grandad gave him a leg up. For all we know, Grandad could have extracted a promise from Dan to look out for Sandra. *Marry* her. Take on the Kingston name. It's been done before today. He certainly felt no woman could run Moondai. Sandra's not even a woman. Just look at her! She's hardly grown since she was ten."

"I have, Bernie," Sandra assured him. "I don't apologise for being petite. You know what they say. Good things come in small packages. I'm all grown-up, *unlike* you. Just so you know I graduated with honours from university with a B.A. majoring in psychology among other things. Consequently I find this theory of yours of considerable interest. Daniel is signed up to be my hero. Is that it?"

"Doesn't look like you're too uncomfortable with it," Berne snorted.

"Well *I* am," Daniel said, his eyes luminous with anger. "You're talking drivel, Berne, but then you seldom talk anything else. I fully expected Mr. Kingston to leave Moondai to your father who could have hired top management to run the station had he wanted. My windfall turned out to be at least as big a surprise. Mr. Kingston never once mentioned his granddaughter to me."

"You expect us to believe that?" Berne was the picture of outraged disbelief. "You always had your

disgust. "Your grandfather always had areas of concern for me to address. They were *all* about station management and business. Which reminds me instead of standing here listening to wild scenarios I should see what's been happening in my absence. The men like to have their duties for the day laid out."

Sandra tried for eye-to-eye contact, failed. "But you haven't had anything to eat, Daniel," she reminded him, loath to see him go.

"Don't worry about me." He gave her a brief salute and turned on his heel.

Sandra made no apologies to the others. She went after him, catching him in the hallway. "I'm sorry about all that, Daniel," she panted. "Bernie has always been a jealous, resentful creature."

"And he talks a lot of drivel. I'd advise you not to listen."

"You're angry?" Carefully she approached him, touching his arm. It was rigid with tension.

"You bet I am!" He stared down into her face. "This isn't going to work, Sandra. I want to help you out, but I'm not going to cop the likes of Berne. Your uncle's arrogance only adds fuel to the flames."

"Why put them before me?" she retorted. "I need

help, Daniel. I need it from *you*. Please tell me I have it?"

"Hell!" Daniel was grappling with her potent effect on him. All this woman magic shouldn't be allowed.

"You're more than a match for both of them put together," she cajoled him, giving him a soulful look.

"No need to pour it on." He stared back challengingly into those blue, *blue,* eyes, his own expression somewhat grim. "The *real* question is, Ms Kingston. Am I a match for *you!*"

CHAPTER FIVE

It was a dismal lunch though the food was good. Meg, looking almost exactly the same, but a little plumper, had come to the library door all smiles. Sandra had no hesitation going into her arms.

"Sandy!" Tears brimmed in the housekeeper's eyes. "It's wonderful to have you back."

It wasn't possible to say, "Wonderful to be back," instead Sandra settled for, "It's wonderful to see you, Meg. I've never forgotten you or your kindnesses to me and my mother."

"I wrote to you, dear."

Sandra shook her head, frowning slightly. "I didn't get any letters."

"I didn't think you did." Meg sounded unsurprised. "Anyway, you're back and I'm thrilled."

"Do we have to listen to any more gushing?" Berne burst out. "I'm hungry."

"You must try to do something about yourself, Bernard," his father said, regarding his son with disappointed eyes. "You'll never get what you

want out of life if you continue to be so belliger-
ent."

"And *you* have, Dad, I suppose?" Berne scowled.

Sandra waited for another reprimand, but none
came.

Meg had set up lunch in the breakfast room which
had a high beamed ceiling and a lovely view of the rear
garden with its stands of lemon scented gums. Roast
chicken was on the menu, cold cuts, potato salad and
a green salad enlivened by a Thai chilli dressing. Sandra had deliberately not chosen the carver at the head
of the mahogany table which could seat ten. She
guessed correctly her uncle had laid claim to that. She
sat to his right with Berne opposite her and Elsa way
off at the other end of the table though Sandra had tried
to coax her to sit closer. It was clear Elsa had made an
art form out of staying near invisible when she could
easily have kicked over the traces and spent the rest
of her time travelling the world, first class.

It soon transpired Uncle Lloyd was set on his
course of reconciliation—or the appearances there-
of—but after a limited amount of time spent on
pleasantries—including kind enquiries about Pamela, once so dreadfully maligned—Berne began to
worry away at Sandra's inheritance and her future
plans like a dog with a bone.

"Obviously you've got some idea what you intend
to do with Moondai?" Fiercely he stabbed at a small
chunk of new potato.

good pilot or I could be dead or in hospital in a coma. As I've already said, I had no idea Grandad would make me the major beneficiary in his will. After all, he sent Mum and me packing, remember?"

"He should never have done that." Elsa startled them by offering the stern comment.

"No, he shouldn't!" Sandra showed her own deeply entrenched resentments.

"Come off it, Sandra." Berne's smile was acid. "Your mother was a real tart! No offence."

His father broke in. "This has gone far enough, Bernard. I insist you keep a civil tongue in your head. Apologise to Sandra right now."

"Dad, you must be joking!" Berne sat back astounded. "Aren't *you* the one who called Aunty Pam every dirty name you could think of? So now you're going to make nice?"

Colour stained Lloyd Kingston's strongly defined cheekbones. "That was in the past, Bernard. I was only teasing anyway."

"Teasing?" Berne shouted with laughter that held no trace of humour.

Sandra for her part felt a swift surge of anger. "My mother suffered from your taunts, Uncle Lloyd. So did I. Now, if *I* am willing to let bygones be bygones I hope you'll do the same. I didn't make myself Grandad's heiress. Grandad did. I have no idea what was going through his mind—"

"Boy, that's rich!" Berne lounged back. "I gave you a reason. Every time I came on Grandad and Daniel they were locked into deep conversation. He'd turned his back on Dad and me. We didn't measure up. He *knew* Dad would sell Moondai like a shot if he got his hands on it. I would, too."

"What about Elsa?" Sandra asked, looking in Elsa's direction. "Elsa is Grandad's widow."

Berne looked stunned. "Elsa could never take over. She can't even handle the dinner menu as I'm sure she'll agree. Meg runs the house."

"Why are you speaking like this, Bernie?" Sandra asked. It was so unkind and disrespectful.

"It doesn't matter, Alexandra!" Elsa said, waving a thin hand.

"But Elsa it *does* matter," Sandra said. "Anyway Meg *is* the housekeeper. Before you married my grandfather you were a successful businesswoman. Didn't you miss it?"

Elsa seemed to shrink in her carver chair. "That was a lifetime ago, Alexandra."

"Does one truly lose one's skills or the need to use them?"

"My cleverness has diminished with the years," Elsa said. "I know you mean to be kind, Alexandra, but nothing Bernard says affects me."

career woman with a ...

wanted a woman who would know her place, not a business partner. That's when you set about turning yourself into a piece of furniture."

"Really, are you any better?" Elsa asked, piercing him with her colourless eyes. "You strut around doing next to nothing while Daniel runs everything. Gutless young men like you disgust me."

Berne's face was a study. "Well what do you know?" he chortled. "She *can* talk."

"Rudeness is what you employ, Bernard, instead of brains," Elsa said gravely. "I have never wished to talk to you."

"Ditto!" Berne retaliated, dark eyes flashing. "I'm lighting out of here as soon as I'm ready. Who am I anyway? *No one!*"

Sandra, amazed by the exchange between Elsa and Berne, felt a sudden rush of empathy for her cousin. "Look, I'm sorry, Bernie," she said. "I'm sorry Grandad cut you out. I'm sorry he did the same to Uncle Lloyd. He was a very strange man."

"He was that!" Elsa pulled more wisps out of her bundle of hair. "He should have been had up for mental cruelty."

"Struth!" Berne dug his fork into a piece of chicken like he wanted to spear someone. "Don't be so ungrateful, Elsa. Grandad's life may not have centred around *you*, but he made sure you were kept very comfortable in your quiet corner. He did leave you rich if not merry."

"Which was only fitting," Sandra murmured.

"If I could I'd send it back to him in hell," Elsa told them bleakly. "It wasn't *money* I wanted from Rigby. It wasn't *money* the rest of you wanted from him, either. It was love and attention. There were only two people Rigby loved in this world. Catherine and Trevor. The rest of us amounted to a big fat nothing."

"Well thank you for sharing that with us, Elsa," Lloyd said suavely. "I must say I too have been missing the sound of your voice. Perhaps Sandra's arrival has brought it back?"

"Why not?" Elsa nodded her head. "I was fond of her father. He was very different to you, Lloyd." Her colourless gaze shifted to Sandra. "It's a great burden you've taken on, Alexandra. This place killed your father."

"Oh for pity's sake!" Lloyd Kingston fetched up a great sigh. "Please don't start on that, Elsa. I won't have it."

"My mother believes to this day my father's death wasn't an accident," Sandra found herself saying although she hadn't intended to.

"And what do you believe, Sandra?" her uncle asked while Elsa turned her head away, looking extremely distressed.

going to forgive you for that, Sandra. That's your mother talking. You were a child. Your mother filled your head with terrible stories. It was a way of getting back at me for the things I'd said about her. A lot of which was true by the way. I loved your father, my brother. I looked up to him. He was everything I wasn't just as Elsa so kindly said. And he had a *heart* which Dad never had. I never regarded Trevor as the enemy. That's blasphemy. I don't regard *anyone* as my enemy."

"Not *me*, Uncle Lloyd?" Sandra asked, quietly.

"Especially not you," he answered without hesitation. "You're Trevor's child."

"Sure about that, Dad?" Berne asked in a taunting voice. "If I were Sandra I'd be worried about what lay behind your sleek mask. No one in this family ever tells the truth."

"How very true," Elsa said in a heartfelt voice, brushing long fingers through her hair. "It is only justice you inherited Moondai, Alexandra. It would have gone to your father."

Sandra bit hard on her lip. After a moment, she rose from the table, saying quietly, "Please excuse me. I'd like to look around this afternoon. I'll take the Jeep out the front if that's okay?" She pushed in her chair, holding the back of it while she got out what she had to say. "I've asked Daniel to move out of the overseer's bungalow and into the house for a while."

As she expected, there was a stunned silence. She might just as well have said the authorities had handed over to her the most dangerous felon in the country to be housed.

Berne finally broke the silence. "You've *what?*"

"Sandra, is that *wise?*" Lloyd asked with less intensity, but he too looked shocked.

Sandra shrugged. "Elsa has no objection. Daniel can have my old bedroom. It's only until I bring myself up to scratch on station affairs. He'll be a big help there as Grandad intended. I'll move into my parents' old suite."

"I'm quite happy to move out of the master suite," Lloyd Kingston offered. "You have only to say the word."

"Sandra isn't going to say it, Dad, just as you were counting on. What you *weren't* counting on was that Sandra is no fool. She wasn't easily fooled as a kid, either."

Sandra was surprised by his support, if indeed that's what it was. She decided to hold out an olive branch. "I don't suppose you'd like to drive around with me, Bernie?"

For the first time he looked uncertain of himself. "You can't want me surely?"

ing to his overload of resentments. ...
we can't!" He shook his head sharply. "Thanks for
the offer. It's beyond me right now to accept."

In the kitchen she spoke to Meg about room ar-
rangements asking Meg to make up some sandwiches for Daniel's lunch. Meg too looked surprised
when told Daniel would be staying at the house for
a time, but in no way did she appear dismayed.
Rather she appeared firmly onside.

"What is it, love? Are you nervous?" she asked
shrewdly, long used to the warring Kingstons.

Sandra gave a wry laugh. "I have powerfully bad
memories of this place, Meg. Daniel is a big de-
pendable guy. I'd like him around. Besides, it's quite
true I'll be relying heavily on him to teach me what
I need to know about the station."

"Well he can do that," Meg said, slicing off some
ham. "Towards the end he was your grandfather's
right hand man. You could say your grandad treated
him as more a grandson than he did Berne."

"That must have been awful for Berne?" Despite
everything she felt twinges of pity for her cousin.

"It wasn't good." Meg shook her head. "It's time
for Bernie to make a life of his own. He's got no di-

rection. It's my belief, excuse me, Sandy for saying this, but inherited wealth is death to ambition. Most times anyway."

It was amazing how quickly it was all coming back to her. Sitting tall behind the wheel of the Jeep Sandra drove out of the home compound taking the broad gravelled drive that wound past the neat and comfortable staff bungalows and bunkhouses. Station employees materialized out of nowhere, roughly lining the track. She began to wave. They all waved back. There were mothers with little children, groundsmen, stockmen, what looked like station mechanics going on their oil stained overalls. Finally she stopped the Jeep and climbed out.

"Hi! Lovely to see you all. I'm Sandra, back home again."

Her youth, the diminutive size of her, the smile on her face and the friendliness of her tone instantly broke the ice. People surged at her, delighted and determined to meet the new boss personally. They had all known she was coming. Mr. Kingston's will—what they knew of it—had been discussed at great length and gasped over. What was going to happen to Moondai, to their jobs? They all knew about the forced landing of the station helicopter in the swamp. Daniel had spoken to his foreman as well as Lloyd Kingston up at the house. The foreman relayed the news to the

stead of leaping briskly out of the way or averting their eyes if their former Boss was about in one of his dark moods, his granddaughter was happy being surrounded by smiling faces. Some faces Sandra remembered and greeted by name. Others, the young wives and the small children were newcomers to Moondai. Sandra found herself nursing babies, which she loved, accepting invitations to morning tea and paying a visit to the schoolhouse where all the children on the station under ten were offered an education by a well qualified teacher. With these open-faced smiling people around her Sandra felt safe.

By the time she drove on she was feeling quite cheerful, not realising friendliness and a genuine interest in the people around them was a side of the Kingston character that had seldom emerged since her father's day.

I could almost build a life here, she thought. That was the voice of her heart. But what of her head? These people liked her at any rate. Drat her family.

One of the station hands had told her Daniel's location. He was out at the crater, a natural amphitheatre caused by massive earth movements hundred of millions of years before. The family had always used that name for the grassy basin which was almost enclosed—save for a broad canyon—by low lying rugged cliffs of reddish quartzite and sandstone. It was quite possible to climb to the highest point which their Kingston forefather had named Mount Alexandra after his wife. The same Alexandra Sandra had been named for. Of course it wasn't a mountain at all. More a hill, but it *reared* out of the vast perfectly flat plains so its height was accentuated. The climb to the summit was a stiff hike too and dangerous with all the falling rubble, but the view from the top Sandra could still remember.

Her father had used to sing to her that they were sitting on top of the world, his arm around her sheltering her from the strong winds.

Why did you go and die on me, Dad? Why? Why did you leave me? It was hard. So hard. Do you know the things that have happened to me? How frightened I was without you to protect me? How much I hated Jem?

She often found herself talking to her father. Not out loud of course, but in her mind. Sometimes she thought he answered. She talked to her little friend, Nikki, too, asking her what it was like in the kingdom of Heaven. Was it all it was cracked up to be? If anyone deserved eternal joy it was Nikki and the children like Nikki who had been so brave and cheerful it had put her own troubles into perspective.

Her father hadn't wanted to die, either. She

needed was the requisite trigger.

The light was dazzling. She pushed her akubra further down over her eyes, congratulating herself she'd had the foresight to buy one from a Western outfitter in Brisbane. It had been hard getting one her size especially when she no longer had her mop of curls to help prop it up. Best quality lens sunglasses sat on her nose, though in the heat they were continually sliding down the bridge. She remembered this extraordinary dazzle of light, blinding in its brilliance, the cloudless skies, the golden spinifex and the blood red sands the wind could sweep into the most beautiful and fascinating delicate whorls and patterns. She remembered the way the desert bloomed in profusion after the rains; the great vistas of the white and yellow paperdaisies she particularly loved; the magnificent sight of the burning sun going down on the Macdonnell Ranges that were always overhung by a hue of grape-blue. These ranges of the Wild Heart were once sand on the beach of the inland sea the early explorers had searched for in vain. She loved the way the wild donkeys came out to graze at sunset and whole colonies of rabbits popped out of their warrens keeping a sharp lookout for any dingoes on the prowl.

Around Moondai all the dingoes had been pure-bred. A wild dingo in prime condition was a splen-did sight, but one always had to remember they were killers by nature.

A big mob of cattle was being walked not far from a waterhole where legions of budgies and perky lit-tle zebra finches were having a drink, indifferent to the presence of a falcon that coasted overhead mak-ing itself ready for a leisurely swoop. Kill and be killed, she thought. There were always predators, al-ways victims. Her mind returned to the question of what had caused the mechanical components in the tail section of the helicopter to work their way loose. Daniel had explained it but it hadn't been all that easy for a nonmechanically minded person like her-self to take in. Had someone deliberately interfered with the control system, or had it simply been an-other case of mechanical failure? So many people over the years had been killed in the Outback when helicopters or light aircraft crashed either soon after take-off, or attempting to land. Some plowed into rugged ranges while others took a nosedive to the desert floor. Flying was a risky business especially over the heated unpredictable air of the desert, but given the vast distances flying was no luxury; it was a way of life.

It was the greatest good fortune that Daniel was such a good helicopter pilot. He had to be equally

was Bernie. She w...

licopter, but he had always held a pilot's licence as had her father and grandfather. It occurred to her it might be a good idea for her to start taking lessons. She had to overcome her fears if she really intended to stay on Moondai. Maybe in the process she would unveil a new aspect of herself?

The drive through the broad canyon was an experience in itself. The walls presented an extravaganza of brilliant dry ochres, fiery reds, russets, pinks, yellows, stark glaring white with carved shadows of amethyst. High up in every available pocket of earth the hardy spinifex had taken root. Because of the recent rains many clumps were a fresh green, most a dull gold. The sandy floor of the canyon was as red as boiling magma, giving vital clues to the mighty explosion that had formed the crater aeons ago. To either side of the canyon long tranquil chains of waterholes already beginning to dry out sparkled in the sun. In the gums nearby, preening or dozing amid the abundant fresh olive foliage were great numbers of the pink and grey galahs who made sure they were always in the vicinity of water. She had grown up with all this even if she had lost contact over the years. Only love of this ancient land was in her bloodstream hence her deeply felt response. Time and distance had not altered the old magic.

The crater, secret to all save the aborigines for tens of thousands of years was a miracle of nature. It attracted massive flocks of birds and wildlife. It was wonderful to look out over the giant bowl of the crater with its protected grasslands then up at the rounded curves, peaks and swells of the surrounding rim.

That afternoon the natural amphitheatre was thickly carpeted in grasses that were liberally strewn with the wildflowers and spider lilies that thrived in the semi-desert environment. Her favourites, the everlastings which didn't wilt when picked, were by far in the majority. In one area she drove through to get to the holding yards they were pink, then a mile or so on, bright yellow interspersed with long trailing branches of crimson desert peas, native poppies, hibiscus, fire bush, hop bush, salt bush, emu bush. There were so many she couldn't begin to name them. She had to leave that to Uncle Lloyd who loved every living thing that grew in the earth far more than people. Cataloguing all this floral splendour was his passion. The ranges at their back door harboured a great wealth of wildflowers, making them an exciting hunting ground for a man who was both amateur botanist and excellent photographer. She remembered her father saying with admiration how his brother, Lloyd, had an encyclopaedic knowl-

into a murderer.

She brought the Jeep to a halt a little distance from the pens. To one side she could see a calf cradle, a ratchet locking device that restrained the calves due for earmarking, branding, dehorning and castration. She slid out of the Jeep and stood with her back against the passenger door watching Daniel stride towards her. Back in the city any guy that looked like him would be mobbed on a daily basis she thought with wry amusement. She had never seen anyone so young exude so much authority. It was strange to think Daniel didn't know who his father was. He had to be a six footer plus, strikingly handsome. From which parent had come those extraordinary eyes? They were the colour of sun on water.

"Hi!" He sketched a salute, forefinger to the brim of his cream akubra.

"Hi, Daniel," she replied, not a whit disconcerted by the way he towered over her. Authority emanated from Daniel, never menace. "When you stalked off, you missed lunch so I brought you some sandwiches."

"Now aren't you kind." He smiled at her, wondering if her beautiful skin was as cool and soft as it looked. "The men are about due for a break. I'll get

Nat to make us a cup of tea. You can meet the men in the break."

"I'd like that," she said, following him over to an area of deep shade. The thick stubby grass that surrounded the tall gums was studded with the all embracing wildflowers, their pretty faces brighter in the refreshing shade. The men had looked up at her arrival, but when she looked back, they had their heads down, hard at work.

Nat turned out to be a wiry jackeroo of around twenty whose duties included making the billy tea for the men when they were out on the job. He had recently perfected an old-fashioned camp fire damper which he offered to Sandra spread with lashings of jam. She accepted tea and the damper with a smile not about to tell him she rarely drank tea and never ate jam. Somehow she'd choke it down.

She and Daniel made themselves comfortable beneath the shadiest tree, Sandra thinking there was no one she'd rather share the moment with. How did one reach such a point so early in a friendship? she thought in some wonderment. All she was absolutely certain of, was, she *had*.

Daniel, oblivious to her soul searching, opened out his packet of sandwiches kept fresh by cling wrap. "These look good," he said appreciatively, getting a kick out of the fact she had thought of him. But then she was thoughtful. And very kind. He re-

beautiful, the crush of wildflowers at their feet were beautiful. The cooling breeze was beautiful, the aromatic smell of the camp fire. *Everything* was beautiful she thought ecstatically.

"You must be hungry?" She stretched out a little, revelling in the vast landscape.

He held a protective hand over the package. "I'll just down a few of these before you start to pinch them."

"It's okay. I had lunch."

"How did it go?" He shot her a sidelong glance thinking her profile was like a perfect cameo.

Sandra swallowed a mouthful of tea, finding it surprisingly good. "Uncle Lloyd was in a conciliatory mood. Bernie was Bernie and Elsa made a few surprising comments that struck home. As a child I couldn't make her out. I can't now. She's so *quiet*, but I have the feeling a lot is going on in her head."

"Well it can't be *good*. She looks positively haunted to me." Daniel picked up another sandwich, deriving a great deal of pleasure in the company of his new boss. Even in the heat of the afternoon she was as bright and fresh as the daisies that ringed them round. She had a tiny beauty spot high up on her right cheekbone just beneath the outer corner of her eye. It emphasized the porcelain perfection of her skin and the natural darkness of her lashes and brows. Quite a contrast with the buttercup coloured hair that clung to her beautifully shaped skull. Not many could look so good with so little hair.

Sandra, while endeavouring to appear not to, was intensely aware of his leisurely inspection and was just as intensely satisfied. She *wanted* him to notice her. She was actively *willing* it. "Why are you looking at me like that?" she asked.

He laughed. "May a cat not look at the queen?"

"I suppose so if it gets the opportunity. This damper is very good but I don't actually eat jam. Would you like it? Then I can have one of those sandwiches."

"Which one?" he asked with an amused look on his face.

"Oh any! I couldn't get my tongue around lunch although I was hungry. Bernie was shouting and shoving his chair around. It put me off."

"I don't want the damper, either," he told her, passing a ham and mustard sandwich and looking Nat's way. "I'll eat just about anything when I'm hungry but *not* damper. It sticks in my chest."

"You'll have to eat it," she said. "We don't want to offend him."

He shook his head carelessly. "He'll get over it. So did you tell them you want me to move into the house?"

took the news with great equanimity. She ___ ___ much fun with Uncle Lloyd and Bernie who, predictably, had serious misgivings."

He drained his mug of tea. "Please don't tell me on a beautiful day like this."

"It *is* a beautiful day, isn't it?" She gave a voluptuous sigh, looking utterly relaxed. A gorgeous butterfly drifted by just to add to her happiness. "You can smell all the wildflowers!" She inhaled. "I used to love Moondai when I was a kid."

"Why wouldn't you? It's a part of you." He was entranced and entertained by her ever changing expressions. She might be small but there was a lot of life in her.

"I know that now. Daniel, why do you suppose my mother thought Uncle Lloyd wanted to get rid of my dad? Uncle Lloyd is a passionate botanist for God's sake."

"I can't imagine him killing anyone, Sandra." While Daniel didn't have a lot of time for Sandra's uncle, he had to say what he believed.

"He wouldn't have to do it himself," she pointed out.

"No." He was deeply sceptical. "Your uncle isn't

the most likable man in the world. He's an appalling snob, but not, I think, a murderer."

"Who then?" she asked. "Bernie has more hangups than I have, but he was just a kid. Elsa? I can't imagine Elsa turning into a homicidal maniac. Marrying Grandad had to be one of the worst decisions she ever made. She mustn't have wanted a man who would play around like her first husband. Sex creates tremendous problems."

Daniel leaned back, the more to study her. "When it's good it beats most things," he offered casually.

"I beg your pardon?" Her heart started to make wild little flutters in her chest.

"You don't agree?" One eyebrow shot up sardonically.

She coloured up. "You keep waiting for me to make a slip."

"I do." He looked at her with a mixture of gentle mockery and indulgence.

"Well you're not ever going to hear it," she promised.

"And here I am the soul of discretion," he said. "Your secrets are safe with me, Alexandra. Anyway we were talking about more momentous things. Who hated your dad enough to want to see him dead? We already know yours is a highly dysfunctional family but I think you'd have to rule them out. It was an accident, pure and simple. Now you're a woman as opposed to the child, you have to accept that. Your mother

away from us, _____
at the bottom of her tin mug as though the _____
arrangement held answers. "Mother was a bad, bad, girl. She's highly susceptible to male admiration to this day. I didn't see it then of course. I heard what Uncle Lloyd was saying but I couldn't understand what he was getting at. Heck, I was only a kid. What I *did* take in was the way he questioned whether Dad was my father or not."

"Now that's really wicked." Daniel gave his judgment. "And just plain wrong."

"Sometimes I wanted to attack him with a meat axe," Sandra confided, watching the beautiful butterfly, a marvellous blue, make another circuit of their heads.

Daniel ran his thumb along his lean jaw. "You're a blood-thirsty little thing. I just hope I never fall out with you."

She jabbed him in the arm. "You must never, *never,* do that, Daniel."

"Even if it's a lot to ask?"

He didn't smile. He appeared to be taking her seriously. "Even then." She nodded as though she could see into the future. "You've signed on for another year. I won't be twenty-one until August. A journey of six months. You have to stick around for another six after that."

"Will do. Hey, sit still," he urged in a hushed tone.

"What is it? What's the matter?"

He sat up straight. "A butterfly has been hovering around. It's alighted on your head. Probably thinks it's a chrysanthemum."

"Oooh!" She drew in her breath and held it. "Is it still there?"

"Want me to catch it?"

"You might damage its wings."

"No, I won't!"

He sounded very sure. Still she shut her eyes. When she opened them again, their heads were very close together, the sable and the golden yellow. "All right, ready?" he murmured.

"Ready."

He opened his hand slowly, revealing the butterfly in all its beauty. It clung to the skin of his hand for barely a second, brilliant blue, yellow and black wings with a glinting yellow body, before it flew off.

"Surely that's a good omen," she whispered, staring into his eyes. They were so close she held her breath. This man was *beautiful!* He made her insides ache.

"I'm sure it is," Daniel said just as softly.

Something in his eyes, in his voice, made a thousand tingles run up and down her spine. Neither of them moved—it was as though movement was im-

hadn't gone away. ~~~~~~~~~~~~~~~~
pressed against the trunk of the tree. "By the way,
Grandad didn't approach you with any deal, did
he?" she asked after a moment.

"What sort of deal, Ms Kingston?" He was all
crisp attention.

"Oh forget it," she said, taking swift note of the
crease between his brows. "Just me being paranoid.
Bernie took one hell of a crack on the head when
he was a kid. Fell off his horse. Maybe that explains
why he too is wandering around in an emotional
fog." She broke off, as the stockmen started coming around for their afternoon tea break. "Time to
meet the men," she said.

"Right you are, ma'am." Daniel stood up, offering her his hand. "Some of them were around when
you left."

"I've already met quite a few people on my way
out here," she told him. Now the tingles spread from
her spine to her hand, to *everywhere!* "I loved the
babies. I've been invited to a getting to know you
morning tea. The schoolteacher wants me to look in
on the lessons. I mean to meet everyone on the station. That includes the aboriginal people who pass
through on walkabout."

CHAPTER SIX

DANIEL had been expecting a bedroom modest in size—or as modest as the rooms at Moondai homestead could get—and furnished in a way that reflected the taste of a very young girl. Maybe not lots of pink, painted furniture, decorations, a collection of dolls and so forth, given Sandra's self confessed tomboy qualities. What he got was the stuff of dreams. Ms Alexandra Kingston's childhood bedroom was very large and very grand. So large in fact she must have been lost in it.

"Think you can get used to it?" She circled the huge four poster bed with its draped canopy, giving the beautiful embroidered silk cover several good thumps while she was at it. "Dressing room adjoining, the bathroom pretty small for a big man but it will do."

"I'm sure." He looked about him with the same sense of wonder he had once felt wandering around an Adelaide art gallery. The bedroom walls were hung with paintings. Not any old paintings. He had

have hidden in it as a child. Maybe even now. A splendid crystal chandelier hung above his head.

"Baccarat," Sandra said nonchalantly, as he tilted his head.

"Of course, Baccarat!" he mocked. He'd never seen anything like it before.

There was a big comfortable cushion laden sofa upholstered in the same gold silk as the bedspread, two armchairs to match and a wing back chair covered in a bold tapestry obviously designed for a man. "I had the wing back chair brought in especially for you," she explained, moving to grace it.

"Not many people have a bedroom like this," he said, brushing long darkly tanned fingers across the pile of a cushion.

"I didn't want my bedroom to look like anybody else's," she said.

His mouth twisted. "You certainly got your wish. What is extraordinary is, you wanted all this when you were what—?"

Sandra rested her bright yellow head against the striking tapestry, the fabric a complementary mix of golds, bronzes and deep crimsons. "Around eight, I guess. I asked my dad if I could have a look around the stuff in the storeroom and he said, 'I'll come with you.' We picked the furniture together. I spotted the chandelier in a big box. Dad had it repaired and in no time at all it was up."

"Where was your mother when all this was happening?" he asked thinking her father's sudden death must have left a tremendous void in her life.

"Oh around," she said vaguely. "Mama said my taste was unbelievable."

"It was very exotic for a small girl."

"That's exactly what I wanted. Exotic, like the old travel books I read in the library. Something from an Arabian bazaar or Aladdin's Cave. Don't you just love the Persian rug under your feet?"

"Don't tell me." He moved backwards so he could study the central medallion and the floral arabesques. "It flies?"

"No, no," she said, laughing. "It's a late nineteenth-century Isfahan. My great-great-great-grandmother, Alexandra, was a rich Scottish lassie who was the big collector in the family. That's her portrait over there." She pointed to a large painting of an aristocratic looking young woman with a thick mane of bright red hair, narrow green eyes, very white skin and a pointed chin. She wasn't a beauty, her features were too sharp, but she was certainly striking as was her richly decorated dark green velvet dress.

"Nice to have ancestors," he said dryly.

"Have you never tried to find out who your fa-

young woman who was right out of his league. Outback royalty no less. Even the ancestor looked impossibly classy. He moved closer to inspect a gilt framed equine painting of a magnificent white Arabian stallion in a half rearing—neck bent stylised pose. In the background beneath a darkening turquoise sky was its dark skinned handler, with a bright red fez on his head. A fine horseman and a great lover of the most beautiful of all animals this was the one painting he coveted.

"French," Sandra said seeing his interest. "Late 1800s. I absolutely love it. Do I take it you tried but got nowhere?"

"Nowhere at all," he said briefly, turning back to face her. Her eyes were like precious gems, so dark a blue in some lights and depending on what she wore, they were violet. Did she know she looked like a painting herself framed by the antique armchair that all but swallowed her up?

"I'm sorry, Daniel," she said, those huge eyes sad and serious.

"I've dealt with it," he said brusquely, wanting yet not wanting her sympathy.

"How?"

"You ask too many questions." He began to prowl around restlessly.

"What happened to your mother?"

He picked up a silver object, put it down again. "She just died. I don't like to talk about it."

"Maybe you should. I hoped you would talk to me. After all I know a lot about death. Your mother must have been very young?"

"She was," he said sombrely, wanting her to leave it alone. "But I can hold on to her memory."

"Yes, you can," she agreed, turning her face more fully towards him. "I remember as clearly as though it were yesterday the afternoon my father was buried. All the Kingstons are buried on Moondai."

"I know." He was familiar with the family cemetery where Rigby Kingston had been buried alongside his first wife, Catherine, who had died of cancer, his favourite son, Trevor, not far away; his ancestors around him. His mother's ashes he had tossed on a desert whirlwind for that was what she had wanted. No trace left.

"Of course, you were *there*," Sandra realized. "My grandfather obviously didn't want me at his funeral. Maybe he was trying to spare me something Lord knows! But I held his hand the day my father was buried."

"Did you?" Daniel took a seat on the huge carved chest to listen to her tale. He had never before he met her considered he might fall under the spell of Ms Alexandra Kingston. She was his employer for one thing. She was too young, unattainable to the

"Mama went to pieces," she explained. "She was crying all the time. I remember someone I didn't know was standing beside her holding her up."

"Man or woman?"

"What do you think?" Her response was laconic. "I remember his glossy black shoes. I held Grandad's hand and he let me even though he didn't like holding hands. Everyone was in black but I wore my best dress, the one Dad liked. It was bright yellow. I tied my hair back with a yellow ribbon. When they lowered the coffin I wanted to jump in with him. I know Grandad wanted to jump in, too. He nearly broke my fingers he held them so tight. Mama was crying buckets, but Grandad and I saved our tears for later."

"What about your uncle Lloyd? Can you remember what he was like that day?"

Sandra shut her eyes tight the better to summon up the memory. "He didn't cry, either, but he looked terrible. He threw something in. Some little leatherbound book. I threw in a letter I wrote and the gold cup I'd just won at a riding competition at the Alice. Mum threw in a red rose. It made Grandad very angry but he never showed it until later."

"That must have been a terrible day for you, Sandra."

She pressed a hand to her fragile temple. "Maybe that's one of the reasons I trust you, Daniel. We both know about terrible days. And we both lost a dad."

"You can't miss what you never had." Daniel shrugged, which was a lie. "At least you were blessed with your memories of him." He stood up abruptly, tall and strong, suppressed emotion in his eyes.

I'm starting to get very good at reading Daniel's face, Sandra thought. Underneath the calmness, the quiet authority and the humour was a passionate man. "Want to see my room?" She whipped herself into sudden action.

"Now that's an offer! I can't refuse." He caught the fresh scent of her as she all but danced by him, light and graceful as any ballerina.

"I want to do lots of things to it," she confided. "It's much too staid. I bet you thought you were going to sleep in baby bear's bed?"

He laughed. "I never thought for a minute you'd let me into anywhere so grand."

"I need you to be happy, Daniel," she said seriously, walking through the open doorway of her parents' old suite while Daniel followed, keeping a few paces behind.

The suite was massive, very traditional in design with a colour scheme of bluish-grey and cream. A few paintings hung on the wall—nothing like the eclectic collection in Sandra's room but a beautiful, eye catching Chinoiserie screen stood beside the

golden ringlets.

"Recognise me?" she asked.

For a moment he said nothing, seized by a violent rush of tenderness that caught him unawares. He wanted to reach out and touch it, study it up close. There was a magical quality about such sweetness and innocence.

"Daniel?" she prompted. He'd had more than enough time to make a comment.

"Let me look at it properly." He stalled for time. "Who painted it?"

"A very clever friend of Dad's who was visiting us. He's a famous architect now. He lives in Singapore."

"It's lovely," he said, after another pause. "And I get to see your curls."

"You can see them better here." She lifted a silver framed photograph off a small circular table which held a collection of other framed photographs and passed it to him.

"This is Nikki?" he asked quietly.

"Yes." Her voice turned husky.

"Thank you for showing it to me." There was a lump in his own throat. He stared down at the recently taken glossy black and white photograph. In it, Sandra's small face was more gently rounded. She was smiling radiantly. A great cloud of blond hair framed her face and tumbled over her shoulders. Her arms were locked around a little girl obviously in the final stages of the childhood leukaemia that had robbed her of life. The child had huge sorrowful dark eyes but a big smile. She was wearing a beanie to cover the cruel effects of chemotherapy.

"How sad can life get?"

Sandra swallowed on a tight throat. "As soon as my affairs are finalised, I'm making a grant to the Leukaemia Foundation for research on paediatric leukaemia."

"You should," he agreed gently. "How did you come to meet Nikki?" He set the framed photograph carefully back on the table.

"It was my last year at uni. A medical school friend rang me one day to ask if I'd consider joining their little group. A few of them entertained sick kids in hospital, played games with them, read to them, sat with them, sang to them, played guitar, anything to take their minds off their suffering. I went along and listened as dying kids poured out their hearts." She broke off a minute to compose herself. "For some reason they wanted to *talk* to me. I think it had something to do with my blond hair and blue eyes. One little kid around four asked Anthony, my friend, who always dressed as a clown if I was an angel. Some of our group cracked up it was all so gut wrenching but I couldn't walk away. The very same day this photo was taken, Anthony

photo of that as we...
ing at the same time."

"Well now isn't this cosy?" A voice rife with sarcasm shattered the moment of closeness. "I haven't
seen so much togetherness in a long, long time."

Daniel threw back his head, his striking face taut
but before he could speak Sandra cut in. "I'm not
surprised, Bernie," she said, turning towards her
cousin. He was smirking and boldly wagging a finger. "Togetherness isn't something I associate with
our family. Do you want something?"

Irritation broke over his face. "Call me Berne," he
protested. "I was Bernie when I was a kid. I'm Berne
now. I prefer it."

"Berne it is," she said crisply. "I was just showing Daniel his room."

"In case neither of you have noticed, this is
yours," he said, acidly, somewhat stunned by the obvious rapport between Moondai's overseer and his
cousin.

"So it is," she returned sweetly. "After all, Uncle
Lloyd has taken over the master suite."

"Why not? He's the rightful master after all,"
Berne retaliated.

"Grandad didn't seem to think so."

"No, he was too busy scheming with Daniel here,
mornings, afternoons, evenings, you name it. Heads

together. Black and silver. Grandad always did cut a fine figure. I always thought—"

"Spare us, Berne," Daniel said, his face strangely impassive. "Your thoughts are way off beam. Your grandfather knew he was dying."

"He told you?" Sandra and Berne spoke together,

Daniel nodded in a matter of fact way. "Yes, he did. I was to say nothing to no one and I didn't. It was his wish and his place to tell his family and anyone else he wanted to know. Some days I suppose he thought he mightn't even last until the morrow. But there were orders to be carried out, decisions to be made. He wasn't going to be around to be in charge. Consequently there was a lot to talk about."

"By God you've kept a lot to yourself." Berne hurled the accusation. "My grandfather was good to you. Why?" he demanded, unable to hide his mountain of resentments. "You got paid well enough, so why the quarter of a million?" More than a touch of challenge had entered Berne's voice. "Was that the dowry price? You could have asked a hell of a lot more."

His intention was clearly to goad Daniel into speaking out and perhaps revealing too much but Daniel had assumed a different guise even as Berne spoke; detached, businesslike, official, pretty much like Rigby Kingston had been as boss. "Maybe I'd better leave. I just know you're going to talk absolute drivel."

guage sent him bac...
for the final word. "Makes sense ...
it, cousin." He shot a glance at Sandra who was ...
ancing some bronze object in her hand as though she
meant to throw it. "Make sense to you? Of course
you won't get anything out of Daniel on the subject,
but denials. But how many girls want to believe
their future husbands were bought for them?"

"You don't think the plan a bit tricky, Berne? As
far as I'm concerned marriage is the kiss of death.
More than half of all marriages today end in divorce.
Quite apart from that, how could Grandad possibly
imagine he could so easily manipulate two people?
Hypothetical question as I don't believe for a minute there's even a grain of truth in your theory."

"There isn't," Daniel confirmed with quiet contempt.

"Don't believe him, cousin," Berne warned,
pleased to have stirred up a hornet's nest. "Listen to
your inner voice. See it my way and it all starts to
make sense. Didn't Grandad love playing God?'

"That he did," Sandra said, wondering if she
could possibly be blinding herself to what she didn't
want to see. After all, it did happen. She raked a
hand through the silk floss of her hair, wanting to
cling to her natural instincts to trust Daniel.

Berne nodded, as though he had won an important point. "You said it. This whole thing smacks of a deal…a marriage of convenience?"

Sandra stared at him while Daniel clenched his fists, looking like he was struggling hard not to lash out. "I'm not bothered by what you think, Berne. Ms Kingston's trust, however, is important to me."

Sandra spoke up. "There's no need to call me Ms Kingston at *any* time, Daniel, I know why you're unwilling to call me by my Christian name in front of the family and staff but it simply doesn't matter to me. I need guidance and I'm willing to take it from you, Daniel. I trust you." For some reason she felt very close to tears, but no way was she going to allow them to fall.

"That's a mistake." Berne frowned fiercely, jealous of her taking sides. "You're a Kingston. *You* own the station. *He's* an employee."

"An indispensable one Berne, lest you forget. I don't have a problem with Daniel calling me Sandra. The *one* person who knew exactly what he intended when he left Moondai to me, was Grandad. Have you bothered to consider he might have wanted to make reparation. After all, he did kick us out."

"With a trust fund," Berne was driven to shouting. "You weren't chucked out into the snow. Grandad didn't want to lay eyes on you and your playgirl mother but he made sure you were provided for."

All trace of colour left Sandra's cheeks. "You're lying."

going to let you ____

schools didn't you? I know you ____

two. You went on to university. Where the hell did you think the money was coming from? Come on tell me. You're supposed to be so bright."

Daniel intervened, holding up his palm to Berne so Sandra could speak. "Did your mother never tell you this, Sandra?"

She shook her head wretchedly. "I was *ten*, Daniel. We always had money. I never knew any other life. My mother told me it was my father's money. I accepted that. Why wouldn't I? When she remarried she married money. That was her way. I had part-time jobs all the time I was at university so I wouldn't be too much of a burden. I never thought Grandad was continuing to look out for us."

"Well he was," Berne said, sounding equally wretched.

"Your mother should have told you, Sandra," Daniel said. "She had a duty to tell you."

"Shameless bitch!" Berne muttered. "Never did tell the truth. All she was ever interested in was herself. Dad was right about her. You should think about it instead of blaming Dad."

"I love my mother, Berne," Sandra said, unable to disentangle herself from the ties that bind.

"Fine!" he fumed. "I know you can love someone and be disgusted with them at the same time. Why did Grandad bypass me for you? Sons and grandsons always have the inside track."

"I know they do," Sandra acknowledged. "Maybe Grandad knew I was the most likely to try to hold on to our inheritance. The Kingston inheritance. Kingstons are buried here, Berne. Do we walk away from Moondai and leave them here?"

Berne gave a strangled laugh. "They're *dead*, Sandra. They're gone forever. They don't know and they don't care."

"But *I* care," Sandra said. "I want to be loyal to my ancestors, to my dad and my grandfather, harsh though he was to us. I don't want to betray them."

"You're too young to be such a sentimental fool," Berne said in disgust. "The dead are dead. No way do they care about our actions. As for Daniel here—" he shot Daniel a glowering look "—he's a fast worker. I'm betting he was offered the deal of a lifetime on a silver platter. He gets Moondai but you're part of the package. He couldn't have imagined such a scenario in his wildest dreams. But a word of caution."

"Okay, let's hear it, Berne," Daniel clipped off, looking like he was more than ready to hear it and deal with it if needs be.

"It's for my *cousin*, pal," Berne emphasized, predisposed to hating Daniel Carson for so many reasons; showing him up without even trying, relating so easily to his grandfather when Rigby Kingston

Sandra sold on him on ~~~~~
and made him doubly aggressive. "We don't ~~~
anything much about you, do we, Dan?" he charged.
"You're a dark horse if ever there was one. Grandad accepted you on the word of a fellow cattleman.
So you did a good job in the Channel Country? I
guess you've always been hell-bent on climbing the
ladder. Personally I think you should be investigated. Most people have things to hide. We know
nothing about your background for instance. Sandra should make it her business to find out."

But Sandra was reeling from Berne's disclosures.
"You think Grandad didn't check Daniel out?" she
asked, staring at her cousin.

Berne shrugged. "It was different with Grandad.
No man had power over him, but from what I can
see Daniel has power over *you* already."

"He must if you say so, Berne." She looked at her
cousin with acute distaste. The charge stung like a
whip because it was *true*.

"Look how you treat him for God's sake!" Berne
wheeled a half circle in his rage. "You've installed
him in the house. It would never have happened in
Grandad's day. Dad certainly wouldn't have allowed it. Daniel is *staff*. He's got the overseer's bungalow. It's good enough for him."

Sandra noted the sharp shift in Daniel's lean powerful body. She moved to stand between them. If there was any physical confrontation she knew Berne would come off second best. "Let's say I want Daniel on call, Berne. Not a good distance away. Yesterday we crash landed in a crocodile infested swamp. Incredibly Daniel was able to bring the chopper down in a clearing the size of a bathtub. The sad thing is, it's my *family* I don't trust. There's a great deal at stake here. You and Uncle Lloyd did handsomely out of Grandad's will as you should, but you're filled with bitter resentments. I understand that. I got the lion's share. But I think most people in my position would find themselves with a few more fears than they started out with. I've made a judgment in regards Daniel. I've elected to trust him."

"More fool's you!" Berne's voice trembled with anger. "It's just as I said. He's got to you already. Just be careful, cousin. That's all I'm saying."

"What have *I* got to gain from something happening to Sandra, Berne?" Daniel asked in a voice that would have brought anyone up short.

"Not now. Not yet," Berne said obscurely, turning to go.

"If you've got concerns why don't you go to the authorities?" Daniel began to move towards him.

"Daniel, please." Sandra grasped his arm. "I will be careful, Berne. I don't need you to tell me. My

if he had been an awful kid, jealous, resentful, always spoiling for a fight.

"That's your stupid mother talking," Berne rasped, his tanned skin turning white. "You might have a little chat with her. You talk about untrustworthy? You can't go past her. Uncle Trevor wasn't supposed to make that trip anyway. It was Grandad." He punched the words out, turned on his heel and stomped off down the hall.

For a moment Sandra couldn't catch her breath. Confusion was growing at such a rate of intensity her mind was in turmoil. "Could that possibly be true?" she managed eventually. "Have you ever heard it?" Her legs felt so wobbly she had to sit down.

"Never." Daniel's voice was rough with concern. "And I've heard plenty of talk. Don't upset yourself, Sandra. You've gone very pale."

"Why would he say it?" She searched those silver-grey eyes.

"God knows." Daniel could see the shock in her. There were far too many revelations for her to handle all at once. "He's been making a lot of wild accusations."

"So that's it, wild accusations?"

He saw the doubts that brushed her expression.

Doubts that made something flare deep in his eyes. "So who should you believe, Sandra?" he asked in a dead-serious voice. "Because it's *you* who has to decide."

CHAPTER SEVEN

In the days that followed Sandra had plenty of time to mull over Berne's revelations. Had it really been her grandfather and not her father who was to have flown to the Kingston outstation that fateful day? Her grandfather had long been accustomed to flying off on regular inspections, often without notice because he took pleasure in catching the staff on the hop. On numerous occasions he had taken her father along with him. As the heir apparent, her father was being groomed to one day take over the reins. Berne had sounded so *sure*. She struggled to understand how, if that were so, her mother had been able to maintain her silence.

She had lost no time ringing her mother in an effort to set the record straight. Just as she feared, immediately she broached the subject, her mother became highly emotional. That was Pam's way of protecting herself from being questioned too closely. Pam invariably resorted to controlled hysteria. She swore she knew nothing of the change of plan. When asked about where their money had come from after they left Moondai, she had flown into a fit of defensiveness saying she had never spoken to Sandra about financial matters because they simply weren't her concern. Whatever lines of credit Rigby Kingston had made available, it was his duty to do so. He was a hateful man. Pam was overjoyed he was dead. Sandra deserved everything that had come her way. Moondai would have gone to her father in any case. Sandra should not upset her like this. That part of her life as a Kingston was long over. Besides, Mickey had chicken pox and needed her attention.

All in all the phone call had been a stomach churning disaster. Her mother had even been crass enough to call her stepfather to the phone to say a few affectionate words, but Sandra had all but hurled the phone down, thinking though she loved her mother Pam was a fool. It made life so much easier if one didn't have to look truth in the face.

The upshot was Sandra felt desperate to get confirmation from her uncle. Daniel had urged her to do so, but somehow she always baulked at the last moment. If Berne's claim was true and not made up on the spur of the moment, it would open up an entirely new avenue of thought. Her grandfather had made enemies over the years. He had never been what one would call popular. In fact a lot of people wouldn't have been upset by his demise.

Lloyd's consuming interest in cataloguing native flora had been a mystery and an irritation to his father, Lloyd had been allowed to make his numerous field trips and tour the country at will. They all lived in what most people would consider, splendour, all financed by Rigby Kingston, notoriously miserly in some areas and surprisingly generous in others.

Mystery piled on top of mystery. It was those closest to Sandra she felt she couldn't trust. Not even Elsa who lived on the periphery of everyone's attention. In some ways Elsa was like a resident ghost, forever hovering about without really being seen or heard. Whatever had happened to the handsome, hardworking, businesswoman of yesterday? Happiness had passed Elsa by. But what had actually happened to cause her to pass from one state to the other? Certainly her grandfather had been an autocratic man but one would have thought Elsa in her mid-forties when they married would have been able to cope with him? There must have been attraction between them for them to have married in the first place. Instead Elsa had turned into a watcher, not a doer as hollowed out inside as if she'd been gutted. That in itself was a mystery. The empty shell of her marriage was now over, but still Elsa made no move to get on with a new and better life.

Sandra on the other hand made a good start on learning about the running of Moondai. As the weeks went by Daniel was able to spend more and more time with her though the amount of time was determined by his own heavy work schedule. She was grateful he was loosening up his routine in order to be able to show her the ropes. It had taken no time at all to discover his workload was considerable. He was on the job at sunup, not returning to the homestead until well after sunset. Consequently she never saw him at breakfast or lunch, meeting up maybe an hour before dinner when they retired to the office. There they read through piles of memos, invoices, letters and documents that Andy, the station accountant had arranged in batches for inspection and signature where necessary. Whatever decisions Daniel came to regarding the business side of running the station he explained the reasons for it, going into quite a bit of detail and not fobbing her off or treating her as if her opinion at this early stage had little value. He treated her like the intelligent person she was. She liked that about him. Her uncle invariably talked down to her. Sandra had never thought of herself as a businesswoman in the making, but she was finding learning about all these financial matters far more interesting than she ever supposed.

Now's a great opportunity to use it.

To that end she and Daniel continued their learning sessions for a couple of hours after dinner. Even dinner had turned into a routine with some degree of normalcy. Her uncle solved the problem of Daniel's presence at the table by addressing the odd civil remark to him but concentrating on his niece. Sandra who had no great knowledge of the desert flora but had always been filled with wonderment at the phenomenon of the vast desert gardens began to avail herself of her uncle's extensive knowledge.

"Don't start him off for God's sake!" Berne had warned when she first started to show an interest.

"You're incapable of appreciating the beauties of nature, Bernard," his father responded, finding he was warming to his niece now that she had become an adult. Sandra had been a very precocious little girl as he recalled. Something both his father and brother had encouraged no doubt to counter Pamela's single digit IQ.

But it was to Daniel Sandra always turned for advice and instruction. It was getting so she couldn't hide her feelings. From herself at least. She prided herself she had the sense not to allow Daniel to see how important he was to her. That might have put him in a very awkward position. She knew she was more than half way in love with him—hell, madly in love with him—which might have been precisely what her grandfather had in mind. Just thinking about it all was interfering with her sleep and her thought processes. To counter her increasing need for him and his company she upped her business-like manner. The last thing she wanted to do was put pressure on him. A girl had her pride. Daniel was there to give her protection, to be her friend and mentor, so that when his year was up she could step into his shoes albeit with the help of a professional station manager they would select together.

End of story or the start of a great adventure?

It was only when she lay in bed at night, thinking about him, she wondered if he were fooled by the briskness of her manner. She was so *aware* of him, every word he spoke, every inflection, the way he laughed, the way he walked, the gleaming glances he sent in her direction, every gesture he made. When their hands brushed, whilst passing documents to one another, little electric shocks zapped through her. There was such a *buzz* around him. No use pretending. She was in *deep*. It amazed and alarmed her, causing her to wonder if her own susceptibility had overtones of her mother? She had seen too much of vulnerable women. She had no intention of becoming one.

* * *

it, a frown or co...

"Well?" Sandra couldn't stand the suspense.

He broke off to look at her. "Nothing much new."

"Damn, are you sure?"

He shoved that errant lock of hair off his forehead. "Of course I'm sure. You can read it in a minute. It's much the same as the preliminary report. Mechanical failure. There's no blame laid, no criticism of the maintenance of the aircraft. In fact a little pat on the back for me for pilot skills."

"Is that all they came up with?" Sandra felt angry and frustrated.

He sighed. "Don't get upset. We survived. The failure of mechanical components is well documented, Sandra. Now we have the chopper back, I'll have the hangar, attended by day and locked up at night. It's never been done before."

"So we drop the whole thing?" Sandra showed her dissatisfaction.

"Nothing else we can do." Daniel shrugged in acceptance. Nevertheless he quietly went about putting new security measures in place.

It didn't take long for a steady stream of visitors to start to call; station people and business people from Alice Springs who wanted to welcome Rigby Kingston's granddaughter back home. Most were good-hearted, Outback people simply wanting to wish her well. A few busybodies came to size her up. Gossip was rife Moondai might very well come onto the market. The wheeler-dealers wanted to be there on the ground floor. Even would-be suitors came to call; some overconfident, dressed nattily, some afflicted by stammering shyness that was painful to behold. None of them fortune hunters exactly—they were all from established families—but young men looking for a suitable wife and future mother for their brood. Sandra's enviable financial standing made her a prize candidate.

The consensus of opinion was made available by way of the grapevine. Alexandra Kingston would make some lucky bloke the perfect wife.

"The word's gone out," Daniel told her, a dry note in his voice. They were sitting atop a fence watching a mob of around thirty brumbies being drafted. For wild horses they had surprisingly well developed muscles and came in varied colours, bay, iron grey, black, big, medium, compact sized, some showing station blood. One liver chestnut beauty was trying its level best to bite a stockman on the shoulder.

"What word?" She turned on him so precipitously he had to grab her to prevent her falling.

"Why your beauty of course, Ms Kingston." His eyes beneath the brim of his hat mocked her.

"And you're the expert?" she asked tartly, to cover

to crush her ...

had happened to her. She was head over heels in love. Then there was the other thing which might or might not have significance but she had to find out from him.

Among the visitors who wished to renew their acquaintance were station people called McAuliffe accompanied by their only daughter, Alanna. Sandra vaguely remembered Alanna, although Alanna was several years older, a vibrantly attractive brunette with a shapely figure and unusual coffee-coloured eyes.

Memories of that afternoon kept coming… After partaking of afternoon tea and complementing Meg on her cooking, Alanna stood up with an appealing, "Do you mind if I go off and find Daniel?"

Sandra had been shocked at her own reaction. She'd wanted to tell Alanna to back the hell off. She was *jealous,* when she had vowed never, never to become a jealous woman.

"I need him to confirm something," Alanna explained. "Would you mind if I borrow the Jeep?" she asked prettily, casting her eyes over the Jeep that Sandra kept parked in the drive for her own use.

Again Sandra couldn't for the life of her wring out a "Please do."

"There's a ball coming up." Alanna looked back,

big eyed. "Daniel has promised to be my partner. He's just so much in demand, I'm thrilled out of my mind it's going to be me."

"Lana's absolutely *crazy* about him," Mrs. McAuliffe piped up, just in case Sandra had missed the message. "Daniel's enormously popular with the girls. There's something about him that makes the knees buckle," she gushed, turning quite pink cheeked herself.

"We're kinda hoping something good might come of it," Mr. McAuliffe tacked on, cracking his knuckles.

Over my dead body!

"Prickly little thing aren't you," Daniel interrupted her recollections, amused by her feisty expression. "It just so happens I *like* it. You must have known you were going to attract every last bachelor from eighteen to eighty in the Territory and beyond."

"I'm relying on you to put it about I'm very bad-tempered," she said shortly.

She had taken off her akubra and damp golden curls clung to her nape. Her hair had grown so quickly Daniel thought, resisting the powerful urge to fluff the gilded halo that had replace the short pet-alled look. No wonder the little kids at the hospital had mistaken her for an angel. But she was more spicy than sweet though she had her sweet moments. A man couldn't ask for more he thought. But it wasn't going to happen to him.

Forget it, Daniel.

"That certainly doesn't apply to your friend Alanna," Sandra retorted, sharper than she meant. *Be careful. Be careful. Don't give yourself away.* "Now there's a sexpot if ever I've seen one. Are you going to the ball with her?"

He laughed, an infinitely attractive sound to her ears. "Though tempted I had to turn her down."

She turned her head to stare at him. He was worth staring at. He had a beautifully structured chin and jawline. She wanted to trace it with her hand. She was painfully aware of the excitement that was throbbing inside her, wishing and wishing she could pass her excitement on to him. "She told me you had *promised.* I'm surprised at you, Daniel. You shouldn't break a promise."

"As it happened, I didn't." He whistled at a hostile horse with a star-shaped white blaze on its forehead. The horse amazingly quietened, ears tipped forward. "Alanna thinks if she wants something badly enough she'll get it."

"And she wants you. Mamma and Poppa made that clear. You better remind her you're working for *me.*"

"Yes, Ms Kingston." He tipped a tanned finger, eyes sparkling. "Anyway what's not to want?" he quipped.

"I suppose. You're very likeable, Daniel," she said

kindly. "What are you going to do with your life? You're so clever and capable."

"You forgot popular." His glance seemed to mock her. "Trying to get rid of me already?"

She wanted to say, you can stay forever but was worried about frightening him off. How could you stop yourself from giving your heart away? It just happened. "The truth is I'm coming to rely on you more and more, Daniel," she said. "Do you suppose—I don't want you to take this the wrong way—but do you suppose Grandad had some master plan in mind?"

Sunlight made a dazzle of his eyes. "For you and me?"

His tone was so highly sceptical she was stopped in her tracks. "Well we all know it wouldn't work. I am resolved not to get married anyway. But I keep wondering why he arranged things the way he did. Berne stirred things up as he meant to. There's got to be some logic to it. Grandad was nothing if not logical. Did he assume in throwing the two of us together some magic might happen? Or more likely did he think we'd see it in materialistic terms? What would undoubtedly advantage you would advantage me as you could successfully step straight into Grandad's shoes. You'd maintain authority and style. You said yourself it made a kind of sense."

His mouth twisted. "Where would I get style from, Sandra?" he asked as though he was burdened

But a good man. . . . . . .
education. He would have let me continue . . .
too determined to pay him back."

"That was Harry Cunningham from the Channel
Country?" she asked with care.

"You've done your homework. What else have
you found out about me?" His tone was astonishingly clipped.

"Don't get mad. It was Vince Taylor who told
me," she said, trying to sound casual when she'd really been pumping foreman Vince, for information.
"Mr. Cunningham must have been a good man."

"The best," Daniel confirmed.

"Obviously. He trained you. As for style, as far
as I'm concerned, style is innate. It's knowing who
you are, not who your dad was; what *you* are. You've
got good blood in you, Daniel."

"The hell I have!" It came out like a soft growl.

"Oh, you've got good blood all right," she insisted. "You'd be at home anywhere."

He gave her a smouldering glance. "Your family
doesn't seem to think so. I'd be lucky if your appalling snob of an uncle addresses two words to me over
dinner."

"I wouldn't have a nervous breakdown about it,"
she said dryly. "Uncle Lloyd is worried *you'll* ask

him something he doesn't know. Think about it. Exactly what does he know about? He's spent his whole life on Moondai but he couldn't possibly run it. His towering achievement is becoming an amateur botanist."

"Well that in itself is something," Daniel said with unexpected approval, given Lloyd Kingston's patronising manner with him. "I'm like you I'm finding the whole area fascinating. I've even taken to looking out for the exquisite little plants tucked away in the canyons. Botany is a legitimate career. Your uncle would have been a much happier man had he struck out for himself. The same goes for Berne."

"It hasn't occurred to you both of them are bone lazy?" Sandra said, marvelling that it was so.

"Now that you mention it, yes. Listen, much as I'm enjoying the break, I must go. I have to do some bull catching this afternoon with a couple of the men. The tallest and the fittest."

"So they can lift the steel panels for the portable yards?"

"Right on." He gave her a little nod of approval. "You might only have been ten when you left but you haven't forgotten much. It's great you've kept up your riding, too." She was, in fact, a natural born horsewoman. He took great pleasure in watching her ride, knowing she loved horses as much as he did.

Daniel swung himself off the fence in one lithe

chest against her cheek.

"Catch me!" she invited, joyous as a child. She threw out her own arms launching her feather light body at him.

But it wasn't a child who landed in his arms. It was a woman who was growing more lovely, more sexually exciting by the day. Just holding her was dangerous. Her skin was perfection even in the strong sunlight. Her buttery curls swept up from her graceful neck. Her full tender lips were curved in a smile but it was her eyes that drew Daniel in. So deep and so sparkling a blue he wanted to drown in their lagoon-like depths.

A woman's beauty and sexual allure was a powerful weapon to render a man helpless. A weapon he couldn't risk putting into her hands. There was no way he could reverse their station in life. She was the Kingston heiress; he was the overseer. He had to hold tight to his pride though he realised had they been on their own and stockmen weren't around, all it would have taken was to tighten his hold on her and lower his head.

Desire swept through Daniel's body like a dark rushing river. He couldn't step back from it. It was on him. All of his senses were astonishingly *keen*.

Sight. Sound. Smell. Touch. They were far too close, their heads bent to one another, both of them seemingly fearing to speak. He could savour the fresh scent of her; feel the heat off her body. She was the very essence of femininity. He could almost *taste* her on his palate.

For one long precious moment he allowed himself to be held in thrall. He couldn't even think straight; just standing there, holding her, drenched in a yearning so powerful, so evocative of something just beyond his reach, it was causing him *pain*. He wondered with an unfamiliar surge of panic what more lay in store for him. What could happen from this point on? This was no fleeting attraction. It was something over which he was losing control. Yet getting her to fall in love with *him* wouldn't be so difficult. He had enough experience to recognise that. He could see the little electric flame in her eyes. What burned her burned him.

Only it wasn't *right*. This was far more than a momentary indiscretion; it was as good as forbidden. She was quite alone. Her family wasn't much use to her. She relied on him; she trusted him. Sometimes she seemed *so terrifyingly* young and innocent. He couldn't possibly hurt her or betray that innocence which he knew instinctively she retained for all that predatory stepfather who deserved to be pummelled into the ground.

Daniel made his decision. Falling in love was not only a powerful emotion, it could come as a body

He rallied sufficiently to make a joke.

"I'll be a butterball in no time," she said, herself faring quite well in regaining her balance. As he turned away she called, "Do you think you could spare me a full hour tomorrow, Daniel?"

"Sure, what for?" He stood in a characteristic pose with his two hands on his lean hips, long fingers pointing down.

She took immense pleasure in his dynamic male aura. "I want to learn how to ride a motorbike," she told him with feigned casualness.

His expression was comical. She might just as well have said she wanted to learn to drive the bulldozer and start ripping up new tracks for the road trains. "Is that a good idea?" He couldn't bear the idea of her coming off a bike, even a minor spill could break bones though he knew her look of fragility was deceptive. She was actually quite strong.

"Heck, Daniel, we're in the middle of nowhere," she protested. "You can show me, can't you or will I get Chris to show me?" She knew she was provoking him. Chris Barrett was a good-looking, full of himself, young jackeroo who was doing a year's stint on the station before taking up a position in the family engineering firm in Brisbane. Hugely enjoying his gap year Chris flirted openly with her though the older stockmen were at pains to make clear to him he was crossing the line.

"Just let's forget Chris," Daniel said dryly. "As a rider I don't regard him very highly, let alone as a teacher. Your grandfather only took him on as a favour to his family. He'll never make a cattleman not that he was ever meant to. Please don't give him any encouragement. He's impudent enough as it is." But harmless, Daniel knew, otherwise he'd have been told to pack up his gear and leave.

"I've forgotten him already," Sandra said airily. "So I can count on an hour tomorrow?"

"Okay," he nodded briskly.

"I'd like to be able to handle the dozer." She kept a perfectly straight face as she said it.

"Forget the dozer," he said, firmly. "It's by no means easy to operate, weighing in as it does at around thirty-eight tons. There's a small tractor I'll let you have a go on one of these days."

"Thank you, Daniel." She gave him a radiant smile. "I've got a lot of learning in front of me. I want to be able to fly the Beech Baron and the helicopter in time."

His answer was serious which greatly pleased her. "Flying lessons can be arranged," he said. "I thought you *hated* flying?"

"So I do and why wouldn't I?" she retorted. "But it was wonderful up there with you in the chopper before we crashed. The best way to get over my

was happening

He nodded his agreement. "It's the only way to get around. I know a very patient and competent teacher."

"You?" she asked hopefully.

He shook his head. "Not me. I'd find that too nerve-racking." He softened it with a smile. "This guy, Paddy Hyland runs the Hyland School of Aviation at the Alice. He's very good, gently spoken and he has the patience of Job."

"So what are you saying, females need to be mollycoddled?"

"Well gentleness makes women feel better, Sandra."

"Plus females need instructors with the patience of Job?"

"Now you're starting to get the hang of it." That engaging dimple flickered in his cheek.

"Have you failed to notice how smart I am, Daniel?"

"Sandra, I haven't failed to notice every last little thing about you," he said with such a note in his voice it turned her insides out. "Have a nice day now!" He sketched a salute. "I'll see you tonight."

Make that every night of our lives!

CHAPTER EIGHT

SANDRA had been going steadily through paperwork since around nine o'clock that morning. It was now eleven and Meg came to the door with a cup of coffee and a freshly baked apple and cinnamon muffin. She stopped for a while chatting—Meg was always cheerful—then went on her way. Sandra had insisted Meg get more help in running the house—it was so big. Elsa did nothing to lend a hand so far as Sandra could see—so Meg had taken two young aboriginal girls under her wing for training. Sandra often heard their infectious laughter issuing from the kitchen and around the house. It brightened up the atmosphere and she was glad of it.

Elsa kept mostly to her suite of rooms—she had not shared a bedroom with Sandra's grandfather for many years—or she took her long rambling walks. The family cemetery was one of her haunts though she hadn't taken to laying flowering branches on her husband's grave as Sandra often did at the grave of her father. In fact Sandra had given instructions for

desolate place. It had been kept in perfect order but an aura of melancholy hung over it. She finished what she was doing, put her signature to the crosses Daniel had marked for her, then decided on the spur of the moment to ride out to the family plot to check on the new plantings. The worst of the heat was over and the desert days sparkled.

On her way she stopped to break off several long branches of the fluffy flowered pink mulla-mulla, a desert ephemeral that threw a blushing veil over the landscape. Some of the branches stood as tall as herself as did the desert grevillea which was one of the most spectacular flowering trees of the Red Centre.

Most of her friends from her student days thought the desert extremely arid, a terrifying, life threatening place, which of course it was under certain circumstances. What they didn't appear to know or had never seen was the desert after the rains; a wonderland on such a scale it made the most beautiful of city gardens, even the botanical gardens, look pocket handkerchief-sized by comparison. What large country garden for that matter ran to the horizon? Where else were there carpets of white, yellow and pink everlastings covering fifty square miles? Her home, Moondai, was a world apart. She had already resolved to hold on to it. Her ancestors lay buried in the lava-red earth.

When she reached the cemetery she slipped off her horse, a highly responsive mare, and tethered it to a branch of an old gum. The gum was almost a sculpture, gnarled and twisted in its endless struggle against the harshness of sun and wind. A short distance away was the iron fenced enclosure with its marble and granite headstones. No one to disturb you here, she thought a melancholy shiver running down her spine.

A great flock of budgerigar, the phenomenon of the Inland, winged overhead drawing her eyes. They were flying in their curious V formation seeking out the nearest water which was maybe half a mile off at Jirra Jarra Creek, its banks graced by a magnificent corridor of red river gums. She took a few moments to watch the squadron of little birds flame across the sky, emerald green and gold, the colours of the nation, then she gathered the mass of pink flowers Outback people called "lamb's tails" and strode off. Once inside the massive gate she noted with satisfaction the bauhinias had responded well to their new home. She had expected to see one or two wilting but they showed their toughness holding their silvery green foliage aloft. Their seasonal flowering was over but come September-October they should be out in all their shining white glory. She had always loved the bauhinias as a child; the

so many generations of

Carefully Sandra paid her respects to her grandfather and the grandmother, Catherine, she had never known, then moved on to the grave of her father, speaking aloud to him as she had as a child. His had been a bittersweet marriage—her mother had never settled in her desert home—but she had always understood her father had deeply loved her, his only child. The happiness and security of her childhood had been destroyed by his death. Her mother, even now, had not apologised for saying her husband's own brother had had something to do with it. She stuck to her claim that Lloyd Kingston was *evil* but though Sandra kept her uncle under constant close observation she couldn't see it. In fact it was starting to seem *unthinkable*. Perhaps her mother had wanted revenge for her brother-in-law's harsh criticism of her own lifestyle? Whatever the reason her uncle should never have used her, a child, as a weapon in their war. *That* had been truly unforgivable even if at some stage he'd believed his claim she wasn't a Kingston. It had only recently struck her, her uncle and her cousin had laboured all their lives for her grandfather's love and approval without ever getting it. Small wonder it had caused such bitterness and driven a wedge between them and *her.* The great irony was the grandfather who had banished her had made her his heir. Should anything happen to her, her uncle Lloyd would inherit the entire estate.

Daniel found her an hour later, sitting in solitude on a stone bench. He tethered his horse beside the mare, watching the animals acknowledge each other with companionable whinnies, before walking towards the enclosure.

"Sandra," he called gently.

She lifted her sunny head that always reminded him of a lovely flower on a stalk, holding up a hand.

How do I withstand her? he asked himself, unnerved at the speed with which she had gotten not only under his skin but right into the deepest cavern of his heart. Sandra Kingston was a dream he had been hankering after all his life. She was also, like a dream, out of reach.

Close to, he could see the track of tears on her satin cheeks. He was deeply moved, thinking he would always hold that little picture of her sitting here, weeping gentle tears.

"Hi, come sit beside me," she invited, moving along the bench a little so he would have room.

"I feel I'm intruding," he commented, his eyes on her poignant profile.

"No, you're not." She gave him a reassuring smile. "I was talking to Dad."

over her eyes. There's...
know, Daniel. Living with my unhappy family these
past months I just can't believe Uncle Lloyd had
anything to do with Dad's death."

"I've *never* believed it." Daniel's eyes rested on
her floral offering, his own wounded heart contract-
ing. "Apart from anything else, he just doesn't have
it in him to take any sort of violent action. As I see
it, your mother was expelled from the family home
in disgrace. She retaliated by accusing your uncle
of a heinous crime. She would have been shattered
at the time. Your uncle had poured endless scorn on
her. There's a limit to what people can take."

"So it *was* an accident?" she asked with a pro-
found sigh.

"That was the result of the inquiry."

"So I've spent more than half my life believing a
terrible lie?" Her blue eyes sought his.

"Some people use up *all* their life believing lies,
Sandra."

"And our accident in the chopper? You had your
suspicions, Daniel?" she reminded him. These moments they spent alone were becoming oddly intense as though it wasn't permitted for them to
become too intimate.

He shrugged, not wanting to increase her sense

of hidden threat. "It just seemed like one accident too many. I jumped to conclusions."

"You don't sound too sure?" She watched his face, wanting to turn his chin a little towards her so she could stare into his eyes.

"Money creates an environment of suspicion, Sandra. In your case a great deal of money."

I've got money for both of us, she cried out inside but couldn't possibly say it aloud. Daniel was fiercely independent and proud.

"Money and passions coexist," he continued. "Anger, bitterness, resentment, shameful, violent thoughts."

"So it would serve my family's ambitions if I didn't get to celebrate my twenty-first birthday?" she asked bleakly.

"Which is fast approaching." He traced the perfect oval of her face with his eyes. She had put a little weight on her fragile frame. It was immensely becoming, the woman emerging clearly from the young girl. "I'll have to start thinking of a present. By the way I have to fly to Darwin, this coming Friday. Joel Moreland wants to meet me."

That name beat against Sandra's brain. "Joel Moreland, the man with the Midas touch? You're not going to leave me for him, are you?" she asked, reduced to near panic.

"Hey, he only wants to meet me, Sandra." For a breathless second he almost pulled her into his

"Yes, I know. I was dismissing Morrissey. "So *why* does a man like Moreland want to meet you, Daniel, unless it's to offer you a job?" Her voice was unsteady with emotion.

"If he does, he does." Daniel shook his head, struggling to retain his own role of employee, friend and mentor. "I have to think of my future, Sandra. Let's face it by the time my year's up, you could either decide to sell Moondai or find yourself engaged to one of the drove of guys who've been calling. Don't for a moment think they haven't got their eye on Moondai as well as the fair maiden."

"Thank you, Daniel," she said crisply, tilting her delicately determined chin.

"Sandra, I've no wish to offend you. As lovable as you undoubtedly are, your rich inheritance would only make them love you more."

"You've made your point," she said acidly. "Or am I supposed to feel flattered they might want *me* at all?"

His mobile mouth twisted. "I just want you to be fully aware of the disadvantages of being an heiress."

"Don't worry. I'll have the lucky man vetted by you."

It distressed him just to hear her say it even in mockery. He locked his strong muscular arms behind his head. "What I started out to say was would you like to come along for the ride? I don't expect to be more than a couple of hours over lunch. You could do some shopping; visit an art gallery. We could meet up later. Actually I'd like you to meet Moreland. It's very handy to know a man like that. He could be a big help to you in the future."

"Well I'll need it, won't I with you planning to pack up and leave," Sandra burst out, startled by her impulse to throw herself into his arms and beg him to stay.

"What did you think was going to happen?" He turned on her, on the surface calm, underneath battling his own complicated needs and wants. Sandra Kingston coming into his life had exposed him to new and overwhelming emotions. Falling in love was the last thing he had seen coming.

"Oh, I don't know," she said. "The two of us surviving that crash entrenched you in my mind as a friend and protector, not just Moondai's overseer which you're determined to be."

"Well that's my job, Sandra," he said tersely. "We're both aware of that. We inhabit different worlds."

"We inhabit the *same* world!" She levelled him with an electric blue stare.

"Don't, Sandra," he said, deliberately using his position as employee as a shield.

Her cheeks flushed with anger. "Don't what?"

"I think you do."

"And you've decided to put me in my place?" she asked raggedly.

"That wasn't my aim." He stood up quiet, but commanding. "What I'm saying is I've decided to remain in *my* place."

"You have a hide!" Her voice trembled. He towered over her with those long legs but for once she didn't find it comforting.

"I'm sorry. You *must* understand."

"Well I don't!" Her vision was blurring with tears. She felt sick to the stomach; ashamed, humiliated. Furiously she blinked the tears away.

Daniel felt his heartbeats thudding like hammers. He was trying so hard to do the right thing. Did she know how much discipline that took? She couldn't, because it was her tears that tore at him and pushed him over the edge.

One moment he was standing stalwart, battling to suppress the emotions that were devouring him, the next he had hauled her headlong into his arms, his blood glittering, passion gripping him like a vise.

He took her mouth hungrily, his arms imprisoning rather than enfolding her. He was smothering her, he thought desperately, perhaps bruising her for days to come but he couldn't seem to loosen his hold much less let her go. Here was beauty, softness, sweetness he had never known. The perfect prize he could never win. His hands began to range over her body, down her back...smoothing, caressing. He had to stay them but his burning desire to know her body was driving him on.

A kiss, one kiss was never enough, but so *precious* because he might never get to kiss her again. He could feel his groin flood with blood, feeding a need so powerful it scared him. What might it feel like to surrender to such desire? To let the force of his passion for her sweep him away?

Her little moans fell audibly on his ears...little expiring breaths. He took it as she was *begging* him to release her. She had placed her hands upon his chest, powerless to push him away.

Immediately Daniel came to himself, afraid of his own strength.

"Sandra, I'm sorry. And in such a place!" With near superhuman control he drew back, setting her free. "Now you know me for what I am. A man like any other."

She shook her head, quite unable to speak. She was stunned by what had passed between them. It had far exceeded even her imagining. When she spoke, her voice was a husky murmur. "I provoked you, Daniel." She brought up her blue-violet eyes.

he said, his expression strained.

"I know that. But you're so high minded you won't let yourself be attracted to me, will you, Daniel?"

"I *can't* be. You know that." Daniel tried to rein in a sudden impotent anger, a railing against the world.

She threw out her arm. "So all this bothers you? Moondai, my money?"

"It's a pretty dazzling legacy, Sandra," he rasped. "You'd have to be one of the richest young women in the country."

"So my inheritance stands between us?" She too was struggling for composure.

"I'm not the man who can ignore it, Sandra. You're so young. There's much for you to see and do. You'll meet plenty of guys. Guys with fine respectable backgrounds. The right man you can trust to stand alongside you, with the strength to help you keep Moondai for yourself and your heirs. You only have to give yourself time."

"And you're *not* respectable, Daniel?" She gave a laugh of sorts.

He sighed deeply. "Of course I am as far as it goes. If you were an ordinary girl…"

"You'd do what?" Sandra challenged, raising her arched brows.

"Let's face it. You're *not!*"

"What if I gave my fortune away?"

"That is totally out of the question," he said with a fierce frown. "Your grandfather gave you the responsibility of holding on to Moondai. He knew you better than you know yourself, because you do *want* it, don't you?"

"I don't want it if it means losing you, Daniel," she said. There, for good or bad, she had come out with the simple truth. Daniel had invested her life with real meaning.

For an instant Daniel was seized by a feeling of joy that carried him right up high. Up, up into the wild blue yonder. Then he fell heavily to earth again with a pronounced thud. All he could do was ram his hands into his jeans pockets lest he reach for her again. "I shouldn't have kissed you," he said as though he took shame in his own weakness.

"I know," she agreed wryly, "because now I'm absolutely *sure.*"

He raised a hand as if to refute it. "You're not sure of anything, Sandra. God almighty, you're not even twenty-one. Maybe *any* guy could have kissed you."

She breathed a great sigh of frustration. "I'm going to forget you said that, Daniel. I might still be a virgin—and that's a little secret between the two of us—but let me tell you I've been kissed plenty of times. The earth didn't move. It moved a few minutes ago."

give yourself time."

When I know right now.

A wry little smile formed on Sandra's mouth. She turned away from him. "You're not going to leave me until your year is up?"

"I'm bound over not to," he replied. "I wouldn't in any case until you felt you were ready. I want the best for you, Sandra."

"But you'd think about it if Joel Moreland made you some kind of offer?" She swung back to face him.

"I don't know *why* he wants to meet me, Sandra."

"Come off it," she said shortly. "You don't have to be too modest. Obviously he's heard good things about you. Every visitor who comes here has nothing *but* good things to say about you. You turned Harry Cunningham's station around. Grandad who was as tough as they come held you in high regard. You're not a *nobody,* Daniel."

"I'm not a fortune hunter, either," he said bluntly.

"Ah, the root of the problem!" She sighed. "You think if you and I grew closer people would think you were?"

He gave her a straight look. "Of course they would."

"No need to sound so outraged." She feigned nonchalance, deciding the smart thing to do was to cloak her emotions from now on in instead of emblazoning them on her sleeve. "All right, Daniel. I can see the wisdom of what you're saying. I'm going to take your advice. I'm going to give myself plenty of time to meet lots of eligible guys. Establishment families of course, stuffy old money, reeking arrogance like Berne. The right blood lines are important apparently. No others need apply. And I *would* like to go along for the ride to Darwin. You can introduce me to Joel Moreland while you're at it. Okay?"

His eyes distant he leaned forward and picked up his akubra shoving it on his head as though he had a dozen pressing reasons to be on his way. "Whatever you say, Ms Kingston."

It was a major shock for Daniel to meet Joel Moreland. For one thing Moreland seemed *familiar* which Daniel didn't think had all that much to do with the fact Moreland regularly got his picture in the papers. It was more a real *frisson* as though he'd met up with someone he'd known in another lifetime. Moreland too seemed overtaken by the same force. He put out his hand with a charming smile, but his eyes behind his dark framed glasses had an intensity far beyond mere interest. "I thought we should meet, Daniel."

"Good to meet *you*, sir." Daniel shook the out-

Bill Morrissey was puzzled.

puzzled.

What was this really all about, Daniel wondered, aware Moreland kept looking at him as they walked to their table. Joel Moreland was a splendid looking man. In his early seventies he was even more impressive in the flesh than in his photographs. Over six feet tall, he had a full head of silver hair and classic features that looked eminently trustworthy. His accent was cultured. He dressed with casual elegance. He looked what he was, a dignified man of real consequence.

Although his interests were huge Daniel was soon to discover Moreland had no hint of elitism or arrogance about him. It wasn't his reputation in any case. He put Daniel in mind of a wise elder statesman, even a revered grandfather, kindly and genial but Daniel couldn't fail to miss the high level of concentration that was being levelled at him. What was it all about? He wasn't a candidate for high political office with Moreland the backer.

Lunch, however, started out well and continued in that vein. Moreland and Morrissey were friends over many years, each comfortable in the other's company. The conversation ranged over a wide number of topics: became focused on the areas of importance to the Northern Territory, its economy and its future. Moondai worked its way into the discussion; Alexandra Kingston's unexpected inheritance over her uncle and cousin, Daniel's position as her overseer.

"She doesn't want to sell then?" Moreland asked, his eyes keen.

"Why, sir, are you interested?" Daniel met the inquiry head on.

Moreland smiled. "As a matter of fact, Daniel, I'm delighted to hear Ms Kingston wants to hold on to her heritage. I knew her grandfather of course and the whole sorry business. It was a tragedy about Trevor. He and my own son were actually friends. Both gone now leaving their families bereft. Rigby changed a great deal after he lost Trevor. He became very bitter. As for his young granddaughter, I'm looking forward to meeting her." Daniel had already mentioned Sandra was in Darwin and had expressed the desire to meet Joel Moreland which seemed to please this great man.

Bill Morrissey excused himself after the main course, having told them he had an important meeting with a Federal Minister, leaving Daniel and Joel Moreland alone.

If it's coming, it's coming now, Daniel thought. An offer of some kind. He'd be a fool if he hadn't cottoned on to the fact Joel Moreland was extraordinarily interested in him. In fact Moreland did

...I'm unsure how...

said, sounding oddly uncertain for him.

"I find that hard to believe, sir," Daniel commented. What could Moreland possibly say that could cause a moment's awkwardness?

"Do you know why I wanted to see you? Lord knows I've heard enough about you."

"To perhaps offer me a job?" Daniel flashed his engaging smile.

"I'd offer you a job tomorrow, Daniel," Moreland replied. "But that's not the reason. I'm looking into your background."

Instantly the smile was wiped from Daniel's face. "I don't exactly have a background, Mr. Moreland," he said, wondering if the meeting was going to end right there. "My mother is dead. I have no idea who my father was. I know one usually knows but my mother couldn't bring herself to tell me."

"Don't upset yourself, son." Surprisingly Moreland put out a large hand, tapping Daniel's reassuringly much like a father figure. "I know the terrible thing that was done to you and your mother. However, I believe there might be a connection with *my* family."

Daniel's silver eyes flashed as though Moreland had made a cruel joke. "That's not possible, sir, I'm sorry."

"Nevertheless I've been looking into it," Moreland said, a discernible tremble in his self-assured voice.

"So this is what it's all about?"

Moreland looked down at his linked hands. "Sometimes guilt or the perception of guilt can cling to the innocent. It's only recently been suggested to me my son may have fathered a child. Imagine the shock, Daniel! I had great difficulty taking it in. I thought I knew everything there was to know about my wife but my sister-in-law tells me otherwise."

Daniel's eyes were like ice. "Why would she wait to tell you now? Forgive me, sir, but your son has been dead for many long years."

"Twenty-eight and I've grieved for every day of it," Moreland said heavily. "My wife died eight months ago. She never got over the loss of our boy. I have a daughter and a beautiful granddaughter, Cecile. They live in Melbourne. They visit me on all the right occasions but I have no one who can step into my shoes. That was Jared's role. Rigby and I always thought there was a parallel. I lost Jared. He lost Trevor. There's Lloyd, I know and Lloyd's boy. Rigby had grave misgivings about leaving Moondai to them."

"He spoke to you about it?" Daniel couldn't keep the shock from his voice.

Moreland nodded. "There was no great friendship between us. Rigby wasn't an easy man to know or like but there was a bond. All he could think of was a way to keep Moondai going."

ing said that most _____ g_____
daughter couldn't possibly run it without a good
man by her side. Young as you are, you managed to
win Rigby's respect. No mean feat. He spoke at
length about you on the last occasion I saw him
which was shortly before he died. I would have been
at his funeral only I was in Beijing at the time as part
of a trade mission."

"So what did you read into it, Mr. Moreland, if I
dare ask?"

Moreland searched Daniel's eyes. "That his
granddaughter had to marry well. I'm not talking
money here. I'm talking marrying a man eminently
suitable to take over the running of Moondai."

"Well there's a sort of logic about it," Daniel said,
his attractive voice turned unnaturally hard, "but
like all things hard to pull off. For one thing it's not
the sort of thing *I* would be party to."

"You mean marry a woman to take a giant leap up
in life and control of one of our finest cattle stations?"

Daniel counted to twenty before replying. "That's
exactly what I mean. I'm no fortune hunter."

"I can see that you're not, Daniel," Moreland
spoke soothingly. "But the Kingstons aside, I want
you to look at this." He reached into the breast
pocket of his linen jacket and extracted a photo-

graph which he handed to Daniel. "Do you know this young woman?"

"Should I?" Daniel's brows knit.

"Have a look."

Daniel took the photograph into his hand, staring down at the young woman's face. For a moment he almost gave way to anger. This wasn't happening. Why was Moreland doing this? Clearly he too was distressed. That fact alone made Daniel get a grip on himself. "What is this?" he asked in a tight voice. "Some skeleton in the cupboard you've let out? This is a photograph of my mother when she was young. The eyes are unmistakable." Large, beautiful dark eyes filled with more sadness than laughter.

"And her name was?" Moreland persisted, his fine face creased with emotion.

Daniel forced himself to answer, memories like importunate ghosts crowding in on him. "Annie Carson."

Moreland nodded, his expression very sombre. "Johanna Carson was a maid in our household for a period of about eighteen months. This was in the late 1970s."

"She obviously had a double," Daniel said his eyes flashing. "My mother was born in England. She came to Australia as a child with an aunt, her guardian. Her parents were killed in a motorway pile-up. That was the story anyway. Her aunt reared her but they split up when her aunt married some-

didn't have the ... y ...

Northern Territory. She is *not* this Johanna Carson. She *can't* be."

Moreland waited until Daniel finished his quiet tirade, before producing another photograph. "Look at this."

"I'm not sure I want to see it," Daniel said. "I'm sorry."

"Please, my boy," Moreland pleaded. "This was my reason for meeting."

"Very well then. I can't say…" Daniel froze in midsentence. Moreland's face had gone from handsome to haggard in a matter of moments. "Are you're all right, sir?" he asked in alarm. "Can I get you anything? You've lost all colour."

"Maybe a brandy," Moreland suggested.

Daniel didn't wait to signal a waiter; he fetched one. The waiter bolted away and reappeared with a brandy on a small silver tray in under twenty seconds.

Moreland took a slow draft then straightened his shoulders which as a young man would have been as wide as Daniel's. The blood rushed back into his face. "Ah, that's better. This isn't easy for either of us, Daniel, but we have to get through it."

To calm him, Daniel took the much newer looking photograph that Moreland had set down on the table.

He pored over it, recognising his own face, albeit the subject was a young woman. "Who *is* this?" he asked, casting a troubled glance at Moreland.

Moreland looked at him in the kindliest way possible. "It's my granddaughter, Cecile."

"She's very beautiful," Daniel remarked, not considering for a moment it followed he had to be very handsome. "How old is she?"

"Twenty-four." Moreland smiled, looking much better. "She's in Scotland at the moment and loving it. She's chief bridesmaid to a close friend who's marrying into Scottish aristocracy if you please. A whole week of festivities is planned."

"One can only wonder at how different her life has been to mine," Daniel said not without a certain bitterness.

Moreland leaned forward, his tone gentle. "I came to ask you Daniel if you would allow a blood test?"

Without giving himself time to think, Daniel shook his head vehemently. "I'm sorry, sir, no. What does it really matter now? My mother was a tragic figure. She's dead now. Personally I don't give a damn who my father was. Whoever he was he didn't want me."

"Have you considered, Daniel, he might not have known about you?" Moreland asked with a sad smile. "Your mother mightn't have been given the chance to tell him she was pregnant?"

"Whomever *he* was," Daniel answered with a

tinue this co...
ing you great upset and ...
In any event it doesn't change an...
rewrite history."

"We can remake the future, Daniel," Moreland said with such a hopeful expression on his face Daniel turned his head away abruptly not wanting to be moved by it.

It was then he caught sight of Sandra, his dream and his desire but as far away from him as the moon. He felt the hot pulsing beat of his blood. She looked absolutely *beautiful* in a summery outfit he had never seen before. She must have just bought it he realized. She hadn't worn it on the plane, nor did he think she had it with her. She was walking buoyantly as a dancer does, threading her way through the tables, a lovely smile on her face.

It was difficult to take his eyes off her but Daniel turned back to Moreland speaking in an undertone. "This is Sandra now. She's looking forward to meeting you. Is someone waiting for you, sir, your chauffeur?'

Moreland laughed softly, correctly interpreting Daniel's look of concern and glad of it. "I've had a shock, Daniel as you have, but don't worry, I'm quite all right. In fact my doctor tells me I'll live to one hundred. Such are the ironies of life. My chauffeur is out the front, yes. We'll talk again when you've had more time to absorb what I've shown you. Meanwhile I want you to take those." He indicated the photographs on the table.

Not quite understanding why he did it, Daniel quickly thrust the photographs into his inner breast pocket, a little embarrassed by how vehement he had become about them.

Both men stood up as Sandra reached their table, looking lit from within. A lot of people in fact were caught up in watching her. Daniel introduced them, Moreland clearly enchanted, but as Sandra sat down for a few moments, she said in fascination, "Surely I've met you before, Mr. Moreland? Perhaps when I was a child?"

Moreland smiled back. "I couldn't possibly have forgotten *you*, Sandra."

"Then how do I explain it?" Her dark blue eyes were full of wonder. "There must be something in this other life business." She laughed.

Moreland stroked his chin. "Millions of people believe in it. Your observation interests me, Sandra. I know your uncle Lloyd of course and your cousin Bernard but I've always thought I should have met you, Trevor's daughter, Rigby's granddaughter. Perhaps you can visit me at my home some time soon. We should get to know one another. Who knows I may be of service? Daniel can bring you."

"Why, I'd love that, thank you." Sandra said, giving Daniel several quick questioning looks. Daniel

They sat talking ...
Eventually Daniel and Sandra ...
Moreland to his car, a stately Bentley. His ch...
who had been in casual conversation with a hotel employee sprang to attention. "But you have a dimple just like Daniel," Sandra remarked in some wonder, turning to Joel Moreland as Daniel momentarily moved off. "The *same* side of your face. You have silver-grey eyes as well. One sees them rarely. Is there some connection? Is that possible?" She stared into those eyes. "There is, isn't there? I feel it in my soul."

Moreland simply smiled. "Women never cease to amaze me." He continued to hold Sandra's hand.

It wasn't just the eyes and the dimple, it was the *charm,* Sandra thought, all sorts of thoughts whirling through her head. A question was about to tumble out only Daniel, who had been stopped by a passing acquaintance, was about to rejoin them.

"Don't forget my invitation now," Moreland said, relinquishing Sandra's hand.

"I definitely won't." Sandra was still rooted to the spot. Just like Daniel, Moreland towered over her in the same reassuring nonthreatening way. "Is this *our* secret?" she asked, her mind racing with powerful intimations.

"We have to work on it, Sandra," he told in a sober voice.

CHAPTER NINE

DANIEL waited for the Bentley to pull away before he turned to Sandra to ask, "Have you had something to eat?"

"You're always trying to feed me, Daniel." She tried a laugh, a little daunted by the gravity of his expression. "I've been shopping actually." She looked down at her dress, hoping that he liked it. She'd bought it to gain his attention.

"You look like a ray of sunlight," he said, but unhappiness touched his eyes.

"You're upset about something, aren't you?" Sandra didn't care what he thought. She took his hand. She *was* his friend, wasn't she? Even if he wouldn't allow anything more. She was still working on it.

"Does it show?" He gave her a wry glance.

"And Joel Moreland has something to do with it? Why don't we have a coffee by the water?" she suggested. "It's a beautiful day. I'd forgotten Darwin Harbour is so immense. The deep turquoise of the water is amazing. You can fit in another coffee can't you?"

made their way ... one could sit outside beneath big blue and white umbrellas. Sandra ordered a cappuccino and a sandwich. Daniel settled for an espresso.

"Are you sure that's all you want?" he asked, sounding concerned coffee and a sandwich weren't substantial enough. She was still light enough for a zephyr of wind to blow her away.

"That's plenty," she said, anxious to get on with what was troubling him. "I want to hear all about your meeting. Please tell me."

"You *know,* don't you?" He leaned forward abruptly, slipping off her sunglasses so he could stare straight into her eyes.

"I don't know *exactly* what it's all about, Daniel," she said carefully, "but I can see a resemblance between you and Joel Moreland."

"Moreland?" Daniel asked in a voice that cracked in surprise. "Then you're seeing a lot more than I can."

Sandra's expression softened. "Whether you can see it or not, there *is.* Don't be distracted by age and the silver hair. I bet his hair was once as black as yours. He has the height, the shoulders, the manner, the charm. You both have a dimple in your cheek and extraordinary silver-grey eyes. They're fairly *rare,* Daniel." She broke off as their order arrived.

Thoroughly unnerved, Daniel took a quick gulp that burned his mouth. "He wants me to take a blood test. I imagine one that establishes DNA."

"Good grief!" Sandra, about to take a bite of her sandwich, put it down again. "This is serious."

"I'm not taking any DNA test, Sandra," he said with considerable firmness.

"Okay." She soothed him. "I don't blame you."

"I know *nothing* for sure," Daniel said, wanting to reach across and take her hand. She offered such comfort. Since Sandra had come into his life he realised he no longer felt he walked alone.

"Well what you *do* know don't keep it to yourself. He must believe you could be family?"

"Who cares!" Daniel said shortly, then made an effort to collect himself. "Once, to have had a family would have mattered a great deal. It doesn't anymore."

"You can't forgive the fact the man who fathered you abandoned your mother and his unborn child," Sandra observed, in an understanding voice.

"Would *you* forgive it?" Daniel threw down the challenge.

"No I would not." Sandra picked up a sandwich and bit furiously into it. "So if you and Joel Moreland are related as it does appear, your father would have been his son who was killed. Jared, wasn't it?"

Daniel's eyes flared as though he couldn't bear the answer. "Here, take a look at these." He with-

vulnerable looking young woman with flashing dark eyes. "This is?" She guessed it had to be his mother although Daniel bore the young woman no easily discernible resemblance.

"It's a photograph of a young woman who worked for the Morelands in the late 1970s," he said in a strained voice. "Her name was Johanna Carson. My mother was known as Annie Carson."

Sandra kept her eyes on the old photograph. "You're Annie Carson's son. You would *know* if this was your mother."

"I'm afraid it is." Daniel sighed deeply as though he didn't want to talk about it. "Everything she told me, I believed *all* of it. I think now, most of it was probably not true. My entire childhood and my whole adult life I've believed what little my mother told me."

"Believing one's mother is an article of faith, Daniel," Sandra pointed out gently. "My mother too dealt in fantasy."

"Maybe it's a problem with mothers," Daniel said. "Tell me what you make of this?" He passed her the second photograph.

Sandra found herself looking at a beautiful young woman who could be Daniel's twin. "How extraordinary! Who is this?" She eyed Daniel cautiously.

"Moreland's granddaughter, Cecile."

Sandra acknowledged that piece of information in silence. "Why produce these photographs *now?*" she asked, tapping the photograph with her finger. "This Cecile could be your twin. What's going on, Daniel?"

Daniel's broad shoulders tensed. "How the hell should *I* know."

"Why decide to acknowledge you *now?*" Sandra frowned.

"Exactly."

Sandra fell into a thoughtful silence. "Do you suppose if Jared Moreland were your father he simply didn't know about you? Maybe he was killed before your mother told him or he was killed before they could do something about it. Maybe they intended to get married?"

Daniel gave an off-key laugh. "My mother worked as a domestic in their house. Moreland has always been a rich powerful man. It's highly unlikely he would have looked on such a union with favour."

"I like him," Sandra said, her blue eyes burning bright. "He seems the nicest, most trustworthy man. I don't want to feel badly about him. I'm sure you don't want to, either."

"No, I don't." Daniel admitted. "He said his sister-in-law only recently suggested the possibility Jared had fathered a son."

strange ~~feel~~ ~~g~~

shook hands. Both of us were upset. ~~In fact he had~~ bit of a sick turn which shook me up as well. All the colour drained from his face. I had to get him a brandy. I got the feeling he wants to make things *right*. Oh God, I don't know, Sandra." Daniel looked away over the glittering marina with its splendid yachts. "Even if he is my grandfather I don't fit into his world. He just can't walk into mine and think I'm going to do anything he wants. I'm not stooping to any DNA test. Not now, not ever! I'm someone else entirely from that. I'm going to make my own way, thank you, not become Joel Moreland's illegitimate grandson, for God's sake. I'm *me!*" he said wrathfully.

"Could I dare put a word in here?" Sandra asked, staring into his taut face.

"Best to stay out of it, Sandra."

"Sorry, Daniel. I'm *in* it, remember? Maybe Mr. Moreland is trying to steal you away from me? It's not on. You're *mine* until your year is up or you've had enough of me."

His stormy expression lightened. "I couldn't ask for a better boss," he said, hoping his smile was on straight.

"You're the boss, Daniel," Sandra said, "but I'm learning."

"You haven't wasted a minute. You're really smart, Ms Kingston."

"Then can you let Mr. Moreland explain?" she urged. "He wants us to visit him some time soon."

He gave her one of his long glittery-eyed looks. "I'll take you any time you want, but the other has nothing to do with you, Sandra, so don't get in the middle of it. If Joel Moreland thinks he's going to recognise me now—subject to a DNA test of course—" he added caustically, "it's all too late."

Sandra put out a hand and grabbed his wrist. "Daniel, will you listen to me for a second?"

"No, I won't," he said in a dangerous voice. "You find it too easy to twist me around your little finger. Eat your sandwiches, Sandra. Your coffee must be cold. Mine is." He put up his hand to signal the waiter. "I'll order fresh."

The sun rose higher. The bush was quiet except for bursts of unrivalled merriment from the blue winged kookaburra perched on the sturdy limb of a red river gum. These majestic trees soared to one hundred and twenty feet and more forming a marvellous corridor of green along Jirra Jarra Creek. It was one of the favourite haunts of Sandra's childhood. Scarcely an inch of the great gums went unexploited much like the multistorey apartment towers in the city. Ravens, hawks, owls, magpies and even the great wedge-tailed eagles nested on the

nesting little birds, insects and tiny reptiles like the fierce little horny lizard. There were more lizards in Australia than anywhere else in the world, the most spectacular of them in her desert home.

Away from the brilliant glare of the plains the peace and cool of this green sanctuary was exquisite. The creek's deep dark green waters were said by the station aboriginals to possess healing powers not only for the health but behavioural problems as well. She and Berne along with the station children had swum here all the time with a stout rope tied to a high branch of a river gum allowing them to *fly* into the water or across the stream like Tarzan and Jane. Berne hadn't benefited much from the sacred waters. He appeared to be the same as he ever was, causing Sandra to believe he would be a whole lot better off starting a new life elsewhere. Her uncle was a lot easier to get on with these days, mollified no doubt by her genuine interest in his encyclopaedic knowledge of Australian wildflowers. He was presently getting ready for another field trip to a remote pocket of Western Australia, a State renowned for the magnificence and sheer abundance of its native flora. A man who loved flowers and plants with a passion couldn't be all bad she reasoned. She was an adult now and thinking like one. Her father's fatal plane crash which her mother had claimed was *murder* had to have been an accident. Only Fate had been responsible.

A little wind blew up, skittering along the green corridor, loosening the olive green leaves and the petals of some dusky pink wildflowers that grew in cylindrical clumps in this oasis-like area. The aboriginal women made a paste of these succulents using it to protect and soften the skin of the face. Sandra knew for a fact the paste was wonderfully soothing on cuts and scrapes. There was so much that was really effective in bush medicine she thought. Arranged around her were the striking dark red sedimentary rocks and boulders that littered the ancient landscape. They formed such a contrast with the cabuchon waters of the creek, the lime-green of the aquatic plants and reeds that shadowed the creek's banks and the smouldering blue of the sky.

She had been sitting there daydreaming for some time now; carrying on a lengthy inner dialogue. There was so much that was problematic in her life. Daniel's life too was as mixed up as her own. Now he was confronted by revelations that had stunned and angered him. Daniel had carried a very bad image of the man who had fathered him. That wasn't going to go away in a hurry. She knew as well as anyone what it felt like to be *unwanted*.

approaching at [s]... peaceful place caused a fligh[t] [of] ducks about to land on the creek's surface, to s[kim] for a few feet before soaring steeply up again; up, up, over the tops of the red river gums seeking quieter waters. The kookaburra held its position, giving way to ribald protest, cackling away for all it was worth without deigning to move off its perch.

"Shut that bloody kookaburra up!" Chris Barrett, the jackeroo, yelled to her. He rode down the track, braking to a flamboyant stop a few feet away from her. Never mind the fact the wheels of the bike tore up scores of wildflowers releasing their faintly medicinal smell. "One of the boys told me this was the likely place you would be." He gave her his cheeky grin; a young man who thought he could always talk his way out of trouble.

"Did they now," Sandra said, watching him dismount. A real show-off was Chris. "So why aren't you working with the rest?"

He took a seat atop a red boulder. "Give me a break. I've been chasing a flamin' stallion all morning. A real stroppy devil."

"I take it he got away?"

"Yes, he did," Chris said ruefully, "but we got the mares and yearlings, even a few foals. It's a fantastic sight watching those wild horses run. I'm going to miss it. Mind if I come and join you for a few minutes?"

"Sure," Sandra nodded, pitching a few more pebbles into the deepest part of the creek. "But you're looking forward to going home, being with your family—surely?"

Chris laughed. "Well yes and no. I've had a great time here. Dan is a marvellous bloke. All the men look to him. No mean achievement when he's so young. These guys are really tough, but Dan has earned their respect. He often used to stand between us and old rubber guts—sorry—" he flushed "—your grandfather. Every other day I expected to be sent packing even though Mr. Kingston and my grandfather knew one another from school days. Dan stood up for us all. By the same token we've all got to pull our weight. Even lightweight old me though I reckon I'm a lot less stupid now. I'm not exactly looking forward to knuckling down in the staid old family firm. I've grown used to all this wonderful *space,* the excitement and adventure, the company of my mates." He stared into her face, hoping he was hiding his tremendous crush. "You're not going to sell the place, are you, Sandra?"

"Almost certainly not, since you ask." Sandra glanced back at the motorbike. "Daniel has been giving me lessons. I'm pretty good, if I say so myself."

"That's the word around the traps." Chris grinned. "Want to show me?" His bright hazel eyes dared her.

loved the ~~~~
pened to know Daniel was ~

"What about I give *you* a spin?" Chris ~~~~
eagerly. "You're game to get on with me, aren't
you?" He pushed to the back of his mind Daniel had
cautioned him never to take Ms Kingston on board
as a pillion rider.

"I don't see why not." She responded to the cocky
grin. "Ten minutes following the stream, then back
again so I can collect the mare. Don't dare take off
like a bat out of hell, either."

Chris rolled his eyes. "The last thing I would ever
do is cause you fright. Daniel would kill me. Climb
on. Just don't tell him about this. I couldn't predict
what he'd do if we took a tumble."

It was Berne who drove into the Five-Mile holding
camp, his handsome face wearing an expression
that could be interpreted as I-told-you-so.

"That fool Barrett has come off the motorbike at
the creek," he yelled to Daniel as though it was entirely *Daniel's* problem.

Daniel strode over to the four-wheel-drive. "Is he
hurt?" Daniel was both irritated and concerned.

"He's broken his arm," Berne offered with little
sympathy. "Sandra is with him. She's all shook up."

"What do you mean, Sandra's with him?" Daniel's face twisted into an expression of alarm. "She wasn't riding pillion, was she?"

"You know Sandra." Berne shrugged with a flicker of grim satisfaction. In their childhood Sandra had always been the favourite, Number One. "She's the same reckless little devil she ever was."

"She hasn't broken anything?" Daniel asked, his voice deepening in dismay.

"Settle down," Berne said, not unkindly. He hadn't wanted his cousin to actually *break* anything. "She's got a few scrapes and bruises but she's okay. She's worried about Barrett of all things and I suppose she got a bit of a fright."

"I'll come back with you," Daniel said, realizing afresh how jealous Berne was of his cousin. He moved swiftly to the passenger side. "I've *warned* Chris never to offer Sandra a ride."

"So I guess he's in contempt," Berne observed, wryly. He'd disliked that smart alec jackeroo from day one.

"You're mad at me," Sandra said as soon as she saw Daniel's taut expression.

"That's correct," he said in a clipped voice, going down on his haunches and feeling for her pulse. She was very pale but not clammy. "Do you feel giddy, any nausea?" It was time for Chris to go back home. He'd make sure of that.

less way he had handl...
Showing off, of course, but they had taken a
spill. "I'm fine," she said, when she was feeling
anything but fine.

Daniel's eyes flashed like coins in the sunlight.
"Well you can thank your lucky stars for that," he
said crisply, turning his attention to the ashen face
Chris who was doing his best not to faint from the
pain. "How's it going?"

"Bloody awful," Chris murmured in a hollow
voice, aware of Daniel's contained anger.

"Why don't we shed a tear?" Berne chimed in
sarcastically.

"Ah, shut up, Bernie." Sandra gave her cousin a
weary glance before addressing Daniel. "I've made
him as comfortable as I can."

"Good." Daniel had already noted with approval
she had padded Chris's lap with their hats and her
rolled up cotton shirt to support the injured limb.
Now she was left wearing a blue cotton singlet that
showed off her delicate breasts.

"It was the best I could do with what was at
hand," she offered apologetically, thinking it a miracle she had escaped more serious injury. Fortunately she had been thrown off onto the sand
whereas Chris's body balanced the other way had

fallen on heavier ground with the bike half on top of him.

"That's fine." Daniel spoke quietly though he felt a mad urge to let off steam. "We'll have to get you to hospital, Chris," he said. "What about the chest area, your ribs? Have you any difficulty breathing?"

"No," Chris gasped. "Look I'm sorry, Daniel."

"Forget that now." Daniel rose to his feet. "You'll need an X-ray to be sure there's no other damage." He looked at Berne. "Give me a hand to get him into the back seat, will you, Berne? We'll try to limit as much movement to your arm as we can, Chris, but be prepared for some pain."

"I deserve it," Chris mumbled, blinking several times to shake off the faintness. "I was pretty well showing off."

"I figured as much." Daniel nodded curtly before turning back to Sandra. "Sit there until I come back for you, Sandra," he said. "You've had a shock and there's a gash above your elbow."

"It's nothing," she said, twisting her arm around to look at something she scarcely felt. "Just bleeding a bit."

"Using up a fair bit of your luck, aren't you?" Berne asked her. "A bloke over on Gregory Downs was killed only the other day when he came off his bike. Broke his neck."

"Would you mind holding those stories for now, Berne," Daniel said, his sculpted features drawn taut.

Chris was airlifted to hospital where ... his arm was confirmed.

"Why did you do it?" Daniel asked Sandra who was slumped tiredly into a planter's chair on the verandah. He picked up the cold beer Meg had brought him and downed it. It was a short while after sunset. The world was for a short time enveloped in a beautiful mauve mantle. The evening star was out. Soon it was joined by a million diamond pinpricks that quickly turned into blazing stars.

"Maybe I have a problem with authority figures?" Sandra suggested, very much on the defensive.

"You mean *me*."

"Yes, you, Daniel. I can see you're angry with me for breaking the rules."

"I'm angrier with Chris," he answered. "I told him not to take you on."

"Surely that's a lot to ask?" There was a slight quiver in her voice.

"No it isn't," Daniel said. "I'm in charge of the men, Sandra. I'm running this station for you until you're ready to run it yourself. Maintaining authority is important. I told Chris not to offer you a ride because I've learned a lot about him since he's been here. He's careless, he's cocky and I can't trust him.

It's imperative to wear a helmet yet neither of you had one on. This is rough country, not a country lane. What if you'd sustained a head injury? What if *he* had? His mother was upset enough when I called her about his broken arm."

Sandra was mortified. "Okay we made a mistake, Daniel I'm sorry. We won't do it again."

"No, you won't," he said with emphasis. "When Chris is well enough he's going home. He's fired."

Sandra sat forward, aghast. "Who do you think you are?"

He drained his beer and set down the glass. "Sandra, I have to have my say out here unless *you* want to fire *me!*"

"Is that an ultimatum?" Her blue eyes started to blaze. She hated falling out with Daniel.

"It is," he said without hesitation. "It's for me to call the shots, Sandra. I'm responsible for the safety of the men and consider how many more times I feel responsible for *your* safety. I'm not objecting to your getting on the back of a motorbike *with* your helmet on. I'm objecting to your doing so with Chris Barrett who thinks he can do as he pleases because he's only fooling around for a time before he goes home to work for his rich old man. I'm not at all sympathetic to the way he acted even if I'm sorry he broke his arm. And you didn't answer my question?"

"What was it?" She sighed, resting back again.

"Next question?"

"How do you feel?" His voice changed and a different light came into his eyes.

"Like a bad, bad, girl. I don't like it when you're disappointed in me, Daniel."

"I don't like it when you give me a fright," he pointed out, remembering the force of his reactions. "The damned fool could have killed you and himself. Berne is quite right. There was a fatal accident on Gregory Downs. All the poor guy did was hit a pothole. His helmet wasn't on properly...it rolled off. Life on the land has its hazards, Sandra. I don't have to tell you that."

"As long as you still love me." She pulled a face at him. "And if you say you *don't,* you're fired!"

A look of amusement crossed his mouth. He allowed his eyes to rest on her as she lay back in the high backed peacock chair. One slender, silky fleshed arm was thrown lazily over the side, the injured arm he had cleaned and bandaged for her resting quietly in her lap. The glow from the exterior lamp mounted on the wall behind her, turned her hair to a glittering aureole. Her skin had the translucence of a South Sea peal. He could never tire of looking at her. *Never!*

"That's blackmail, wouldn't you say?" he asked, managing to sound casual.

"Whatever it takes, Daniel," she answered.

CHAPTER TEN

LLOYD KINGSTON had to seek his niece's permission to have either Daniel or Berne fly him to Perth, the capital of the adjoining vast State of Western Australia where he would be staying with a long-time friend, the well-known botanist, Professor Erik Steiner who was going to accompany him on his expedition. Daniel couldn't afford the time, so it was decided Berne would fly the Beech Baron into Perth.

"I wouldn't mind staying on for a week," Berne remarked to his cousin rather tentatively for him, "that's if you can spare the Baron. I know you can spare me. I've always liked Perth. I've got quite a few friends there."

"You'll have to check with Daniel, Berne," Sandra said in a calm, helpful way. "If it's okay with him it's okay with me. A week mind. We've got the helicopter but one never knows when the plane might be needed."

"True," Berne acknowledged. "Daniel's got to be

very important around here, hasn't he?" he added, almost sadly.

"Well he *is* running the place, Berne." Sandra was careful to answer reasonably. "*You* don't want the job."

"No way!" Berne threw up his hands as if to show that was way beyond his ambitions.

"What would you like to do?" Sandra asked, sounding like she really wanted to know and perhaps help him.

For once he saw her sincerity. "Something to do with aircraft," he said. "I'm a good pilot. Ask Daniel. Maybe not as good as him but good all the same. I love flying. I'd love to captain a jumbo jet flying all around the world."

"Can't you train for that?" she asked, surprised he wasn't already doing it if that was his ambition. "Heavens, you're young enough. You have the money to support yourself through your training. Seize the moment, Berne. Make enquiries in Perth. Jumbo jets aside, you could start your own charter business if you wanted to. Elsa could help you there. Surely she and her first husband were among the first to pioneer Outback charter flights?"

"Yeah." Berne thought for a minute. "She can fly, did you know? She's let her licence slip for years now but she can fly a plane. In fact she knows a hell of a lot about aircraft. She's very secretive, Elsa. She likes to act the dotty old lady. God knows why. I was

"Maybe not, but she could. There are a lot of things you don't know, cousin. Why would you? You were only a kid when you left. Your sweet mother did everything she could to paint Dad in the worst possible light. You can't imagine what it did to him, her claiming he sent his own brother to his death. If your mother could have had Dad convicted she would have. No wonder he hates her."

Sandra could see that would be the case. "I'm sorry about that, Berne," she said, all sorts of emotions swirling around inside her. "In many ways you, me, Uncle Lloyd and Elsa too have had a tough time. Elsa must have gone into marriage with Grandad thinking she was going to get something out of it. I don't mean material things, but whatever she craved, she didn't get it. Looking back I'm sure it wasn't *all* Grandad's fault. I've never acknowledged that before but I can see now it might have been true. What happened to Elsa is a mystery. But I want *you* to know if you'll let me I'll be your friend."

Berne had a sudden overpowering need to believe her. "You really want that? We never got on. I was jealous of course. You got all the attention."

"Didn't last long Berne," she sighed. "We were

both deprived kids. Neither of us got enough love or attention. We suffered in our own way. But there's no need to be jealous of me any more. You can have your own life. A different life, one that suits you. Spend all your energies on becoming an airline pilot, as that's what you want. Shake on it, reconciliation?"

"Sure." Berne gripped her outstretched hand, drawing a deep, shaky breath. "I guess it is better to have you onside, Sandra."

"You bet it is." Sandra smiled.

They were on their own! Sandra couldn't believe her good fortune. Elsa and Meg were in the house of course, but essentially they were on their own. It was a *sumptuous* feeling and she was determined to take full advantage of it. During the day she joined Daniel as often as she wanted. The evenings were spent over a leisurely dinner, a short walk around the grounds afterwards, then they retired to the study where the intensive but stimulating learning sessions continued. There was so much to learn about the business and Sandra was anxious to make her contribution.

Midweek something strange happened. Sandra awoke with the unnerving feeling *someone* was in or had just left her room. Not only that there was a faint rattling noise. She sat up quickly in the bed, her eyes trying to pierce the gloom. There was no moon to send its illuminating rays across the verandah and into her room. She desperately needed light.

though she was...

order. She was a naturally tidy person. Everything was in its place. Just a bad moment she thought. Some lingering dream. She'd had a full day joining in on a muster for clean skins the men knew they had missed in dense scrub. She'd enjoyed the experience but in the end the heat and the physical exertion had gotten to her. Before bed she'd been forced to take a couple of painkillers for her headache. Elsa had rustled them up from her stockpile.

Her accelerated heartbeats were slowing. She breathed deeply, punching her pillows a few times to get them into the right shape. A glance at her bed-side clock told her it was 3:00 a.m., the witching hour. The temptation to get out of bed and go across the hallway to Daniel was so acute she groaned with the pain of it. She could tip toe across his room, rest her hand upon his sleeping shoulder.

"Daniel, it's *me!*"

He'd awaken; recognise the scent of her, draw her wonderingly down onto the bed. He would gather her into him, his body against hers, telling her he wanted her urgently. His beautiful mouth would un-erringly find hers. She would open it to him... His hand was on her breast. She's holding on to him, clutching him. One of her arms is locked around him, the other is buried in the raven thickness of his hair. Delicious shudders are passing through her. She's guiding his hand, wanting his fingers to slip inside her. God, she's been thinking about it all the time, wicked girl!

Only it wouldn't happen like that at all. She sobered abruptly, ashamed of the illicit pleasure she was taking. Daniel would bundle her up and escort her back to her room. No seduction scenes for Daniel. If it were ever going to happen he wouldn't let it happen in her own house. Daniel had *huge* problems with making love to her. She knew that. It was almost as if he were up against a serious taboo or he was heeding lots of signs tacked up everywhere saying, Keep Off. It is just stupid, she thought, when we both want it. She wasn't such a fool she didn't know how he watched her.

Better check the door.

She knew perfectly well it was locked. She had gotten into the habit of locking it even with Daniel in the house. If it looked like she didn't trust her family, she didn't care though these days her anxieties seemed absurd. Her mother's perspective had been warped. She slipped out of bed and padded across the room, listening for noises in the house. Not that she would hear them. The old homestead had been built of stout timbers, mahogany and cedar.

She was halfway across the spacious room when she paused, staring at the floor. There was some-

...dow...
in all. Jade bead...
in her room hit her like a pul...
turned on the chandelier flooding the bea...
light. She found one more bead closer to the door.
They had poured off a necklace. Sandra reached for
the brass doorknob. The door was still locked. So
how then had someone come to stand in the deep
shadows watching her?

She started to think of an intruder coming by way
of the verandah. There was a white lattice door at
the end of the wing, usually locked. The other day
she'd found a tiny scrap of fabric impaled on it but
hadn't thought much of it. It could have come off
one of Meg's dresses or even one of the house girls'
Meg was training.

When a dingo's mournful howl carried on the
desert air her nerve broke. Sandra unlocked her door
and fled across the hallway to Daniel's room, as-
suming it too would be locked but it wasn't. She
burst in. She couldn't help it, not doing anything appalling like screaming but rushing towards the bed,
calling his name.

"Daniel, Daniel, wake up!"

Something *huge* was in her way. Hell, a damned
chair! She swore fiercely, holding a hand to her
throbbing shin. "Daniel!"

"Sandra, what the hell!" Daniel sprang to his feet,

straight as a lance. He had thought that voice belonged in his dream. But no, she was *there*, in his bedroom swearing her head off.

"Where's the light?" she was yelling. "I don't want to run into another great hulking chair. What's it doing in the middle of the room anyway?"

Immediately he switched on the bedside lamp seeing her standing in the centre of his room *irradiated*. She was wearing the flimsiest little nightdress he could ever imagine. No concealing robe. Not even slippers on her feet. She was clutching something in her hand.

"Sandra, what are you doing here?" he asked, all his senses instantly raised to the nth power. "Do you know what time it is?"

"What's time got to do with it, Daniel?" She looked at him with highly critical blue eyes. Not that there was anything to criticise. He could have posed for a Calvin Klein ad for boxer shorts for that's all he was wearing. Brief navy boxer shorts with a white stripe down the side.

"It's the only few hours I get to sleep," he explained.

"When you promised me you'd be on call." She moved to close the distance between them and he sprang back.

"What's the *matter* with you?" She eyed him sternly. "Anyone would think I was going to give you an electric shock."

"Allow me to put some clothes on would you,

"I must. Swiftly .... zipped them up. "I don't mean to criticise your be-haviour in any way—you are after all my boss—but is there something you want?" They faced one an-other again, Daniel's dark polished skin gleaming in the light.

He had a light V shaped mat of dark hair on his chest that disappeared into his low slung jeans.

"Well it's not *sex* if that's what's worrying you," she snapped. "I mean would I do anything so crass as to jeopardize our friendship?" she added causti-cally. "No, the thing is, Daniel, someone was in my room just now."

"You're kidding!" He was in something of a daze. This *was* happening, wasn't it? She was in his bed-room in a sheer little nightie with her tousled cap of buttery curls and her eyes blazing like sapphires.

"I found these beads on the floor. Look."

Now she moved right up to his shoulder. His heart leapt. She might be pocket sized but she packed such a powerful sensual punch unless he was very strong she could defeat him easily. "Show me." Daniel forced his breath to stay even. "Jade, aren't they? Or nephrite." He stared down at the small polished olive-green beads. "Maoris use it as a talisman of protec-tion. The Chinese believe it blesses all who touch it."

"I'm not trying to *sell* them to you, Daniel," she said testily.

Such a tart tongued glowing creature! "Let's take a look in your room then," he suggested. "You might like to put something on."

"Anyone would think you had to fight off my advances," she started muttering as she stalked into her bedroom, making a beeline for her yellow Thai silk robe. "There, feel safer now?" she asked tartly, tying the sash with exaggerated movements.

"You aren't the sweetest girl in the world, are you?" He looked around, frowning in concentration. "Where were the beads?"

"On the floor, just about here." She moved to the spot rubbing the pile of the Perisan rug back and forth with her bare toes. "I woke with the panicky feeling someone was in the room or just leaving it. I thought I heard a rattling sound. I knew my door was locked. I must have been dreaming. It wasn't until I decided to double-check the door when I saw them. They certainly weren't there when I put out the light. Someone was in the room, Daniel."

"You don't think you could have missed them earlier? They blend in with the rug strangely enough."

"Then how did I miss not *walking* over them?" she asked as if she'd produced the trump card. "One was actually near the door."

"And it was locked?"

"The only [...] and Meg. I can't thi[...] dle. You'll have to leave *me* ou[...]

"Because of your vow?" She stared a[...] huge challenging eyes.

"What vow?"

"The one you made as soon as we met. *Never lay a finger on her!*"

"So you know about that, do you?" he asked dryly.

"There's no logic to it, Daniel."

"Really? I consider to break it would be more like men acting badly. Now, shall we get back to the problem at hand? Your nocturnal visitor could only be Elsa or Meg or the resident ghost. I can't see Meg or Elsa paying you a call unless one of them sleep walks. Come to think of it, it does happen."

"Yes, like once in a blue moon," Sandra scoffed. "I didn't imagine any of this, Daniel."

"Hang on." He hesitated for a second looking down at her, then strode out onto the verandah.

She raced after him. "I found a scrap of material pinned to the lattice a few days ago," she told him breathlessly. The door was unbolted. She watched him as he shot the bolt home.

"It could easily have come off Meg's dress. Go back to bed, Sandra. I'll leave my door open and a light in the hall. No one is going to bother you."

"Well I *am* bothered," she said huffily.

"We'll leave it until morning to ask questions." They were back in her room, staring at one another. "Meg would never do anything to cause you concern. Elsa genuinely cares for you. You're sweet to her."

"I feel sorry for her, that's why. But she's just the type to do spooky things," Sandra felt a sudden chill. "No mouse could be quieter, though I can't think she'd wish to harm me. Can I ask you a question?"

"Fire away." He gave a single abrupt nod of his head.

"Do you wear jade beads?"

He didn't deign to answer.

"Just a thought. Would you like to stay with me, Daniel?" For some reason she had the wicked impulse to taunt him. "It's an awfully big bed. Our bodies wouldn't have to connect at all."

"Impossible, Sandra."

"I know, I'm ranting. I'm sorry." She stripped off her silk robe and threw it around one of the bedposts.

"You're not at all self-conscious of your body, are you?" he said, desire for her lashing at him like stockwhips.

"Well I'm not exactly a glamour model," she answered tartly. "What's to *see*?"

"Are you completely mad?" he rasped, astonished she could say such a thing.

Sandra spun around, furiously hurt. She rushed him very fast, hitting him in the chest. "How *dare* you say something like that to me, Daniel!"

back.
around her lifting
ing her onto the bed with such

"Daniel!" She sat up in astonishment a

"You have to stop playing games with me." He
was breathing hard through flared nostrils, his powerful body tense, a vertical frown between his black
brows, luminous eyes stormy.

"I will. I will," she promised. Fear didn't come
into it. She wanted to *calm* him. "I'm sorry, Daniel.
I wasn't trying to turn you on. Not *then* anyway."
She couldn't lie to him.

"Well you did!" He knew it was wrong, but he
was too tanked up with desire to be able to turn off
the engine.

"Come here!" He swooped on her, dragging her
up against him feeling her fingers sink into the mat
of hair on his bare chest.

"Daniel!" She made a soft yielding sound, pressing herself against him.

For an instant he was worried his beard might
rasp her lovely skin. "Little *witch!*" he said hotly.
"You should be using those little fists on me not urging me on." He clamped her small slender body still
closer against him, revelling in her female softness
and the alluring scents of her hair and skin. He
wanted to know the *whole* of her…so badly…so
badly. With a shudder he speared his fingers into

those buttery curls pulling back her head so he could take her mouth. It seemed like an eternity since he had last kissed her. He had never stopped thinking about it, how beautiful it was. He had her *now!*

His mouth covered hers, not hard but voluptuously. He found the touch and the taste exquisite, to be savoured. A primitive adrenaline was pumping through his blood, assisting his sense of mastery. His hands had a life of their own. They strayed over her throat and delicate shoulders, moving towards those small tantalizing breasts. The V neckline of her nightgown had fallen low; low enough for him to fondle her naked flesh. Her nipples came erect under his urgent fingers while a little moan came from the back of her throat. She arched her back making it easier for him to take first one then the other into his mouth. He lifted his head. Watched her face. Her eyes were closed but the lids were flickering with sensation.

He pulled her in tight, wanting her wild and wilful on the bed. She had a little wildness in her. He *knew* it. He wanted to strip that lighter than air nightdress from her. He wanted her to feel his hands all over her, exploring that sweet tender body that gave off a million sparks when touched.

She was making sounds, little kittenish *mews* he found incredibly erotic. There was a heat inside him he had never experienced before. Did she know those little mews were pushing him further along the

was permissible between lovers.

Wasn't that what he wanted to be, her lover? Her *only* lover.

"Daniel!" Bright little explosions like stars were going off in her head. She was literally swooning in his arms.

Daniel misread her ecstasy. To him it sounded like the fevered gasp of the tortured.

He recoiled sharply. What the hell was he doing? Ravishing a virgin? Ravishing this slip of a girl he had sworn to protect? That jolted his heart.

He released her so abruptly, she pitched forward, her head whirling while she tumbled to the floor. "Sandra!" He was stunned; sick with shame. He picked her up bodily, embracing her, before he laid her on the bed. "I hate myself if that's any comfort to you."

"It isn't!" Her voice was shaken, the sound vibrating inside her head. "You're a caveman."

"I don't doubt it. But you've made me. You're an enchantress."

"Daniel, do you *mean* that?" Suddenly she was full of hope. If she could enchant him she was really on to something.

"Listen, I'm going." Daniel read the swift speculation in her huge blue eyes. "I wanted to *ravish* you. I stopped just in time. Don't you realise that?"

How to convince him she was ready? "Wherever you want to take me, Daniel, I'm prepared to go," she said, mind and body flooded with love for him. "I never thought I was going to fall in love. I didn't even think I would *want* a man too near me. I thought the way my creep of a stepfather behaved towards me I was somehow damaged. I hated being the object of *lust*."

"Did you now!" Daniel was breathing fast, thinking if he stayed any longer he would really unravel. Her loveliness, her desirability was overwhelming. How was he supposed to combat all that? "I have to tell you, Sandra," he gritted, "*I* lust after you, too. There's a warning in there somewhere but you don't want to hear it."

"Then get out of my room if that's how it is!" She felt bitterly rejected.

"Don't worry, I'm going." He speared his fingers through his thick pelt of hair, dragging it back from his tense face. "It's damn near daybreak anyway. I'll leave my door open. I won't leave the homestead in the morning either until we find out exactly what went on here. Okay?"

"Morning can't come soon enough," she cried and punched the pillow.

CHAPTER ELEVEN

S*ANDRA* slept so heavily she might have been drugged. In the morning Meg had to wake her to say they couldn't find Elsa. She wasn't in the house, nor anywhere in the home compound. Daniel had already sent out a search party to scour her usual haunts.

"She's getting on you know." Meg pleated and re-pleated the edge of her white apron in her agitation. "Never sees a doctor and she should. She's often short of breath. Occasionally she wanders in her mind. You must have noticed that."

"Of course I have, Meg." Sandra was out of bed, fishing out clothes to put on. "She likes to visit the family cemetery. I hope Daniel will try there."

"I don't know about *likes*." Meg looked dubious. "More like she's *driven*. She does go there a lot. I'll let you get dressed, love. I've got a bad feeling about this."

It was when Sandra was halfway out the door she spotted out of the corner of her eye, a dark grey envelope that lay on top of the highboy.

"Wait a minute," she said aloud, though no one was listening. She retraced her steps reaching for the envelope. It was addressed to her.

"Oh, God!" Sandra knew at once it was from Elsa though she wasn't familiar with Elsa's handwriting. A sudden wave of nausea rolled through her, which was odd. She took up a position on the nearest chair opening the envelope and withdrawing its contents; two handwritten sheets of a lighter grey paper embossed with Elsa's initials EGK. Sandra found herself slumping back against the chair overtaken by a peculiar feeling of weakness and fatigue. She knew now from the bitter taste in her mouth and the unfamiliar sluggish feeling Elsa had given her not painkillers but some kind of sedative, maybe sleeping pills. It had been Elsa in her room, Elsa's broken beads. Elsa gliding around the house like a ghost.

What she read in stunned horror and disbelief was Elsa's *confession*. Her last words to anybody.

Alexandra, my dear, I find I can no longer continue. I know you will hate me now you learn the truth. I deserve your hatred. It was I who was responsible for your father's death no matter Trevor was the last person in the world I intended to harm. Trevor was always kind to me as you are. It was your grandfather, my husband, I wanted to see punished for the uncaring way he treated me. I wanted love. I

me; your grandfather did the rest. It was Rigby who was to visit the outstation that day. Rigby sent Trevor at the very last minute. I had known what to do to the Cessna to cause it to crash. I did it without a qualm. Not much of a motive I know, but I was different then. Afterwards I was changed forever. The guilt stripped me of my sanity. I've suffered terribly for my crime, Alexandra. But there must be an end. Scatter my ashes far away from Moondai. Far away from your grandfather. I never belonged here. The sea might be the place. I never meant your father harm. I've visited his grave countless times begging his forgiveness. But my crime is unforgivable. I'll be made to suffer for it in the next life I'm sure. There's no escape.

Elsa.

Lloyd and Trevor returned to Moondai the very next day, the family closing ranks on the sudden death of a senior member. The cause of death was given as myocardial infarction or more commonly heart attack. It was noted, had Mrs. Kingston received emergency medical assistance or been close to a hospital she might have survived but she had chosen to take a long walk that day without telling anyone where she was heading. That alone had greatly lessened her chances of survival. It seemed Elsa had ignored many of the symptoms of heart disease for some considerable time without seeking help.

Whether Elsa had helped her death along, given her stated intention, Sandra would never know, but she couldn't withhold Elsa's secret from the family. They had a right to know.

"Poor Elsa," Lloyd said afterwards, without any sympathy at all. "She started going to pieces from that day on. As well she should. Her problems were all of her own making." He looked in a kindly fashion on his distressed niece. "My father did his best but pandering to a neurotic woman wasn't in his nature. It was the first husband leaving her that really destroyed Elsa. At least *I'm* in the clear," he added ironically.

"Tell me you forgive me," Sandra begged.

"Nothing to forgive." He patted her shoulder. "You were a child. You believed what you were told. Forgiving your mother is another matter. Are you going to tell her?"

Sandra shook her head. "I can't see any point in making this public, either. Elsa had her secret. I think as a family we have to keep it, otherwise we start up another pointless scandal. Elsa is dead. It's all over. Shall we take a vote on it?"

"Does Daniel know?" Berne asked.

the world we've lost a dear family member ... all sad which of course I'm not."

"So much of life is sad," Sandra said, thinking she would never get over the shock of it. "Elsa wanted her ashes to be scattered at sea."

"I'll take care of that," Lloyd offered. "She was my stepmother though she never took the time to be one. In many ways she was quite simply, *mad*. I'm going back to Perth as soon as I can. Berne can come with me. The trip will do him good. I understand he wants to be an airline pilot."

"Sure do." Berne smiled across at Sandra.

"Then good luck, my boy. You'd better get on with it. You'll have a lot to learn."

"No problem!" Berne appeared entirely comfortable with the idea.

There was a memorial service for the late Mrs. Elsa Kingston in Darwin. Dying so soon after her husband, people acquainted with the family shook their heads in sympathy prepared in death to overlook the fact the marriage had been a disaster.

Outside the church people pushed forward to introduce themselves, or reintroduce themselves, offering a word of condolence or respect. From time to time Daniel touched Sandra's elbow, dipping his dark head to murmur the names of people she didn't know. The healing process with her own family had started, but Daniel was the one person Sandra wanted beside her.

"It's Joel Moreland coming this way," Daniel alerted her, easily spotting Moreland's distinguished silver head among the crowd. "He has a lady with him. Seventies, beautifully dressed. The sister-in-law I'd say."

They approached, a handsome couple. Moreland looked even more impressive in his dark clothes. He certainly was a splendid looking man Sandra thought as introductions were made and respects paid. The lady *was* Moreland's sister-in-law, Helen, widow of a younger brother who had never enjoyed good health and died prematurely at fifty-six.

Helen Moreland tried, but couldn't conceal her shock at meeting Daniel, indeed her expression crumpled into tears.

"Now, Helen," Moreland took her hand in a comforting grasp. "It's all right, my dear."

"I just can't believe it that's all," Helen Moreland said, staring into Daniel's eyes. "He looks *exactly* like you at that age, Joel."

"I'm not sure I want to speak about this, Mrs. Moreland," Daniel said, very quietly.

She put her hand on his arm. "But you must, my

suggested. ...
eyes resting on her as though she ...
ful ally.

"I'm sorry, sir," Daniel said, courteous but firm.

Sandra turned to him immediately. "Perhaps you should, Daniel," she urged. Secrets turned into terrible burdens. The best thing Daniel could do was let Mrs. Moreland tell him what she knew.

"*Please,* Daniel." Helen Moreland lifted her gentle eyes that nevertheless missed nothing to his face. "Did you know Joel was christened Daniel Joel Moreland? His father was Daniel too so somewhere along the way to avoid confusion Daniel got to be Joel. Jared was christened Jared Joel Moreland."

"Where is this leading, Mrs. Moreland?" Daniel asked, intensity in his voice.

"Why don't we follow a bit later on?" Sandra smoothly intervened. "Any taxi driver will know where you live."

"If that's your wish." Joel Moreland inclined his silver head. "Or I could send my man back for you."

"I don't seem to have much choice, do I?" Daniel turned away from an intense scrutiny of Sandra to ask in an ironic voice.

"It's all *for* you, Daniel," Helen Moreland said.

"Perhaps an hour, Mr. Moreland," Sandra said

quickly, linking an arm through Daniel's and holding on.

Moreland, the man with the Midas touch, nodded, seemingly content to let a twenty-year-old girl handle things. "As you wish, my dear."

The fact they had reached a decision gave Sandra a new sense of purpose. Resistance, however, was coming off Daniel in waves. She knew and sympathized with the intensity of conflict going on inside him but she trusted her feminine intuition. The crowd had dispersed and the two of them had wandered off finding the same coffee shop they had visited once before.

"You don't want to go, do you?"

Daniel had removed his dark jacket in the heat. The dazzling white of his shirt made a striking contrast with his tanned skin. "You know damn well I don't," he replied, tersely, thinking he had done nothing but drink coffee over the last few days. "Though I've taken great note of the fact you seem determined to get me there."

"Maybe it's where you *belong*, Daniel," she said. "Ever thought of that?"

He dismissed that with a cursory wave of his hand. "I don't exactly belong anywhere. Most certainly not with the man with the Midas touch."

"Even though he could be your grandfather?" she asked, covering his hand with her own.

"Sandra." ~~He~~ without looking up. She couldn't ~~keep telling~~ she loved him otherwise he could never go away.

"No need to be embarrassed," she said cheerfully. "You know me. I rush in where angels fear to tread. You don't have to love me, okay? I can see you're obsessed with standing alone, but you need a little bit of a hand with this. I'm the right woman for the job."

He lifted his head again, finding those electric-blue eyes. "And a *little* hand is what you've got." He raised it to his lips and kissed it.

"People are looking, Daniel," she pointed out, love for him invading every part of her body.

"Fine. Who cares?"

"I thought you did?"

His eyes glittered. "How many people do you think know you're the rich Alexandra Kingston, mistress of historic Moondai station?"

"You want to pretend I'm not?"

"I wish with all my heart you weren't," he said, with intense feeling.

"Then I wouldn't be *me*, Daniel, would I? I know you care about me."

"I wouldn't be heading for the Moreland mansion if I didn't," he told her a shade harshly. He was lashing out in frustration when he loved her. Hell he knew it, but it was impossible to say. What could he offer her? Maybe in a year or two when he had time to get going. Hope reared its head. She looked so beautiful, so exclusive. She was wearing a little black suit with gold button detailing, a white silk blouse beneath the jacket, sheerest black stockings—he had never seen her in stockings—with a pair of high heeled black shoes on her feet. The shoes matched her handbag. No hat. Just her radiant curls that were growing longer and thicker by the day. He knew the outfit had been air freighted in. She'd told him she had nothing she could wear to a funeral in her wardrobe. Well she wore this outfit with considerable chic. She looked what she was: a lovely, fashionable heiress and thus way out of his league.

The meeting with the Morelands passed with far less difficulty than Daniel had anticipated. Helen Moreland who recognised Daniel was there to please Sandra more than anyone else, lost little time telling her story while Joel Moreland and Daniel, sat forward in their respective armchairs, their heads bent at *exactly* the same angle.

"I want to tell you the truth, Daniel," Helen Moreland began, "you know, the truth, the whole truth, nothing but the truth as I know it. The story is as old as time. A secret arrangement between two women. One powerful, one of lower station. The young

the girl packing while her husband was away on business and her son was enjoying what should have been a fun week with his friends which took in the Alice Springs annual rodeo. What tragic event happened next pushed all thought of a dismissed servant out of a wildly grieving mother's mind. For almost four years Frances was literally off her head with grief. She adjusted to the harsh reality of life in time but had never fully recovered. Frances adored her only son. She had such plans for him. She genuinely believed no blame could be attached to her for getting rid of a girl she considered little more than an opportunist. It wasn't until Frances lay dying that she told me she had a feeling—just a *feeling*—the girl could have been pregnant. She said she did try to trace the girl—this was some five years after Jared's death—but Johanna Carson had simply vanished with the money Frances had given her to disappear. But that *feeling*, remained. It must have haunted her, particularly as she kept it all to herself. After Frances died it took me quite a while to work up the courage to tell Joel. He'd had enough to bear but what if there was some truth in this feeling Frances had? Joel set an investigator to find out. The rest you know."

Joel Moreland looked up as his sister-in-law's voice faltered. "We have ample reason to believe you're Jared's son, Daniel," he said. "The son he never knew about because you were in your mother's womb. Knowing my son the way I did he would have stood by Johanna no matter what. As Helen said, my wife had great plans for Jared—she worshipped him almost to the exclusion of our lovely daughter—she already had a girl picked out for him. She would have been determined not to allow Johanna, your mother, to ruin those plans. God knows what would have happened only Jared was killed. It was all too late. And it *would* have been only Frances couldn't keep her secret to the end. She knew not to tell me. I would have been shocked out of my mind. We're talking my grandchild here! She chose to tell Helen."

"I tried to get her to tell you Joel," Helen said, emotional tears springing into her eyes. "But she was adamant you should never know. You would never have acted as Frances did. I believe Frances had *more* than a feeling Johanna was pregnant but she was already condemned as not being good enough for her son."

"A *nice, compassionate* woman," Daniel observed grimly.

"Your grandmother, Daniel," Joel Moreland reminded him, sadly. "I know how you feel, son. I understand perfectly. Perhaps if Jared had lived

sack her. I don't remember Johanna...
I'm sorry. I was so busy all the time, travelling around the country and overseas. Nothing worked for your mother, I'm afraid. Nor for you because of it. My wife's punishment was not only the loss of her son but her only grandson. That's *you*, Daniel. I know I asked you to allow a DNA sample but I didn't really want to anyway. I *know* you're my grandson."

"So do I," Helen Moreland added with untrammelled joy. "You're the image of Joel at the same age. You also have a look of Jared, though you have Joel's eyes. Cecile has them too. No one seeing you and Cecile together would doubt you were family."

"So what *is* it you expect me to do, sir?" Daniel addressed Joel Moreland directly.

A look of agonised longing passed over Moreland's distinguished face. "I want you to take your rightful place as my grandson, Daniel. Be in *no* doubt I would never have let Johanna go, knowing she was carrying my grandson. Your father would never have permitted it either. If you doubt it, you don't know me," he said emphatically.

Daniel believed him without hesitation. "How many people know about this?" he asked.

"For *sure,* only the four of us. Sandra—" Moreland turned his head to smile at her "—recognised the resemblance right off but then I sense she's very close to you?"

"Aren't you forgetting something, sir?" Daniel asked bleakly. "Sandra is the Kingston heiress. I *work* for her."

Joel Moreland nodded. "I understand your feelings, Daniel. Your sense of pride and decency, but *you're* the Moreland heir. Don't you *want* to be?"

The question saw Daniel on his feet, obviously upset. "I'm sorry, sir. It's too much to handle." He shook his head.

"I understand that as well." Moreland rose to his full height, laying his hand on Daniel's shoulder. "You need time, Daniel. Time is on your side. Unfortunately it's not on mine."

"You're not ill?" Daniel asked with a rush of dismay.

"No, no," Moreland reassured him swiftly, "but I'm not young anymore. I'm not even middle-aged even if I don't feel so old. I'm a septuagenarian, Daniel."

"Like me." Helen Moreland smiled at them both, wondering how *anyone* could fail to see the resemblance. "I couldn't be more thrilled to meet you, Daniel. It's like a dream come true. Thank you so much for bringing him to us, Sandra." She reached out to take Sandra's hand. "Now that we've met, you can't go away, either."

the overseer's bungalow.

"We're in the middle of nowhere, Sandra," he told her as they rode out to the holding yards. A road train was due in around noon to transport a mob of prime cattle to market. "There's not a single soul on the station who would harm a hair of your head. Your uncle and cousin have left for Perth. They were never any threat even if they've been damned unpleasant up until very recently. It was all in your mother's mind, sad to say although she was right about one thing. The crash was no accident. Meg is in the house and I'm near enough for you to yell if you want me. I'd be with you in a trice. I can't stay in the house, you can see that?"

"Certainly," she answered mockingly, watching a small group of nomadic emus feeding on some dry seeds in the ground. Emu oil had been used for countless centuries by the aboriginals for a variety of ailments. These days it was having great success easing the pain of arthritis. She had to think about that one. Lord knows there were enough emus running wild on Moondai. "You're scared I'll barge into your room." She turned her head back to Daniel. He looked marvellous in the saddle, all lithe athleticism, a superb horseman.

"You bet I am," he said. "I'm scared what I might do."

"Could I believe...consider having sex?"

"It's okay for you, to joke. By the time you got around to yelling *stop,* you'd have pushed me right over the edge."

"There's a cure for being a virgin, you know. I think that's what's worrying you."

"You want to stop teasing, Sandra," he warned. "In my book there are certain rules of behaviour."

"Does this mean you're going to keep me at arm's length until we're married?"

"You can stop that right now," he admonished, noting the cheeky mocking look on her face. "Besides, did I ever mention I love you?"

"If you had any brains you would," she answered, smartly. "Sandra, I love you more than life itself!" She assumed a melodramatic voice, quickly reverting to her normal tones. "*That* would be nice. And that's not *all,* as any good salesman would say. There's an added incentive. The house comes with me. There's tons of room for future kids. Try to see it my way, Daniel. There's only one word for us. It's *soul mates!*"

He gave a short laugh. "Then this soul mate has a lot of soul searching to do."

"I know," she sighed, riding her mare in closer. "Daniel there's nothing wrong with admitting to being Joel Moreland's grandson. He's a lovely man. A lovely, *lonely* man. You could think of him."

went through. But had she lived, I think she would have told you to deny this relationship. In a way it's a vindication of all the sacrifices that went before. Frances Moreland paid for what she did. I just don't think you and your grandfather should have to suffer her mistakes any longer. It's not as though I'm doing myself any good, saying this. You become a Moreland, where does that leave me? I'm sending you off to join the competition when I desperately *need* you."

"I'll be here as long as you need me, Sandra," he promised, a flash coming into his eyes. "When I get my life straightened out we can talk."

Well at least we've got *that* cleared up, Sandra thought. She knew she only had to sit still and she'd get her way in time. She *loved* this man, this Daniel. She was more than prepared to put up a good fight for him.

EPILOGUE

HER mirror told her she looked dazzling. This was the eve of her twenty-first birthday. A big party was being held downstairs in her honour. Moondai was a much healthier, happier place than it had been for many long years. Daniel continued to manage the station wonderfully but the time was rapidly approaching when she felt in her bones he would go to his grandfather. For Daniel with a good bit of coaxing from her had cemented his relationship with his grandfather. She could take extra credit for the fact Daniel had bowed to his grandfather's dearest wish to allow Moreland to be added to his name. These days Daniel was known as Daniel Carson-Moreland but everyone knew it was only a matter of time before the Carson was dropped. Maybe Daniel C. Moreland she'd suggested to him? She was after all, a terminal do-gooder.

The entire Outback had taken in its stride the revelation that Daniel Carson was actually Jared Moreland's son. Stories like that might have happened all

tragically and needlessly. Such a wast~~~
was universally liked and approved of, a fitting heir
for his grandfather.

Neither Lloyd Kingston nor Berne resided at
Moondai anymore. Berne was continuing his intensive training and doing extremely well. Lloyd had
taken up residence in Perth, a city he had always
liked, close to his academic friends. He had also acquired a lady friend he brought back with him to
Moondai to celebrate Sandra's twenty-first. Festivities were to last the entire weekend. Sandra had invited all her old friends, especially those who had
formed the hospital entertainment group. Vinnie,
her former next door neighbour was invited, too.

Several members of the Moreland family had
been invited, Sandra having met them on previous
occasions. Sandra had taken to Cecile Moreland at
once as Cecile had taken to her. It was very heart-
warming to have such glad-hearted acceptance. It
established them as friends who wanted to carry
that friendship further. But then it was difficult not
to be drawn to Cecile when she was so much like
her cousin, Daniel.

Time to go downstairs! Sandra took one last look
at her reflection, aware there was the sheen of tears

in her eyes. Excitement was running at full throttle, fuelling every fibre of her being.

And always and always... Daniel. If I'm beautiful, I'm beautiful for you!

Her cloud of hair had been tamed with exquisite, star shaped diamond pins, heirloom pieces from her grandmother, Catherine's, collection which was now hers. Her dress was truly lovely, very romantic, white chiffon hanging from shoestring straps, the bodice tightly draped, decorated with glittering beads, crystals and sequins, the skirt dreamy for dancing.

She inhaled deeply to calm those tumultuous nerves. *Oh, Daniel, please say you love me!* Didn't he know his name was written indelibly on her heart?

When they were together love seemed to be all around them, but still he hadn't spoken, true to his own standards. She knew his mother's trauma, left pregnant and quite alone to rear a fatherless child had affected him deeply. Responsibility was Daniel's middle name. She quite liked that really.

She was almost at the door when someone outside, knocked. Probably her mother. Her mother and her stepbrother, Michael were staying at the homestead, but she had gotten in early telling her mother she preferred it if her stepfather didn't come. Her mother had expressed dismay but Sandra had remained firm. Her stepfather would never be permitted to cross her threshold.

called, she would fly t̶o̶

"Only me." He stared at her for the long̶ ̶
then barely containing his feelings breathed ardently, "You look a dream come true, birthday girl."

"Thank you, thank you." Colour bloomed in her cheeks. She smiled up at him, her eyes a burning violet-blue. "You look splendid too. How much did that dinner suit set you back?" she asked lightly, aware they were both highly emotional on this special night.

"I hired it."

"Did you really?" She studied the perfect fit, the set of his shoulders. "You didn't."

"Of course I didn't." He gave her his marvellous lopsided smile. "But I won't be able to afford another in a hurry. May I come in for a moment?"

"Certainly." She stood back to let him pass.

He paused in the centre of the room; turned to face her. "You've turned into a beautiful woman right in front of my eyes."

"You're saying I wasn't much to look at when you met me?" She adopted a teasing tone.

He laughed softly. "You were the prettiest youngster. But *not for long!*"

"I put my heart into getting beautiful, Daniel," she said. *All for you.*

"Well you made it," he said, with considerable feeling, thrusting a hand inside his dinner jacket.

"What are you doing?" Her voice wobbled.

"I'm giving you your birthday present now, okay?" He looked up, a silver flame in his eyes.

"I just hope it cost a lot of money," she tried to joke. "Just fooling, Daniel."

"I know. That was one big fat cheque you wrote for the Childhood Leukaemia Foundation."

She nodded her satisfaction. "Joel has agreed to match me. I really love him, you know. My grandad didn't inspire a lot of affection. Your grandad is the kind of man one loves."

"He is," Daniel agreed with obvious affection, then with sudden intensity, "What about *me*?"

"I've told you I love you a number of times. I won't be tempted again."

"So I'll send this back then?" he asked, waving a small velvet box about.

"After I've seen what it is." A swarm of butterflies took flight in her stomach.

He moved towards her with his characteristic athletic grace, going down on one knee. "I've got to do this properly." He looked up at her with half smiling, but deeply serious eyes. "Alexandra Mary Kingston," he said with burning formality, "would you do me the great honour of becoming my wife?" He didn't wait for an answer but put out his arms and gripped her slender body to him. "Dar-

with joy. "Oh, ~~D~~
cry," she whispered, her two hands cupping
loved head. "I dare not. I'll spoil my makeup. Oh,
Daniel, I never believed you'd ask me."

He rose to his feet, bending to kiss the creamy
slope of her shoulder. "How could you not?" he
asked gently. "You know how *I* feel just as I know
how *you* feel. We love each other. We were meant
for each other since we were born." Swiftly he
opened the box in his hand. "Here is my gift to you,
your engagement ring. It comes with my solemn
promise to love, honour and protect you all my life.
Give me your hand, sweetheart."

Sandra raised it, but overcome by emotion,
squeezed her eyes shut. Precious metal slipped
down her finger.

"You can open your eyes now," Daniel said in a
gentle loving voice.

"Oh, Daniel!" She stared down at her precious
ring, a glorious sapphire flanked by baguette dia-
monds. "I feel like I'm going to bawl my eyes out."

"Not now, you can't," he reminded her. "You can
cry in my arms when the party is over."

"Is that a promise? I don't think I can contain myself so long."

"Well we have to. I don't dare muss you, you

look perfect. Tears, lots of cuddles and kisses are allowed later, but though it's *excruciating* and a real test of my control, we're not going to bed together. Not until the first night of our honeymoon which I personally guarantee will be the most wonderful night of our lives. Do you trust me?"

She smiled radiantly. "Trust in you wraps me like a security blanket. I've always trusted you, Daniel. From the moment I laid eyes on you at the airport. Now, having said that, I don't want to pester you, but *when* is this honeymoon going to be? It's a good time to put pressure on you because I don't mind telling you I'm in an agony of longing."

"You think *I'm* not?" He linked his arms around the waist. "I'm ready to start it *immediately,* but what I want even more is to see you as my shining bride. The woman I love and honour. That said, what about as soon as possible in the New Year? Would a few months give you enough time to get organised? I don't think we're going to get out of a big wedding, do you?"

"The biggest!" In an ecstasy of joy she started to whirl around the room all the while holding her beautiful engagement ring up to the light.

"Like it?" He caught her to him, commanding her to a stop.

"Love it. Love you."

"That's what I want to hear." He allowed himself several kisses that trailed from behind one small

your eyes."

"Are you going to kiss me anywhere else?" she whispered.

His brilliant eyes rested on her mouth. "Don't tempt me. One kiss and it would all get out of hand as you very well know. We'll store the kisses up until the early hours of your birthday morning. Meanwhile I'll kiss those delicate fingers." He brought her hand to his mouth, running the tip of his tongue over her smooth knuckles.

"Daniel," she said weakly, just about ready to dissolve.

"This is *nothing* to what I'm going to do to you," he told her in a low thrilling voice.

"I *know!*" She gave an expectant shiver. "I'm going to pieces already."

"Me, too!" Ardently he touched a finger to the little pulse that beat in the hollow of her throat. "We'll have a lifetime together, Sandra." His voice was full of the wonder of being deeply, truly in love. "Just think of it!"

An enormous lightness of being seized Sandra. She linked her arm through his as they walked to the door. "From this day forward!"

"From this day forward," he repeated, looking

down at her with his spirit, exultant, in his eyes. "You and me on life's journey."

For a long lovely moment they were sealed off in a world of their own.

I'm getting what every woman prays for, Sandra thought, an expression of utter bliss irradiating her face. I'm getting the thing in life that really matters: Having a wonderful man love me as I love him.

Only with Daniel could this happen.

*****

Look out for Cecile's story.
Coming soon!

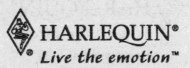

Superromance.
A *big* satisfying read about unforgettable
characters. Each month we offer *six* very different
stories that range from family drama to adventure
and mystery, from highly emotional stories to
romantic comedies—and much more! Stories
about people you'll believe in and care about.
Stories too compelling to put down....

Our authors are among today's *best* romance
writers. You'll find familiar names and talented
newcomers. Many of them are award winners—
and you'll see why!

If you want the biggest and best
in romance fiction, you'll get it
from Superromance!

Emotional, Exciting, Unexpected...

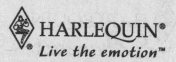

HARLEQUIN®
Live the emotion™

Historical Romantic Adventure!

From rugged lawmen and valiant knights to defiant heiresses and spirited frontierswomen, Harlequin Historicals will capture your imagination with their dramatic scope, passion and adventure.

Harlequin Historicals...
they're too good to miss!

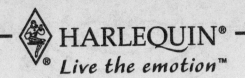

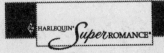